MAYA CREATION MYTHS

Mesoamerican Worlds: From the Olmecs to the Danzantes

After Monte Albán, Jeffrey P. Blomster, editor

The Apotheosis of Janaab' Pakal, Gerardo Aldana

Carrying the Word, Susanna Rostas

Commoner Ritual and Ideology in Ancient Mesoamerica, Nancy Gonlin and Jon C. Lohse, editors

Conquered Conquistadors, Florine Asselbergs

Empires of Time, Anthony Aveni

Encounter with the Plumed Serpent, Maarten Jansen and Gabina Aurora Pérez Jiménez

In the Realm of Nachan Kan, Marilyn A. Masson

Invasion and Transformation, Rebecca P. Brienen and Margaret A. Jackson, editors

The Kowoj, Prudence M. Rice and Don S. Rice, editors

Life and Death in the Templo Mayor, Eduardo Matos Moctezuma

The Lords of Lambityeco, Michael Lind and Javier Urcid

The Madrid Codex, Gabrielle Vail and Anthony Aveni, editors

Maya Creation Myths, Timothy W. Knowlton

Maya Daykeeping, John M. Weeks, Frauke Sachse, and Christian M. Prager

Maya Worldviews at Conquest, Leslie G. Cecil and Timothy W. Pugh, editors

Mesoamerican Ritual Economy, E. Christian Wells and Karla L. Davis-Salazar, editors

Mesoamerica's Classic Heritage, Davíd Carrasco, Lindsay Jones, and Scott Sessions, editors

Mexico's Indigenous Communities, Ethelia Ruiz Medrano, translated by Russ Davidson

Mockeries and Metamorphoses of an Aztec God, Guilhem Olivier, translated by Michel Besson

Negotiation within Domination, Ethelia Ruiz Medrano and Susan Kellogg, editors; translated by Russ Davidson

Rabinal Achi, Alain Breton, editor; translated by Teresa Lavender Fagan and Robert Schneider

Representing Aztec Ritual, Eloise Quiñones Keber, editor

Ruins of the Past, Travis W. Stanton and Aline Magnoni, editors

Skywatching in the Ancient World, Clive Ruggles and Gary Urton, editors

Social Change and the Evolution of Ceramic Production and Distribution in a Maya Community, Dean E. Arnold

The Social Experience of Childhood in Mesoamerica, Traci Ardren and Scott R. Hutson, editors

Stone Houses and Earth Lords, Keith M. Prufer and James E. Brady, editors

The Sun God and the Savior, Guy Stresser-Péan

Sweeping the Way, Catherine DiCesare

Tamoanchan, Tlalocan, Alfredo López Austin

Thunder Doesn't Live Here Anymore, Anath Ariel de Vidas; translated by Teresa Lavender Fagan

Topiltzin Quetzalcoatl, H. B. Nicholson

The World Below, Jacques Galinier

Maya CREATION MYTHS

WORDS AND WORLDS OF THE CHILAM BALAM

TIMOTHY W. KNOWLTON

UNIVERSITY PRESS OF COLORADO

Published by the University Press of Colorado
5589 Arapahoe Avenue, Suite 206C
Boulder, Colorado 80303

First paperback edition 2012
Printed in the United States of America

AAUP 1937 / 2012
The University Press of Colorado is a proud member of
the Association of American University Presses.

The University Press of Colorado is a cooperative publishing enterprise supported, in part, by Adams State College, Colorado State University, Fort Lewis College, Metropolitan State College of Denver, Regis University, University of Colorado, University of Northern Colorado, Utah State University, and Western State College of Colorado.

∞ This paper meets the requirements of the ANSI/NISO Z39.48-1992 (Permanence of Paper).

Library of Congress Cataloging-in-Publication Data

Knowlton, Timothy W.
Maya creation myths : words and worlds of the Chilam Balam / Timothy W. Knowlton.
p. cm. — (Mesoamerican worlds : from the Olmecs to the Danzantes)
Includes bibliographical references and index.
ISBN 978-1-60732-020-3 (hardcover : alk. paper) — ISBN 978-1-60732-198-9 (pbk. : alk. paper) — ISBN 978-1-60732-021-0 (e-book) 1. Maya mythology. 2. Maya cosmology. 3. Creation. I. Title.

F1435.3.R3K63 2010
299.7'842024—dc22

2010036028

Design by Daniel Pratt

For
Ron Duncan-Hart

Contents

Figures

Acknowledgments

Initial travel to conduct the research presented in this book was funded by grants from the Mesoamerican Ethnohistory Fund of Tulane University. Intermediate and final stages of research and writing were supported by a Dumbarton Oaks postdoctorate fellowship in spring 2006 and a faculty summer stipend from Berry College in summer 2008, respectively. The successful completion of my research would not have been possible without the generous assistance of the staffs of the Latin American Library at Tulane University in New Orleans, of the Ayer Collection of the Newberry Library in Chicago, and of the Archivo General de la Nación in Mexico City. I extend a warm thanks to Markus Eberl and Elissa Ferguson for preparing some of the line drawings included in this work. I also thank E. Wyllys Andrews of the Middle American Research Institute; David Zeidberg of the Huntington Library; Charles Greene, AnnaLee Pauls, and Ben Primer of the Princeton University Library; and Nuria Moreu Toloba and Carolina Notario Zubicoa of the Museo de América (Madrid) for permission to reproduce images from pre-Hispanic and Colonial Maya sources. Geneviève Le Fort generously facilitated permissions for reproducing some translations and arguments in Chapter 4 published elsewhere (Knowlton 2009). I am grateful to the staff of the University Press of Colorado, especially Darrin Pratt, Laura Furney, and Daniel Pratt, whose efforts and enthusiasm have enabled the manuscript to see the light of day. Throughout the process of research and writing, I have benefited greatly from discussions, comments, and suggestions from many wonderful people, including Anthony Aveni, Alfonso Lacadena, Judith Maxwell, Dennis Tedlock, Gabrielle Vail, Gretchen Whalen, and especially Victoria Bricker. Most importantly, I owe a deep debt of gratitude to my wife, Stacy Dunn, for her support, both intellectual and emotional, throughout the process that resulted in the present work.

Foreword

The final page of the Dresden Codex, a pre-Columbian Maya document, displays a scene showing the end of the previous world creation. Water is vomited from the mouth of a celestial caiman, poured from a vase by an old woman deity, and discharged from eclipse glyphs appended to the sky beast's body, all of the action displayed against a dark and somber background. The severely eroded glyphic text that accompanies this vivid portrait of destruction by deluge reads in part, "Storm, black sky . . . first year" (*Dresden Codex*, p. 74). Parts of alphabetic narratives in the colonial Books of Chilam Balam of Tizimín and Chumayel paint a virtual word picture of the ancient flood scene documented in the codex, referring specifically to the celestial caiman deity as well as the various ways the sky gods have chosen to let loose their aqueous burden.

Students of the Maya are prone to pluck passages out of the colonial literature to demonstrate cultural continuity, to argue how Christianity impacted and transformed pre-Columbian religion and world view or to bolster their ideas about world ages and the cross-cultural unity of mythologies. Rarely does one encounter a treatise on Maya myths that combines a knowledge of both literary tradition in the codices and the ideological doctrine of those who first encountered the native population, the Spanish missionaries. Tim Knowlton argues that the *dialogue* between these realms is what set the backdrop for the reinterpretation of ancient wisdom by the guardians of the Chilam Balam books, the local Maya elite. To understand what these myths meant in pre- and early post-contact times and what they mean today, one needs to know about Mayan language, epigraphy, pre-Columbian history and cosmology, literary theory, and a good deal about the history of Old World religion.

Tim Knowlton's work fills the bill. His is a well-grounded, skillfully argued study of the Maya myths, which he analyzes case by case; for example, he explores the dialogue between *katun* (score of years) prophecies in the Chilam Balam books and biblical apocalypticism, and the destruction of earlier Maya people via catastrophes like the one pictured on Dresden 74 and the biblical account of the Fall of Man.

Cast in a style accessible to students of all the disciplines he broaches, Knowlton's dialogic approach breathes new life into old stories. But more than this, his interdisciplinary approach to mythography renders *Maya Creation Myths* a hallmark text for this series.

ANTHONY AVENI

MAYA CREATION MYTHS

CHAPTER ONE

Introduction

There is no Classical Yucatecan Maya word for "myth." But around the close of the seventeenth century, an anonymous Maya scribe penned what he called *u kahlay cab tu kinil* ("the world history of the era") before Christianity came to the Peten, the land of the Maya. In this he collected numerous accounts of the cyclical destruction and reestablishment of the cosmos; the origins of gods, human beings, and the rituals and activities upon which their relationship depends; and finally the dawn of the Sun and with it the sacred calendar Maya diviners used (and in some places still use today) to make sense of humans' place in the otherwise inscrutable march of time.

Today, we call these accounts "creation myths" and refer to their collector as a "mythographer." But for the Maya scribe who brought together this compilation, these accounts were drawn from two native genres: *kahlay*, meaning "annals" or "history," and *kay*, meaning "song." This compilation of myths itself eventually became part of a larger handwritten copybook, occupying pages 42 to 63 of the colonial manuscript known today as the Book of Chilam Balam of Chumayel.[1]

Balam or "Jaguar" was the surname of a *chilan*, a pre-Hispanic oracle or "prophet" from the town of Maní in the northwestern portion of the Yucatán peninsula, in what is today southeastern Mexico. In Colonial times (ca. AD 1540–1821) this Chilam Balam was believed to have foretold the arrival of the Spanish conquistadors and the new religion they aggressively promoted, Christianity. Chumayel is the name of the particular Maya community, or *cah*, to which this specific copybook belonged. Located to the northeast of Maní, Chumayel is one of many Maya communities that had handwritten manuscripts called the Books of Chilam Balam. These books were compiled, copied, and recopied throughout the Colonial period. The Books of Chilam Balam are usually distinguished according to the town in which they were first encountered by scholars, such as Chumayel, Kaua, Chan Kan, and Ixil. Two other such documents are referred to by the names of the scholars who collected them, the Códice Pérez (after Juan Pio Pérez) and the Morley Manuscript (after Sylvanus Morley). These manuscripts contain materials on topics as diverse as cosmology, history, calendrics, astronomy, divination, medicine, religious doctrine, ritual, riddles, and tales drawn from both Mesoamerican and Renaissance European traditions, of which only a few texts are explicitly attributed to the books' namesake, the Chilam Balam.[2] These community manuscripts are written primarily in the Classical Yucatecan Maya language using a modified version of the Latin alphabet, although isolated words and short sections in Nahuatl (Aztec), Spanish, or Latin occasionally appear, sometimes garbled because of the authors' imperfect bilingualism. These books served as a major medium for recorded tradition once overzealous Christian missionaries had seized or burned many native books and had dismantled the temple-schools that in pre-Hispanic times taught hieroglyphic writing, calligraphy, and the Maya arts and sciences (Landa 1978 [ca. 1566]:12–13, 82).

The Books of Chilam Balam are an indispensable source of Maya literature and lore. As the *Eddas* are to knowledge of pre-Christian Norse culture, so these Classical Yucatecan Maya language manuscripts are to our understanding of this great Native American civilization. Like the K'iche' (Quiche) Maya narratives contained in another Colonial period alphabetic manuscript, the *Popol Vuh* (D. Tedlock 1985, 1996; Colop 1999, 2008; Christenson 2003a, 2003b), much within these Classical Yucatecan Maya texts has its roots in ancient Maya civilization. Maya arts and sciences flourished during what archaeologists call the Classic period (ca. AD 250–900), and despite major societal upheavals they continued to be maintained throughout the Postclassic period (AD 900–ca. 1540), as evidenced by the few illuminated barkpaper codices that have survived, despite the unforgiving tropical environment and their seizures at the hands of religious zealots.

However, also like the Old World *Eddas* and the New World *Popol Vuh*, these Classical Yucatecan Maya texts reached their present form during a period in which many indigenous elites had recently converted to Christianity. The extant cosmogonic texts contained in the Books of Chilam Balam represent different historical stages of the colonial redaction of mythic narratives, stages spanning the entire length of the Colonial period and drawing on traditions of knowledge from both sides of the Atlantic that predate the colonial encounter. Since scribes not only were guardians of tradition but served or were themselves elites, obvious Christian references appear in the mythological texts. Furthermore, because the Franciscan missionaries who first evangelized the Yucatec Maya less often accommodated to local culture by assigning indigenous terms to Christian theological concepts than did the Dominicans who transmitted alphabetic writing among the K'iche' Maya (D. Tedlock 1985), the creation texts of the Books of Chilam Balam contain more obvious Spanish loanwords than the *Popol Vuh*. These historical contingencies of language use are only one of several challenges facing interpreters of Classical Yucatecan Maya creation myths.

DECIPHERING THE MYTHS OF THE BOOKS OF CHILAM BALAM

The last several decades have witnessed revolutions in our understanding of ancient and colonial Maya societies. The decipherment of Maya hieroglyphic writing has opened an unparalleled vista onto the world of the ancient Maya (see Coe 1999 for one history of Maya epigraphy). Although attracting less publicity, the emergence of the New Philology in postconquest Mesoamerican ethnohistory has resulted in a flurry of high-quality scholarship based on indigenous language sources (see Restall 2003 for a review of the development of research in this area). In the midst of these breakthroughs, less emphasis has been placed on the Books of Chilam Balam than in previous generations. As the late Munro Edmonson (1982: xiv) remarked, the language of the Books of Chilam Balam often presents considerable challenges to the translator, resulting in considerable variation from version to version. Scholarly translations in English of these documents go back to the pioneering work of Daniel Brinton (1882), and the entire Book of Chilam Balam of Chumayel alone has appeared in two, at times very divergent, English translations. The edition by Ralph Roys (1967) was first published in 1933, followed many decades afterward by Edmonson's (1986) own poetic translation.[3] Mexican scholars such as

Barrera Vásquez and Rendón (1948) attempted to overcome some of these challenges facing translators by positing the existence of an original *ur*-text reconstructed from the various redactions available across different books of Chilam Balam. While a productive approach, this method tends to overlook the possibility of meaningful variation by treating alternate redactions as corruptions of the "original" text or ascribing alternate readings to scribal error. Given the challenges of arriving at accurate, readable editions of these documents, book-length studies of Maya myth and cosmology in recent decades have suggested that mythic literature from colonial Yucatán is either too sparse (Taube 1993:67) or too opaque (Freidel, Schele, and Parker 1993:45) to figure significantly in their diachronic investigations.

Even with accurate translations, the significance of a given text is not necessarily clear, as the authors wrote not for us but assumed an audience familiar with their metaphors, mythic characters, and motifs. Also, because of the environment of suppression and the clandestine nature of these manuscripts, their transmission, and their performance, we often lack the reliable dates of composition otherwise available for the official documents written by colonial Maya scribes, such as testaments, or the readily available dates of publication of Mayan-language Christian doctrinal works. Such hurdles hinder the kind of chronological precision one conducting an ethnohistorical study of the composition of creation myths in the Books of Chilam Balam would like to have. In its absence, scholars endeavoring not only to translate but to interpret these Classical Yucatecan myths in their sociohistorical context must take into account what evidence is available in order to access the local meanings, the process of transmission, and performative contexts of the myths. What I adopt here is a case study approach focusing on features internal to the individual texts (deixis, reported speech, evidentiality) as well as intertextuality. By *intertextuality*, I am referring to the interrelationship between these myth texts and other texts that formed the basic resources and shared knowledge necessary for both the composition and interpretation of that text by their authors and their audiences. Intertextuality is conceived of differently at various points in this study depending on the case at hand, as broadly as allusion and shared motifs and as narrowly as the systematic comparison of multiple redactions of the same text or the usages of the same word or phrase between roughly contemporaneous documents. As we will see, the Maya maestros responsible for compiling, guarding, and performing the Books of Chilam Balam did so by drawing on a web of knowledge that had its origins in Classic Maya societies and the Postclassic Mesoamerican world system, a network that in some ways expanded as the Maya were increasingly integrated into the Spanish colonial empire. This web of knowledge consisted of traditions of oral and written texts and iconography deriving from Maya and Central Mexican sources (embodying perhaps even older, pan-Mesoamerican themes), as well as popular European language writings and Christian doctrinal works composed in Classical Yucatecan Maya.

So in preparing the translations of Classical Yucatecan creation myths that form the basis for the interpretations in this work, I first rendered the myths in lines that accord with the natural discourse features of the language, such as the initial particles and terminal enclitics that mark where an individual utterance begins and/or ends in Classical Yucatecan. This ethnopoetic method for discerning line division based on particles was pioneered by Dell Hymes (1980, 1981), who applied it to native North American Indian texts. Although punctuation marks do exist in the original manuscript (Gordon 1993 [1913]), the use of punctuation throughout the manuscript is inconsistent, sometimes disregarding not only clause but even morpheme divisions. Therefore, I have not systematically relied on it in determining line divisions, although I do believe the patterns of punctuation in these documents deserve further research. I have departed from Ralph Roys's (1967) practice of providing the text in blocks of prose, for I believe this obscures for the reader those poetic elements such as parallelisms, chiasmi, couplets, and triplets, and so forth that are present and would have been heard in the myths' performance. At the same time, I have not straightjacketed the entire text into a sequence of parallel lines, as Edmonson's (1982, 1986) translations do. I believe my work is closest to the format employed by Bricker and Miram (2002) in their annotated translation of the Book of Chilam Balam of Kaua, whose line divisions enable the reader to pick out poetic devices where present without forcing the entire composition into an artificial model. The resulting transcription and translation is the text of Classical Yucatecan creation myths that provides the basis for the interpretive essays that make up this study.

In this work, I apply an interpretive approach that addresses the emergence of Classical Yucatecan creation myths as Maya peoples dealt not just materially but intellectually with the colonial situation. The intellectual resources the Maya had to draw upon included their access to both popular European and Christian sources as well as the cosmogonic traditions resulting from their previous position in the Postclassic Mesoamerican world system. Oriented in part by the works of Mikhail Bakhtin (1968, 1981, 1984) and the field of dialogical anthropology (Tedlock and Mannheim 1995), I am concerned with how the authors and redactors of Classical Yucatecan Maya cosmogonies give (and suppress) voice and how these voices reveal different discursive positions relative to received and emerging mythological traditions and the authors'/compilers' sense of identity. These colonial creation myths, neither precise replicas of pre-Hispanic belief nor confused compromises of European religion, themselves constituted the genesis of a heteroglot colonial world of novel cultural categories and possibilities.

I hope to shed light on both the diversity of Maya mythic traditions and the uniquely Maya discursive strategies emerging during the Colonial period. If Classical Yucatecan Maya myth has previously been considered too sparse or opaque for useful analysis, I suspect it is in part because many of our scholarly models are poorly suited for adequately addressing the mélange that makes up mythic discourses in colonial settings.

COSMOGONY AS DIALOGUE

Scholars have long considered how creation myths, as foundational stories, establish and/or reinforce other fundamental cultural categories, serving as a charter for the organization of society (Malinowski 1948) and the basis of a moral order (Lovin and Reynolds 1985). However, mythology typically has not been the anthropologist's first choice of phenomena to examine when addressing questions of cultural dynamics and hybridization. Often set apart from other cultural forms of discourse, myth and its kin ("worldview," "cosmology," "cultural logic") traditionally rested beyond history in that garden preserve of *la pensée sauvage* kept by academic disciplines involved (more self-consciously to be certain) in mulching alterity. Myth in anthropology, like poetry in Bakhtin's sociological stylistics, is too often considered to be "by convention suspended from any mutual interaction with alien discourse, any allusion to alien discourse," and only to "reflect lengthier social processes, i.e., those tendencies in social life requiring centuries to unfold" (Bakhtin 1981:285, 300).

In recent decades, however, several studies have undermined the old myth/history dichotomy (e.g., Bricker 1981; Guss 1981; Sahlins 1981; Taussig 1984). Furthermore, multiple mythic discourses exist simultaneously in many, if not all, societies. From ancient Mesopotamia to pre-imperial China and contemporary Guatemala, multiple cosmogonies have existed side by side within a single society, each discourse with its own system of categories and resultant behavioral norms and practices, either compatible or in competition (Lovin and Reynolds 1985). In the search for structural regularity, this privileging of centripetal forces, we have often defined our object in such a way that constructed variation is not as significant as structural regularity, blinding ourselves a priori to those centrifugal forces acting on culture. Perhaps nowhere is this more apparent than in the study of myth. Barth's (1987:8) critique of several anthropological approaches to myth and cosmology is that they are "linked with the premise of an encompassing logical order" and that "once this premise has been adopted, local variation becomes essentially uninteresting." Barth sees this as a problem of those approaches descended directly from either Durkheim or Lévi-Strauss; in other words, the assumptions of a great many anthropological approaches to myth and cosmology. Instead of operating at a level of abstraction in which "local variation must be reduced and controlled," Barth (1987:8) admonishes us that "we must always struggle to *get our ontological assumptions right*: to ascribe to our object of study only those properties and capabilities that we have reasonable ground to believe it to possess." Barth's (1987:84) own study focuses on the meaningful variation to be found in New Guinean Ok cosmologies when examined "as a living tradition of knowledge[,] . . . allow[ing] us to see the events taking place in a tradition as incidents of the very processes that shape that tradition." Barth found that different "schools of thought" within Ok villages no more lack meaningful variation than do the different schools of British social anthropology (Barth 1987:18–19); both are the effects of people historically transmitting (perhaps radically) different traditions of knowing about a shared object. For example, according to Barth's argument, it would be as indefensible empirically to analyze Ok traditions only in terms of their common denominators as it would be to lump together the theoretical arguments of Radcliffe-Brown and Leach on the basis that both address the subject of kinship. Barth (1987:85) does recognize that the specific method employed in his monograph is best restricted to variation within relatively isolated autochthonous cultures ("an exploration of meanings in the folk tradition of a society which has long been incorporated in the economic and political world system would have to proceed along very different lines"). Nonetheless, his focus on the social processes of knowledge transmission, and embracing rather than suppressing messy variation, is a much needed corrective to previous approaches to myth.

The difficulty anthropologists and other scholars have had in arriving at adequate interpretations of myth and culture change, and the Classical Yucatecan Maya cosmogonies of the Books of Chilam Balam in particular, may in fact result from an intellectual heritage we share with the original Spanish colonial missionaries to the Americas. This intellectual heritage is to be found in our theories of language, society, and culture. Bakhtin (1981:271) argues that the poetics of unitary language (and therefore of structuralism) are historically those of "Aristotelian poetics, the poetics of Augustine, the poetics of the medieval church," and the scholarship of European nationalism. He vividly describes the ends of such unitary linguistic projects as "the supplanting of languages, their enslavement, the process of illuminating them with the True Word, the incorporation of barbarians and lower social strata into a unitary language of culture and truth." The beginning of the Spanish colonization of the Americas in 1492 was accompanied in that same year by the publication of Antonio de Nebrija's *Gramática Castellana* as part of the Spanish Crown's program of creating a nation from the linguistic, religious, and ethnic diversity of the newly reconquered Iberian Peninsula. Following Bakhtin's critique, in structural linguistics and anthropology we can perceive the remnants of the colonial project embedded in our theoretical assumptions even as we, as scholars, seek to understand those elements of human diversity repressed under the colonial project (see also Mignolo 2003).

The present study attempts to address the mélange of mythological discourses apparent in colonial settings. I attempt to incorporate Barth's theoretical critique by approaching creation myth not so much as an object but as an *interactional* communicative event, both sociologically and historically. I follow Bakhtin (1981:291) in asserting:

> Thus at any given moment of its historical existence, language is heteroglot from top to bottom: it represents the co-existence of socio-ideological contradictions between the present and the past, between differing epochs in the past, between different socio-ideological groups in the present, between tendencies, schools, circles and so forth, all given a bodily form. These "languages" of heteroglossia intersect each other in a variety of ways, forming new socially typifying "languages."

In this study, I consider mythological texts as a species of discourse, by which cultural knowledge emerges during its negotiation via one or more *languages*, languages being historical and social verbal-ideological systems that may or may not coincide with our traditional concept of unitary "national" languages. A dialogical approach provides an alternative to the structural view of language and culture as unitary entities internalized in an individual whose unique expressions appear in practice. Instead of assuming meaning exists within the structure of a unitary language and the practice of a unitary individual, dialogical anthropology recognizes "the word in language is half someone else's" and that "every utterance participates in the 'unitary language' (in its centripetal forces and tendencies) and at the same time partakes of social and historical heteroglossia (the centrifugal, stratifying forces)" (Bakhtin 1981:272). Rather than taking the categories of things and persons simply as socially given, these categories are considered to be cultural phenomena. To be truly cultural, they must be shared. And in practice, categories are shared to the extent their meanings are the subject of implicit or explicit negotiation among persons, of dialogue. As we shall see, a dialogical approach is particularly appropriate in the case of Classical Yucatecan Maya creation myths, which frequently employ the discursive strategy Bakhtin (1984:110) refers to as syncrisis, "the juxtaposition of various points of view on a specific object." By accounting for both centripetal and centrifugal forces in verbal-ideological life, a dialogic anthropology may proceed unencumbered by those philosophical categories underlying structural anthropology that are ill-equipped to account for the variation, heteroglossia, and syncretism so characteristic of colonial creations like the Maya myths in question.

CONTENT AND METHODOLOGY

In the chapters that follow, I have several related goals, for which I apply several related methods. I wish to ground both the cosmogonies (creation myths) and their interpretations in the changing sociohistorical circumstances from which the Book of Chilam Balam of Chumayel ultimately emerged. Chapter 2 provides a brief overview of ancient Maya society and cosmology and presents an argument for the existence of two metaphysical discourses discernable from extant Maya hieroglyphic texts. Prominent in this argument is the couplet metaphor *c̄hab akab*, which I translate as "genesis and darkness," a phrase that refers to the creative power of penitential sacrifice and gift-giving. This phrase is part of the discourse of ancient Maya theogonies (myths of the birth of gods) and continued to be in use for more than a thousand years, where we will find it again in reference to sacrifice and the birth of gods in Classical Yucatecan accounts.

Moving forward from the pre-Hispanic documentation of Maya cosmogonies, Chapter 3 places the creation myths of the Book of Chilam Balam of Chumayel in the context of the social and cultural upheavals of the Colonial period. With indigenous institutions of religion and learning suppressed or destroyed, the legend of the Chilam Balam provided a quasi-legitimate voice in which newly Christianized Maya elites could attempt to continue their literary tradition and maintain their intellectual culture. The preface to the mythography in the Chumayel is analyzed in terms of what we can learn about the identities, motivations, and likely sociohistorical context of its compiler(s). Contemporaneous Maya- and Spanish-language sources are interrogated for what they can tell us about the transmission and performance of Classical Yucatecan creation myths. Finally, the relationship between Christian missionary works and the Books of Chilam Balam is discussed, with special emphasis on the anxiety of Christian authorities about the existence of handwritten copybooks (*cartapacios*), like the Books of Chilam Balam, versus those printed works that were subject to oversight by the Inquisition.

Chapter 4 is the first of several concerned with the individual myths themselves that make up the Chumayel mythography. The Katun 11 Ahau myth is unique in the Chumayel mythography in having cognate versions in other Books of Chilam Balam. Comparisons among the different redactions are made not for the purpose of reconstructing an *ur*-text but for what this might tell us about the redactional history of the myth and the idiosyncrasies that mark the Chumayel redaction. Episodes in the myth are interpreted in light of Mesoamerican mythological motifs found in lowland Maya, highland Maya, Nahuatl, and Spanish sources. Finally, the distinctive eschatological frame that the Chumayel redaction of the Katun 11 Ahau myth contains is interpreted in light of the popular European apocalyptic literature known to have been translated into Classical Yucatecan Maya during the early Colonial period.

The creation myth of Chapter 5, the Ritual of the Angels, lacks extant variants like those available for the analysis of the Katun 11 Ahau myth. So instead its analysis focuses on what we can learn about the ritual context and transmission of the myth and its Maya-Christian cosmology and theogony from the use of reported speech and markers of evidentiality internal to the text. Scholars have studied reported speech in Yucatec in particular (Lucy 1993; V. Bricker n.d.), and, more generally, reported speech is of special interest because of the importance often attributed to instances of divine speech in cosmogonies. God is frequently represented as the unique "NAME" or "WORD" in the Old World exegesis of Judeo-Christian cosmogonic traditions (Janowitz 1993) like those diffused by missionaries, and as we shall see, the name and speech of divinity are a pertinent issue raised in this colonial Maya theogony as well. The text is also interpreted in light of near-contemporaneous Yucatec-language Christian doctrinal texts and reports of indigenous religious belief and practices by non-Maya clergy in order to establish the role of such a myth in the life of colonial Yucatec Maya communities.

The myth of Chapter 6 is introduced in the Chumayel manuscript by an anthropomorphic illustration of Death. This account addresses the creation of the First People and the origin of death and disaster as dramatized in the "Itzá" song of the collapse of the ancient city of Chichén Itzá. This narrative occasions a discussion of Colonial period Mayas' approaches to suffering, illness, and death, as well as a critical evaluation of scholarly interpretations of indigenous ontologies during the pre-Hispanic and Colonial eras.

Chapter 7 analyzes the "Birth of the Uinal," a cosmogonic "song" (*kay*) set within the "chronicling" (*tzol*) of the days of the 260-day Maya divinatory calendar, or *tzolkin*. In this text, the Maya myth-singer juxtaposes Maya and Christian cosmologies in a composition of beautiful syncrisis, while simultaneously undermining the claims of some European clergy and catechism texts that divine truth is a monologue to the exclusion of Maya voices. Chapter 8 concludes with a reflection on dialogism in Classical Yucatecan Maya creation myths as well as suggestions for future research.

NOTE ON ORTHOGRAPHY

As this study incorporates Maya texts in different languages and scripts from different time periods, determining how to consistently represent these in a way intelligible for audiences from different backgrounds has been a challenge. For the transliteration of hieroglyphic texts I have followed the guidelines of the series *Research Reports on Ancient Maya Writing* (*RRAMW*, Number 15, May 1988). However, to facilitate comparison of the transcriptions of the language of the hieroglyphic texts with Colonial era Maya texts, I have adapted those transliterations to the modified orthography also used for Classical Yucatecan Maya alphabetic texts throughout:

b	voiced, glottalized bilabial stop
tz	voiceless, plain alveolar affricate
dz	voiceless, glottalized alveolar affricate
ch	voiceless, plain alveo-palatal affricate
cħ	voiceless, glottalized alveo-palatal affricate
h	voiceless, laryngeal spirant
j	voiceless, velar spirant
c	voiceless, plain velar stop
k	voiceless, glottalized velar stop
l	voiced, alveolar lateral
m	voiced, bilabial nasal
n	voiced, alveolar nasal
p	voiceless, plain bilabial stop
ꝑ	voiceless, glottalized bilabial stop
z/s	voiceless, alveolar fricative
x	voiceless, alveo-palatal fricative
t	voiceless, plain alveolar stop
th	voiceless, glottalized alveolar stop
u/v	voiced, labiovelar glide
y	voiced, palatal glide
a	low, central, unrounded vowel

e	low, front, unrounded vowel
i/y	high, front, unrounded vowel
o	low, back, rounded vowel
u	high, back, rounded vowel

Since a scholarly consensus regarding the significance of synharmony and disharmony in the ancient Maya script has yet to emerge at the time of this writing (V. Bricker 2004:1056; Houston, Stuart, and Robertson 2004; Lacadena and Wichmann 2004; Robertson et al. 2007), I refrain from imposing any particular proposal on transliterations of hieroglyphic texts contained herein. Furthermore, tone is not usually marked in Classical Yucatecan alphabetic texts and is therefore not represented in transcriptions of these texts either. Neither are vowel length and the glottal stop usually represented in Classical Yucatecan alphabetic texts; when a vowel is represented by two letters (*aa*, for example), this may represent either V'V or a long vowel. Consonants f, d, g, and ñ occur in Spanish loans. Line divisions in the original manuscripts are marked by a slash mark (/). Transcriptions in this study utilize /y̧/ to represent the abbreviation of the Yucatec conjunction *yetel* 'and' that occurs frequently in the colonial documents.

The names of Guatemalan Maya ethnic and language groups in this text follow the orthography approved by the Academia de las Lenguas Mayas de Guatemala.

NOTES

1. Page number citations for the Book of Chilam Balam of Chumayel manuscript follow Gordon (1993 [1913]).

2. Restall (1997:chapter 21) refers to the Books of Chilam Balam as a "quasi-notarial genre," meaning the language of the Books of Chilam Balam shares similarities with notarial genres such as titles and land records. This is certainly correct in the case of a few sections of the Books of Chilam Balam (like those cited in Restall 1998:chapter 7). However, given the wide diversity of materials actually contained in the Books of Chilam Balam, many with obviously closer links to other genres such as Christian doctrinal literature (e.g., see Knowlton 2008), it is clear Restall's original and insightful analysis provides an important, but only partial, perspective of the genres that are part of these manuscripts.

3. Edmonson's translation (1986) has been criticized on a number of counts (Hanks 1988).

CHAPTER TWO

Aspects of Ancient Maya Intellectual Culture

As with traditions of knowledge everywhere, the creation myths written in the Book of Chilam Balam of Chumayel were composed in dialogue with the voices past and present, even (or especially) with those voices that conquistadors and missionaries attempted to appropriate or suppress. In this chapter I provide a brief orientation to some aspects of ancient Maya civilization, with special reference to what is documented in pre-Hispanic hieroglyphic texts regarding Maya intellectual culture that served as discursive resources at various stages in the dialogical emergence of Classical Yucatecan Maya creation myths.

ANCIENT MAYA SOCIETIES

The area in which ancient Maya societies emerged encompasses territory in what is today southern Mexico, Belize, Guatemala, El Salvador, and western parts of Honduras. This ecologically diverse region consists of Pacific coastal plains, volcanic highlands, and tropical lowlands. Yucatecan-speaking Maya peoples have long occupied the relatively flat and dry northern subdivision of the lowlands. Surrounded by Caribbean seacoasts, the karstic landscape of the Yucatán peninsula is characterized by shallow topsoil, with the principal sources of surface water being large natural wells called cenotes (Yucatec: *dzonot*), near which human settlements are frequently located.

Archaeological and epigraphic evidence establish that by AD 250–300 (the beginning of the Classic period), Maya peoples were organized in numerous independent city-states sharing certain aspects of elite culture. Individual states were ruled by hereditary kings (*ahau*), or more rarely queens (*ix ahau*) (Martin and Grube 2000:81). Textual evidence surviving on carved monuments at the remains of Classic period cities at Yaxchilan and Piedras Negras indicates the presence of a double-descent kinship system among the nobility like that later attested for colonial Yucatec Mayas (V. Bricker 2002a). Although these kings were the predominant subjects of those monumental inscriptions that survive, the Classic Maya political structure was also populated by a number of lesser officials such as the *sajal* (provincial governor) and the *ah kuhun* (possibly a royal clerk; see Jackson and Stuart 2001). Furthermore, in the shifting alliance system of ancient Maya city-states, kings could be the clients of other kings. An expression often occurring in the surviving inscriptions identifies historical personages as *y ahau* 'his (client) king' (for a detailed account of the dynasties of several individual Classic Maya city-states, see Martin and Grube 2000).

In the Late Classic period (AD 600–900), literate Maya civilization was mostly concentrated in the southern lowlands. Politically balkanized, lowland Maya city-states nonetheless shared a common hieroglyphic writing system that may have expressed a Ch'olan Maya prestige language unifying peoples speaking numerous vernaculars (Houston, Stuart, and Robertson 2000; Mora-Morín 2009). During the Late Classic period, political and ritual functions appear to have coalesced in the person of the *kuhul ahau* 'divine king.' Monuments were frequently erected commemorating rituals in which these divine kings, sometimes along with their wives or other political officials, participated with gods or as gods (Houston and Stuart 1996). The civic monuments erected by the divine kings utilized numerous calendrical systems of historical, divinatory, astronomical, and other timekeeping concerns. In one of the most elaborate calendrical commensurations in world history, these were combined into a single "Initial Series" calendar. The space devoted to this Initial Series commensuration makes up a large portion of a given text on numerous ancient monuments. Given the great amount of space and intellectual labor involved, the motivation behind the Initial Series calendar was much more profound than those of us in the contemporary West attribute to timekeeping today.

In ancient Maya civilization, belief in calendrical divination meant that proper timekeeping was essential not only to tracking astronomical and seasonal phenomena but to the very success of all those human activities, episodic or quotidian, necessary for subsistence, material production, and social reproduction.

For multiple reasons whose relative importance is still debated among scholars, the traditional polities of the Maya lowlands unraveled during the Classic to Postclassic transition (AD 750–1050) (Demarest, P. Rice, and D. Rice 2004). The concentration of lowland Maya population and its civilization shifted from the southern to the northern lowlands, a transition completed during the Late Postclassic period (AD 1200–ca. 1540). First the Terminal Classic city of Chichén Itzá (A. Andrews, E. Andrews, and Castellanos 2003; Kowalski and Kristan-Graham 2007), followed by its successor Mayapán (Milbrath and Peraza Lope 2003; Aveni, Milbrath, and Peraza Lope 2004), emerged as important centers serving within Yucatán as core zones of the Postclassic Mesoamerican "world system" of economic and cultural interaction (Smith and Berdan 2003). Such regional polities continued to dominate Yucatán until the end of Mayapán's power around 1440 (Kepecs and Masson 2003). Hieroglyphic evidence suggests the *kuhul ahau* title, although present at some sites such as Ek Balam, was eventually reduced to simply *ahau*, and instances of persons with the *sajal* title abound in the texts from the northern lowlands (Grube, Lacadena, and Martin 2003; Grube and Krochock 2007). Colonial period alphabetic documents purportedly relating events of the Postclassic period continue to refer to prominent leaders simply as *ahau* 'king'; the *halach uinic*, literally the 'true man' or regional ruler; and the *ah tepal* 'sovereign,' this last term ultimately of Nahua origin (Justeson et al. 1985).

Geopolitical decentralization appears to have been the rule from the end of the Mayapán league until the establishment of the city of Merida by the Spaniards in 1542, a period one scholar has referred to as the "Segmented Century" (Restall 2001:338). Until recent years, the understanding of the political organization of the lowland Maya on the eve of the Spanish invasion held to pioneering ethnohistorian Ralph Roys's (1957) model of a peninsula divided into sixteen geographically bounded provinces. However, more recent research by several scholars (Quezada 1993; Okoshi 1995; Restall 1997) has radically revised this model. The fundamental unit of Yucatec Maya society in the Late Postclassic and Colonial periods was the *cah* 'town' (Restall 1997), with the members of a dozen *chibalob*, or patronym groups, such as the Canul, Cocom, and Xiu holding the most offices of *batab* 'governor' in various towns during the sixteenth century (Restall 2001). Maya nobles, or *almehen* (literally meaning 'children of women, children of men' in reference to the double-descent kinship system), continued to promote both their status and territorial boundaries within the Spanish colonial system through the composition and maintenance of primordial titles (community or dynastic histories with mythological overtones) and related accounts (Restall 1998). Therefore, the extent to which an indigenous writer of Classical Yucatecan Maya emphasized patronym group, region, class, or ethnic identity in their compositions varies considerably and needs to be taken into account before assuming a homogenized Maya voice for any given composition, including creation myths.[1]

Numerous changes in Maya intellectual institutions and culture occurred during and after the Classic-Postclassic transition. In contrast to the previous predominance of combined political-religious offices in monumental texts, specifically religio-intellectual offices of the *ah kin* 'divinatory priest' and the *matz idzat* 'educated sage' also appear (Grube 1994). The discrete historical and divinatory calendar systems—the *katun* and *tzolkin*, respectively—were now used more frequently as independent timekeeping mechanisms, and the unified Initial Series calendar gradually fell into disuse (Grube, Lacadena, and Martin 2003). Also at this time, the Yucatecan Maya vernacular began to be recorded in hieroglyphic texts in addition to the Ch'olan prestige language (Lacadena 1997; Vail 2000a; Wald 2004). The extant versions of priestly divinatory manuals and astronomical tables, written on barkpaper in Maya hieroglyphs, were composed during this period, although part of their content was drawn from Classic period precursors (H. Bricker and V. Bricker 2007). Extant Postclassic Maya and Mexican codices show evidence of exchange across ethnic and linguistic divisions, marking participation in a shared intellectual culture during this period (Boone 2003; Vail and Aveni 2004).

DOCUMENTS OF PRE-HISPANIC MAYA COSMOGONIES

The breakthroughs by scholars in the decipherment of hieroglyphic writing over the last several decades have opened new windows onto pre-Hispanic Maya cosmology (H. Bricker and V. Bricker 1992; Schele 1992; Looper 1995), theology (Lounsbury 1985; Ringle 1988; Taube 1992; Grube and Nahm 1994; Houston and Stuart 1996; Vail 2000b), and ontology (Houston and Stuart 1989, 1998; Houston, Stuart, and Taube 2006). Specialists in ancient Maya writing, most notably the late Linda Schele (Schele 1992; Freidel, Schele, and Parker 1993), have attempted to identify episodes of pre-Hispanic Maya creation mythology. Extant hieroglyphic texts, however, are often frustratingly terse. Despite this, interpretations of pre-Hispanic hieroglyphic texts are particularly relevant for establishing the themes and categories that may have been involved in the dialogic emergence of colonial Maya creation myths.

For the ancient Maya, there had been several creations prior to the one in which we live, with the genesis of the present creation occurring on the calendar round date 4 Ahau 8 Cumku, or August 11, 3114 BC, in the Gregorian calendar (a discussion of the ancient Maya system of calendars follows). According to the analyses of terse hieroglyphic texts by Schele and others (Freidel, Schele, and Parker 1993:61–75), several events occurred on this 4 Ahau creation date. Two pre-Hispanic Maya constellations, the First Hearth and the Turtle (each of which consists of sets of three stars in the Western constellation of Orion) appeared in the heavens. A pair of canoeing deities known to scholars as the Paddler Gods established three stone thrones, which are bound by the creator god Itzamna at the First Three Stone Place. As hearths in traditional Mesoamerican domiciles consist of three stones, this First Three Stone Place may be synonymous with the First Hearth constellation. Also, some Late Classic ceramics illustrating the chthonic merchant God L presiding over his court relate that seven (or more) deities were "placed in order" at the mythological location Black-Is-Its-Center (Kerr no. 2796; Coe 1973:109; see also Miller and Martin 2004:58–62) on that date. In the Postclassic Dresden Codex we are told that a "human being" (*ah uinic*) was also "formed" (*patah*) on this date (Schele and Grube 1997:139). Many other important mythological events that occur shortly before or after the 4 Ahau creation date include the beheading of the Starry Deer Crocodile and the *c̈hab* 'engendering' or 'genesis' (see the following discussion) of the gods known as the Palenque Triad.[2]

This compilation is not meant to be exhaustive, as new discoveries will undoubtedly continue to add new texts and iconography to help flesh out our understanding of ancient Maya cosmogony. What this list of mythological references does provide is a datum of epigraphic sources of motifs and characters explicitly documented in pre-Hispanic texts that may or may not have parallels in the mythologies of later periods. Certainly "symbolic" applications of ethnographic analogy not complemented by a critical ethnohistorical methodology can be problematic as scholars attempt to reconstruct and interpret aspects of ancient Maya religion (see Behrens et al. 2004, for a recent attempt to address this problem). What is intended here is that, from the reference point of terse texts alluding to a larger body of cultural knowledge about creation events, we may better recognize the dialogical processes also involved in the emergence of Classical Yucatecan Maya cosmogonies.

ANCIENT MAYA METAPHYSICS: CORRELATIVE MONISM

To this brief list of themes documented in explicit "creation texts," I wish to add the total corpus of Maya texts demonstrating the presence of two different, if complementary, metaphysical orientations in pre-Hispanic Maya civilization. I conceive of these metaphysical orientations not as archetypal structures for praxis so much as discourses that, while facilitating sociocultural reproduction and transformation, are themselves specialized knowledge systems whose composition and existence are subject to both a historical chain of transmission and imaginative innovations.

By the Late Classic period, ancient Maya civilization had developed one of the richest humanistic traditions in the world. Its logosyllabic writing system communicated the sound and meaning of human speech in beautiful calligraphy. Its painters and sculptors signed their subtle and elaborate carvings, murals, and painted vases by name. Its historians chronicled changing political fortunes of their city-states and traced royal genealogies back to the dawn of the present era. Its astronomers tracked and mathematically predicted the movements of the heavenly bodies and correlated them with the seasonal phenomena into tables, calculating recurring celestial cycles from time immemorial far into the future.

This flurry of cultural activity was certainly not without cause or reason. So much of what was accomplished was explicitly under the patronage of the divine kings. But one would go too far to argue that all these accomplishments were simply the results of a campaign of royal propaganda to buttress their authority ideologically. Again, that would reduce all of Maya civilization to simply an ideological apparatus of state, an argument that fails to account for the sustained cultural activity that survived the demise of those states during the calamities of the Classic collapse as well as the Spanish Conquest centuries later. Instead, it appears that something just as fundamental to the human experience as the vanity of the powerful is required to make sense of these phenomena. Regardless of the patrons who attempted to direct or control these cultural activities, I argue that one motivation was the pan-human need to make meaning from experience. I will refer from here on to a particular mode of meaning-making activities by people in response to phenomena as a philosophy. Elements within ancient Maya philosophy that express theories of nonempirical causation resulting in an empirical effect I refer to as a metaphysics.[3]

The textual evidence of the pre-Hispanic period suggests *at least* two philosophical orientations and respective metaphysics existed prior to the arrival of the Spanish. In their own way, each orientation deals with the duality of social thought and action that anthropologists have recognized as a concern of peoples across the globe (Maybury-Lewis and Almagor 1989). In the first orientation, familiar to scholars who understand the Maya system of calendars, mathematics is employed to interpret all phenomena as interconnected at a single fundamental plane. This single fundamental plane is time. From movement in the heavens, meteorological events, treatment of illness, political fortunes, down to the quotidian activities of weaving, fishing, and carving, all had their effect within this single system. The correlation of celestial and terrestrial events according to divinatory calendars was the method by which persons in ancient Maya society acquired the knowledge necessary to better harmonize human activity with the temporal rhythm of the cosmos to effect greater success. It is reasonable to conclude this orientation from the commensuration of the great many calendars that compose the Initial Series, the calendrical apparatus that dominates the text of a large portion of ancient Maya monuments. A related metaphysics of the relationship between cosmos and human action also underlies the operations of the tables and divinatory almanacs in the surviving pre-Hispanic Maya books. I refer to this aspect of ancient Maya metaphysics as correlative monism.

To understand how this philosophy of correlative monism is discernable from the hieroglyphic record, it is essential to understand the peculiar way in which the Classic Maya innovated upon ancient pan-Mesoamerican practices. Ancient Maya almanacs record numerous kinds of prognostications and historical occurrences in terms of the 260-day divinatory calendar. This divinatory calendar, called the *tzolkin* by scholars of the ancient Maya, was composed of thirteen numbers paired with twenty day names. These divinatory calendar dates were frequently paired with corresponding dates in the Mesoamerican 365-day vague year, which Yucatec Mayas still refer to as the *haab*. The *haab* was composed of eighteen months of twenty days, with a final nineteenth month of five days preceding the new year. Any single combination of divinatory (*tzolkin*) date and vague year (*haab*) date occurred only once in a 52-year period. This system of temporal reference, called the Calendar Round by Mesoamerican scholars, was used from the Valley of Mexico to the highlands of Guatemala in pre-Hispanic times (Edmonson 1992).

In addition to the Calendar Round system, the Maya used yet another calendar, called the "Long Count" by scholars. A Maya Long Count date is typically composed of five elements. The smallest unit is the *kin* or 'day'; twenty *kins* equal one *uinal*. In pre-Hispanic hieroglyphic texts the 20-day-period *uinal* is actually pronounced *uinic*, the word for 'human being.' This probably reflects the practice of counting the body's twenty digits (fingers and toes) in addition to a symbolic association between divinatory days (*kin*) or time (*kinil*) and its influence on the *uinic* or human person (Aveni 2002). Eighteen such *uinals* compose the fundamental Long Count unit of 360 days known as a *tun*. Again the calendrical term has broader symbolic associations, *tun* referring to both the period of time and the commemorative stones that were erected at the completion of these larger calendrical cycles.

The Maya continued the count with twenty 360-day *tun* composing one 7,200-day *katun*. The *katun* was a frequent historical marker in the Classic period and the principal unit of historical reckoning in the Postclassic and Colonial periods, especially in the *kahlay* 'histories' contained in the Books of Chilam Balam. Every *tun*-derived date corresponds to an *Ahau* 'King' day in the 260-day divinatory calendar. The Maya practice of identifying a *katun* by its place as one of thirteen possible *Ahau* dates (referred to by scholars as the "Short Count") provided a mechanism for enlarging divination to the historical scope; that is, for prophecy. In the Classic period at least, twenty *katuns* composed the largest calendrical unit in common use, the 144,000-day *baktun*. Each complete *baktun* cycle is composed of thirteen *baktuns*, or a total of 1,872,000 days. Mesoamericanists represent Maya Long Count dates in positional notation from left to right, beginning with the number of the *baktuns* and ending with the number of *kins*, with the number of each unit separated by a period. For example, the beginning of the present calendrical cycle was on 13.0.0.0.0. Although the *baktun* cycle of the Long Count is ultimately cyclical like all Mesoamerican calendar systems, the length of the cycle is so great that, for all practical purposes, it functions as a linear system for reckoning historical time. For example, the present cycle, which began on 13.0.0.0.0 4 Ahau 8 Cumku, or August 11, 3114 BC, in terms of our Gregorian calendar, has yet to expire at the time of this writing.

But for the purposes of the Classic Maya, it seems the historical precision of the Long Count and the explanatory power of the divinatory cycle were still insufficient. A great number of Classic period monuments contain a vast correlation of Long Count, Calendar Round, and numerous other calendrical systems into what scholars call the "Initial Series" because of its typical position at the beginning of monumental texts. Several of the systems forming the "Supplementary Series" to the Initial Series are poorly understood, although moon ages, a lunar synodic calendar, and a series of tutelary deities are among them (Morley 1916; Linden 1986, 1996).

The Classic Maya calendrical apparatus is so vast that not only was it the subject of the lion's share of pioneering work in Maya hieroglyphic studies but prior to Proskouriakoff's (1960) breakthrough, Maya texts were thought to be composed almost exclusively of the calculations of peaceful calendar priests for esoteric ritual matters (Coe 1999). Of course, this myopic view of Maya society was shattered by the discovery of ancient Maya political history accessible in the wake of the syllabic decipherment of the writing system (Knorosov 1958). Nonetheless, the implications of the tremendous intellectual effort required for the maintenance and transmission of the calendars and their concomitant social institutions, as evidenced in texts of surviving stela and the almanacs and tables of the codices, are in keeping with a strong philosophy of correlative monism. Given the available evidence, it would be difficult to overstate the significance the cultural imperative to correlate various temporal, celestial, biological, and sociohistorical phenomena all within the explanatory system of the count of days had for the ancient Maya. As Barbara Tedlock (1992:196) notes regarding the possible implications of contemporary K'iche' Maya calendrical ritual for interpreting ancient Maya practice, "It appears that Mayan peoples used differing systems of timekeeping in the separate provinces of their biological, astronomical, psychological, religious, and social realities, and that at some point in the past, these various systems underwent a process of totalization within the overlapping, intermeshing cycles of their calendars."

ANCIENT MAYA METAPHYSICS: COMPLEMENTARY DUALISM

The second philosophy, although familiar to scholars of Nahuatl (Aztec) literature (León-Portilla 1963), has only recently received attention from specialists in the pre-Hispanic Maya literature. This apparently widespread philosophical orientation perceives phenomena as composed of dualities: day and night, sky and earth, cloud and rain, female and male. Other phenomena are the effects of these fundamental pairings. This metaphysics corresponds to a widespread and enduring Mesoamerican literary device, the couplet metaphor or diphrastic kenning (León-Portilla 1963; Knowlton 2002; Hull 2003).[4] As we will see, the efficacy of some ritual activity among ancient Maya royalty is related in terms of one such dualism: *ch̄ab akab* 'genesis and darkness.'

The Maya philosophies of correlative monism and complementary dualism are not mutually exclusive, but as we shall see they are two different modes with their own unique historical transformations in the Colonial period. But first, since the idea of complementary dualism as a philosophic mode is relatively undeveloped in Mayanist scholarship, a detailed discussion of this mode (and the ancient Maya concept of "genesis and darkness" in particular) is needed.

The ancient Maya were part of a pan-Mesoamerican intellectual milieu in which statements concerning the fundamental nature of reality are expressed in the form of poetic metaphor (León-Portilla 1963). At least as early as the Classic period in the Maya lowlands (and perhaps in Central Mexico as well), philosophically salient concepts were expressed in what scholars of Aztec literature have referred to as diphrastic kennings: couplet metaphors (or, more precisely, metonyms) expressing poetically a third referent (Garibay K. 1953–1954, 1:19; see also Maxwell and Hanson 1992). In simplest terms, diphrastic kennings are couplets that equal more than the sum of their parts. In Maya hieroglyphic texts, for example, the couplet "flint and shield" refers not only to the physical objects themselves but also to the more amorphous concept of military efficacy; "mat and throne" refers to political authority, and "land and well" is the expression for an inhabited territory. Constructed in the same fashion, there is also a wealth of diphrastic kennings relating the count of time as celestial, meteorological, and gendered complementary oppositions (Knowlton 2002:13). Although these kinds of tropes would later compose the repertoire of the *tlamatinime*, or Aztec poet-philosophers of Central Mexico, their earliest documented usage occurs in lowland Maya hieroglyphic texts from the Classic period (Knowlton 2002).

Compared to the voluminous metaphysical musings attributed to individual poet-philosophers recorded in colonial Nahuatl documents (León-Portilla 1992), the available hieroglyphic evidence for the Classic Maya is admittedly slim. The barkpaper books on which such poems or treatises might once have been recorded have long since decayed in the tropical forest; often all that remains are those tropes inscribed on surviving stone monuments (or, more rarely, painted on ceramics) as part of an otherwise mundane text recording the dedication date of a house or name-tagging a family heirloom. Nonetheless, much can still be discerned from the terse contexts in which diphrastic kennings survive. Late Classic Maya rulers, as *kuhul ahauob* or 'divine kings,' regularly performed and had recorded their ritual, political, and sometimes economic activities. Although the extant textual evidences are few, it is in the manner these ancient texts attribute efficacy to those actions and interactions they described (whether ritual, political, and economic) that we can elicit something of the ancient Mayas' own understandings of the fundamental processes underlying reality. And it is through the contextual usage of the diphrastic kenning *ch̄ab akab* 'genesis and darkness' in these public discourses that we can take steps toward an emic understanding of ancient Maya metaphysics.

Epigraphers routinely refer to Maya hieroglyphs by their "T" numbers, in reference to J. Eric S. Thompson's *Catalog* (1962). In hieroglyphic texts, the diphrastic kenning *ch̄ab akab* is composed of the T712 glyph reading

2.1. "Genesis and Darkness": The *c̆hab akabil* diphrastic kenning. Copan Stela 7 Back, A10 (photograph by author).

c̆hab and the T504 glyph reading *akab* (Figure 2.1).[5] Like other diphrastic kennings, their couplet format is discerned by the instances in which the glyphs are separated by pronouns and/or prepositions. However, in Classic texts there are many instances of the T504 *akab* sign infixed into the T712 *c̆hab* glyph (Thompson 1962:303), a stylistic option of the ancient scribe that makes the glyphs' couplet format less obvious to modern observers. The potential ambiguity of this condensed variant, however, is clarified by the fact T504 almost always carries the suffix *-il* when paired in the couplet, deriving from "night" the word *akabil* 'darkness.'

Although the T712-T504 couplet has been glossed in the scholarly literature as 'to let blood' (Schele and Freidel 1991:190), this is at least imprecise when it is not inaccurate. *Čhab* alone is attested to in a number of Mayan languages as meaning "to fast" (Kaufman and Norman 1984:118), but both the variety and kind of contexts in which the complete diphrase appears suggest something more or other than fasting is meant. In Classical Yucatecan, the Motul Dictionary translates *čhab* as both 'to create' and 'to do penance,' with its early colonial compiler noting that the latter definition "es vocablo antiguo" (Ciudad Real 2001:207). I understand *čhab* to indeed refer to the pre-Hispanic Maya form of penitence, which included bleeding the body from, among other places, the genitals (Landa 1978 [ca. 1566]:47). Although the iconic referent of the T712 glyph was long ago suggested to be an obsidian lancet (Proskouriakoff 1973:172), some scholars have noted that its flaccid shape is more suggestive of male genitalia than any stone implement (Stross and Kerr 1990:352). Furthermore, the T712 glyph is also an element of the not yet fully understood "child of parent" phrases (Schele 1998:41), again suggesting some association with biological reproduction in contrast to any sort of creation ex nihilo. Although there is no equivalent English word encompassing all of these associations (penitence, genital bloodletting, and sexual creation), for our purposes I choose to translate Classic Maya *čhab* as 'genesis,' in my estimation the most nuanced term available in English.[6]

The iconographic referent of T504 *akab* is most likely, in my evaluation, a stylized representation of the inside of the human mouth. This is a visual play on the term *ak* 'tongue,' which Victoria Bricker (1986:74) originally suspected the glyph to mean. Bricker (1986:73) also noted the couplet format of T712 and T504 in her work on hieroglyphic grammar, as well as the fact that T712 [T504] occurs iconically in plates containing autosacrificial blood offerings depicted on monuments from Yaxchilan (Figure 2.2). Also, well-known monuments such as Yaxchilan Lintel 17 (Graham 1977) depict bloodletting as gender-marked activity, with royal males engaging in genital bloodletting while royal females let blood from the tongue, *ak*. This division may suggest that the iconic referents of both T712 and T504 glyphs are likewise gendered, with a complementary dualism of "male" and "female" as underlying the visual expression of the *čhab akab* kenning. This gendered construction might also play upon a homophony documented in Classical Yucatecan, for dictionaries translate *ak* not only as 'lengua' or 'tongue' but also as 'la crica de la mujer' (Ciudad Real 2001:60) or 'clitoris' (Barrera Vásquez et al. 1995:7). This pattern of pairing complementary dualisms to construct diphrastic kennings is consistent with those examples previously identified for the Classic period (Knowlton 2002).

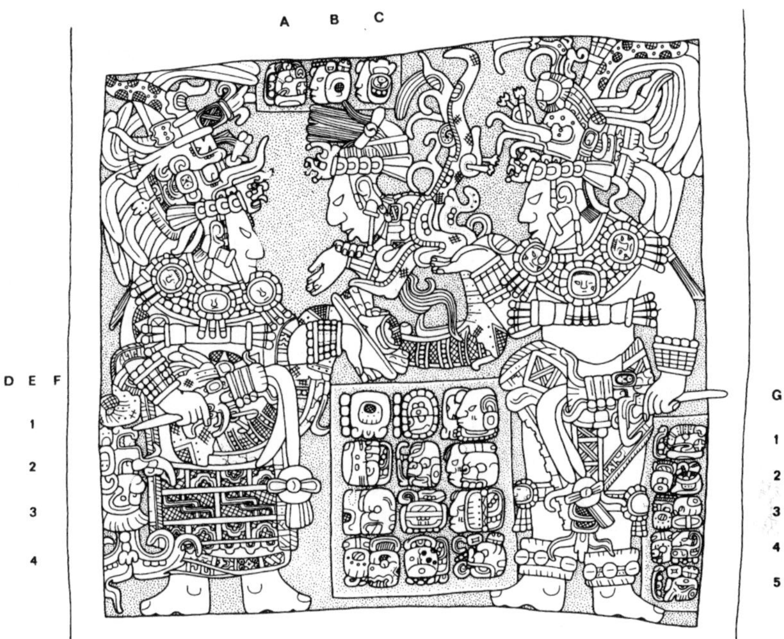

2.2. Offering plate marked with T712 [T504] glyphs reading *c̄hab [akab]*. Yaxchilan lintel 14 (drawing by Ian Graham).

Furthermore, scholars have argued along quite different lines of evidence than those presented here that the Classic Maya expressed gender in terms of complementary, rather than hierarchical, dualism (Joyce 1996).[7]

METAPHYSICS OF RITUAL POWER

Having explored the possible iconic roots of T712-T504 as a gendered complementary duality, we now examine its discursive contexts. As recorded on wooden Lintel 3 from the royal funerary Temple I at Tikal, on August 6, AD 695 (9.13.3.7.18, 11 Edznab 11 C̄hen in the Classic Maya calendar system), Jasau Chan Kauil I of Tikal defeated Yic̄haac Kak, king of the region's dominant polity Calakmul (see "Note on Orthography" in the Introduction for the conventions applied throughout this work). This event marked a turning point in Classic Maya history, a victory that ushered in the revitalization of Tikal as a preeminent polity in lowland Maya politics (Martin and Grube 2000:44). Two *uinals* (twenty-day months) later on September 15 of that same year in the Gregorian calendar (9.13.3.9.18, 12 Edznab 11 Sac), as part of his triumph, the king Jasau Chan Kauil "conjures divinity by his genesis, by his darkness" (*u tzac kuh tu chab ti y akabil*) as part of this celebration.[8]

That the T712 [T504] glyphic compound represents the *chab akab* diphrastic kenning both textually and iconically and is not necessarily only associated with bloodletting or accouterments like obsidian lancets is supported by references to Classic period fire-drilling events. An unprovenanced lintel (Mayer 1995:plates 264–265, A2–B4) depicts a T712 [T504] iconic "offering" being presented while *jochoj kak u cahiy yax hun uinic kuhul ajau [Yaxchilan]* 'fire is drilled under the auspices of Yax Hun Uinic, the holy lord of Yaxchilan.' The text of a looted panel currently at the Museo Municipal in Emiliano Zapata, Tabasco (Mayer 1995: plate 249–250), reads **OCH-chi K'AK' tu CH'AB ti AK'AB**, *ochi kak t u chab ti akab* "fire entered in his genesis, in darkness." Dedication rituals involving fire or incense often appear in Classic Maya texts (Stuart 1998), and this passage may refer to a fire-drilling ceremony by Ah Kuna Kak Chaac prior to his arrival at the tomb of Chac Bolon Chaac, king of Tonina (Martin and Grube 2000:179). *U chab y akabil* likewise occurs in another ritual text, Kuna-Lacanja Lintel 1 (D6), accompanying an illustration of what is probably an incense-burning ritual utilizing the object known to iconographers as the Double-Headed Serpent Bar. From these examples it is clear that *chab akab* can be related, both iconically and textually (in a prepositional phrase), to events involving *tzac* 'conjuring' and *joch* 'ritual fire-drilling.' Therefore, whatever its iconic roots, the *chab akab* diphrastic kenning must refer to a more broadly applicable range of ritual performance and not just to sacrificial bloodletting.

In addition to these ritual references, a large number of *chab akab* references appear to refer to both captive sacrifice and autosacrificial bloodletting. The text of Tikal Column Altar 1 frankly captions the depiction of a bound captive as **U B'AH U? CH'AB [AK'AB]**, *u bah u chab akab* 'his self [as] the genesis, the night' (A3–A4). Houston and Stuart (1998) argue that *u bah* is a reflexive statement meaning "his self." This argument assumes that the syntax of clauses utilizing this reflexive noun is like those denoting ownership of an object (Matthews 1979; Houston, Stuart, and Taube 1989). The reflexive use of *bah* in "name-tagging" an object is illustrated, for example, by the text incised on a carved bone recovered from a burial in Temple 23 at Yaxchilan (Martin and Grube 2000:126). However, in addition to those contexts in which it serves as a reflexive noun, the T757 *bah* glyph may appear taking verbal suffixes in the clause initial position (V. Bricker 1986:138). The T757 sign may have more than one meaning or be polyphonic. Future research by epigraphers may resolve these ambiguities.

A good example of a more lengthy text witnessing the relationship between *chab akab* and captive sacrifice is Yaxchilan Stela 18 (Tate

1992:246). Following the capture (*chucaj*) by King Itzamnaaj Balam II of Ah Pol Chay Ah Payal Mo'ol, the latter is henceforth (A9) referred to as *u bac* (his captive), A10–13 states: *tu ch̄ab ti y akabil ch̄ahom-Ø* '[Itzamnaaj B'alam] is a scatterer in his genesis, in his darkness.' Given that captives are at times referred to as *ch̄ab akab*, it appears that the king of Yaxchilan becomes a *ch̄ahom* 'scatterer' (of liquid; presumably blood) by means of his newly acquired captive and not by autosacrifice. Ritual activities involving autosacrifice on the part of the actor may be marked by statements of *u bah u ch̄ab y akab* 'himself, his genesis, his darkness.' In fact, a number of T714 *tzac* 'conjuring' events occurring with *u bah u ch̄ab y akabil* are documented epigraphically at Copan (see Thompson 1962:302–304).

The examples cited thus far demonstrate that ritual events such as fire-drilling and conjuring occur *tu ch̄ab ti y akabil* 'in his genesis, in his darkness.' This prepositional phrase indicates that "genesis and darkness" is the affective medium of ritual action. Furthermore, contextually, *ch̄ab akab* may refer to a captive, a royal personage during the act of autosacrifice, or the medium by which a royal personage becomes a sacrificer (i.e., by a newly acquired captive). In these particular instances, it is the sacrificial products of the human body, one's own or by proxy, through which ritual is efficacious. But we have seen as well that rituals not necessarily involving blood sacrifice, such as fire-drilling, are also accomplished "in the genesis, in the darkness."

LANGUAGE OF GIFT AND SACRIFICE

Another discursive realm in which *ch̄ab akab* appears is that of political economy, in reference to gift exchange and tribute between Classic Maya elites. Anthropologists have long recognized the relationship between gift and sacrifice. In the anthropological classic *The Gift: The Form and Reason for Exchange in Archaic Societies* (1990 [1925]), Marcel Mauss established the logical and historical relationship among sacrifice, contract, and exchange. Mauss (1990 [1925]:16) observes that "one of the first groups of beings with which men had to enter into contract, and who, by definition, were there to make a contract with them, were above all the spirits of the dead and of the gods." Mauss (1990 [1925]:15) recognized that such exchanges often occurred among ritual specialists who were the "masked incarnations" of these spirits. Mauss (1990 [1925]:74) goes on to argue that, like sacrifice, gift exchange establishes reciprocal yet hierarchical relationships between "chiefs and vassals," just as sacrifice does between gods and worshipers.

Mauss's early observations are still productive for Mayanists today for interpreting Classic society. Judging from Late Classic Maya texts and art, the *kuhul ahauob* 'divine kings' of Maya polities did in fact take on the identities of gods through masking during ritual (Houston and Stuart 1996). Further, Mauss's theory of sacrifice, contract, and exchange has informed approaches to Mesoamerican religions emphasizing "covenants" between people and supernatural forces (Monahan 2000). An enduring contribution of *The Gift* is how Mauss's concept of archaic exchange as "total prestations" crosscut modern Western definitions of the economic, religious, and political, providing an explanation for how social relationships are forged and maintained. Perhaps unsurprisingly then, there is evidence that the ancient Maya used *ch̄ab akab*, the diphrastic kenning for the affective element of ritual (i.e., sacrifice), to describe exchange that cemented the reciprocal yet hierarchical relationships among Maya elites in addition to the ritual interactions between people and supernaturals discussed earlier.

One illuminating example is the text and image on the unprovenanced codex-style ceramic Kerr 4113 (Figure 2.3). This vessel relates the "arrival" (A1: **HUL-li-ja**, *hulij*) of a subordinate lord *y ahau* from an otherwise unknown "Star" or "Venus" polity *Ek* (A2). He is further described as *u sajal* 'his subordinate noble,' apparently of the lord seated in authority to the right. This *sajal* is shown presenting his patron with *u bah u ch̄ab y akabil* 'itself, his genesis, his darkness' (C2–C4). Rather than the sacrificial exchange via penitential blood sacrifice, the caption refers to the exchange of a large face-shaped olla, the contents of which are not recorded.

Being cognizant that royal gift exchange or tribute can be referred to as *ch̄ab akab* allows for the reevaluation of familiar, if less understood, texts. One instance is the captions of the Tablets of the Scribe and Orator from Palenque. As Stephen Houston and David Stuart (1998:88) observed, these captions employ the rare second person *a-* pronoun as direct speech by the sculpted figures who are "addressing someone on the throne or the stairway on which it rests . . . the perforated clothing and submissive gestures underscore their subordinate states." The captions accompanying both images refer to *a ch̄ab akabil* 'your genesis [and] darkness' (Tablet of the Orator B1; Tablet of the Scribe C1). The Orator caption makes reference to the king of Palenque, Kinich Acal Mo' Naab III (r. AD 721–736), and the figures on the tablets have been identified from the adjacent text (Orator E5–6) as perhaps two views of the same person, a *sajal* of the Piedras Negras king Yo'nal Ac (Martin and Grube 2000:146, 172). The quote from the "Scribe" flanking the opposite side of the staircase seems to refer to a "presentation," perhaps of a "gift" (although admittedly the use of **si** here might simply be for its syllabic value), referred to as the Palenque king's "genesis and darkness": **ILA-hi a-ba ma-ta-wi-AJAW u si-?-na a-CH'AB AK'AB-li**,

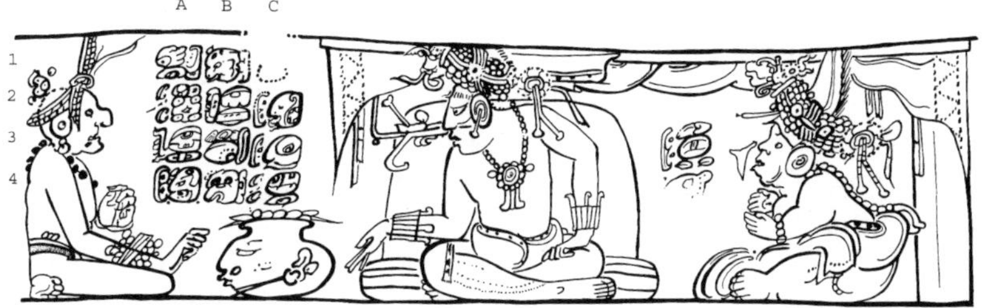

2.3. Elite gift described as *u bah u chab y akabil.* K4113 (drawing by Markus Eberl).

ila-h-i a-ba(h) Mataui(l) Ajau, u si-(?)-na a-chab akabil; '[it] was witnessed [by] yourself, Matauil Lord, his gift(?) your genesis and darkness.'

There are several reasons to believe the best interpretation of *chab akab* in these texts is that it refers to tribute rather than simply the Piedras Negras *sajal* himself. First of all, grammatically one would expect the first-person absolutive pronoun *-en* to suffix the phrase *a chab akab* if the speaker (i.e., the captive *sajal*) was referring to himself. Furthermore, it is known that the Palenque military commander Chac Suudz waged a successful campaign in the Piedras Negras region in AD 725, providing the occasion for the presentation of tribute by the defeated polity. Another panel at Palenque, dated AD 731, depicts Acal Mo' Naab III and others handling a large tribute bundle, tribute apparently occupying an important place in this Palenque king's sculptural program (Martin and Grube 2000:172–173). Perhaps most importantly, the two panels are located flanking a stairway leading up to a throne, the place we know from numerous sources where tribute was presented at a Maya court (Stuart 1998:410–414).

GENESIS AND DARKNESS IN THEOGONY

The above examples demonstrate that the diphrastic kenning "genesis and darkness" is part of the ancient Maya vocabulary of metaphysical efficacy. I approximate the Maya conceptual domain of *chab akab* as that of the "generative gift"; I include the adjective "generative" because this takes into account the meaning of *chab* as "to engender" and the gender complementarity of the iconic elements composing the diphrastic kenning. Furthermore, in Classic Maya texts, the generative power of ritual is not restricted to historical actors but features in the birth of the deities themselves in the theogony of the present creation. Both the Temple of the Cross Tablet (Robertson 1991; C16–D16, E3–F3) and the South Panel of the

Platform of Temple XIX (Stuart 2005:80–81) at Palenque relate that one of the establishers of the present creation, the god GI **U B'AH U CH'AB AK'AB-li**, is *u bah u ch̄ab akabil* 'himself, the genesis, the darkness' of the Triad Progenitor, the primordial founder of the Palenque royal dynasty. GI is the same deity who is said to have dedicated the eight partitions of the sky (Temple of the Cross Tablet C10–C13) and set the heavens in motion (Temple of the Cross Tablet D15–D16). According to Palenque's Tablet of the Sun (Robertson 1991), the younger brother of GI, GIII, is likewise *u bah u ch̄ab* of the Triad Progenitor (C11–D13). Therefore, there is a sense of (re)productive power inherent in the iconic roots and contextual usage of *ch̄ab akab* that extends even to the birth of the gods of the present creation, the gods whose cosmogonic activities set in motion the world as the ancient Maya experienced it. In later chapters, we will return to usages of the verb *ch̄ab* and the diphrastic kenning *ch̄ab akab* 'genesis and darkness' where they occur in the Classical Yucatecan Maya texts of the Books of Chilam Balam, as well as in the medical incantations of manuscript known as the *Ritual of the Bacabs* (Roys 1965; Arzápalo Marín 1987).

ECHOES OF ANCIENT VOICES

It is certainly too much to argue that this brief discussion gets "into the minds" of the ancient Maya. At best I hope to have highlighted some themes in ancient Maya elite discourses discernable from those fragments surviving a millennium of decay in the tropical forest, the onslaughts of religious fanaticism, the desperation of looters, and the greed of their patrons. Although relatively terse, these texts are nonetheless invaluable, as the logosyllabic writings of the Maya are so far our most extensive documents from the pre-Hispanic Americas recording language phonetically. Several of these documents share episodes of ancient cosmogonies. Others bear tribute to two different modes of philosophical discourse in that ancient civilization, that of correlative monism and complementary dualism. The metaphors embedded in discourse help shape human beings' understanding of experience (Lakoff and Johnson 1980). In our extended discussion of *ch̄ab akab* 'genesis and darkness,' we find even a single trope could be used to express the efficacy of ritual, the substance of political economic relations, and the birth of gods.

The arrival of the Spaniards and resultant disruption of autochthonous institutions had a profound impact on the maintenance and transmission of pre-Hispanic philosophies. With the indigenous priesthood at least formally abolished (but see Chuchiak 2001), education was increasingly the occupation of Maya *maestros*, educated by Franciscan friars as well as clandestinely conversant in the ancient lore. In the aftermath of the Spanish clergy's extirpations of idolatry, much ancient Maya natural philosophy, metaphysics, and cosmogony was, literally, in ashes. Colonial documents of Maya philosophies necessarily emerged in the dialogic tension with multiple sources of European world views. Catechisms, histories, popular almanacs, and cosmological treatises all marked the dialogical frontier of colonial Yucatán. Within a century, it was not so much the historical provenance of a cultural object that most distinguished it as Maya or Spanish in origin, but rather the differing devices applied within the colonial dialogue itself. In few places is this process as pronounced as in the composition of the mythography contained in pages 42 to 63 (folios 24r–34v) of the Book of Chilam Balam of Chumayel.

NOTES

1. Restall (2004:64) rightly problemizes the issue of Maya ethnogenesis, although his assertion that the Maya during the Colonial period "did not call themselves that or any other name that indicated they saw themselves as members of a common ethnic group. Nor did Spaniards or Africans in colonial Yucatan refer to the Mayas as 'Mayas'" is phrased too strongly to be consistent with the documentary record. See Knowlton 2010.

2. See Stuart (2005:chapter 6) for a review of previous research and new proposals regarding the mythology at Palenque.

3. By employing the term *metaphysics*, I do not mean to suggest that the ancient Maya attributed ontological priority to spirit over matter. As described in this text, the Mayas' metaphysics is thoroughly non-Western.

4. For northern European texts, the term *kenning* generally refers to a metaphorical term or pair of terms substituting for a noun. In the Mesoamerican case of *difrasismo* or the diphrastic kenning, I am extending the typical usage of *kenning* to refer to these pairs of complementary metonyms that create a meaning for which there is no individual Maya noun.

5. The reading of T712 as *c̈hab* is established by the presence of the **ch'a-** phonetic complement prefix (e.g., on Caracol Stela 3, B19b) and the **-b'a** phonetic complement suffix (see Mora-Marín 2001:145–151 for a thorough discussion of proposed readings and known examples of phonetic complementation). The glyph is most likely to have been pronounced *c̈hahb*, but since at the time of this writing a scholarly consensus regarding the significance of synharmony and disharmony in the Maya script has yet to emerge (V. Bricker 2004:1056; Houston, Stuart, and Robertson 2004; Lacadena and Wichmann 2004; Robertson et al. 2007), I refrain from imposing any particular proposal on the data. The reading of T504 as *akab* is established by several lines of evidence. First, T504 takes **ya-** rather than **U-** as the third-person pronoun prefix. Second, it takes the **-b'a** phonetic complement suffix on Dresden Codex page 46, C2. Finally, T504 frequently forms a semantic couplet with T544 *kin* 'sun, day.'

6. Given one meaning of *c̄hab* as 'to create,' "genesis" might also be seen as an appropriate translation given the word's association with cosmogony in the Western tradition via the Greek translation of the Hebrew Bible, the Septuagint. However, it is crucial to understand that in actual textual contexts, the Maya *c̄hab* does not refer to creation ex nihilo (although the Christian compiler of the Motul attempted to recast the term in that manner in his dictionary). Instead, *c̄hab* refers to an act of sexual creation, with *sihsah* 'to give birth' being the female counterpart of *c̄hab*. Therefore, I prefer the English translation 'genesis' over simply 'to create' not because of any Judeo-Christian parallel but because this translation takes into account the sexual aspect of the Maya glyph's iconographic and contextual bases through the etymological relationship between the "genesis" and other English words such as "to engender," "genital," and "progenitor."

7. Interestingly, Joyce (1996) argues from archaeological and iconographic evidence that the *kuhul ahauob* 'divine kings' would adopt elements of both male and female costume when performing rituals alone, thus consolidating gender-marked ritual power in their persons.

8. The glyphic phrase on Lintel 3, C3-C5, is **u TZAK K'UH tu CH'AB ti ya-AK'AB-li ja-sa-wa CHAN-na K'AWIL**, *u tzac kuh tu c̄hab, ti y akabil Jasau Chan Kauil* 'Jasau Chan Kauil conjures deity by his genesis, by his darkness.'

CHAPTER THREE

Clandestine Compilations and the Colonial Dialogue

Pages 42 to 63 of the Classical Yucatecan Maya–language manuscript known as the Book of Chilam Balam of Chumayel is a collection of Maya creation myths dating to years following the Spanish invasion of the Americas. Although individual creation narratives and related accounts written in the Classical Yucatecan Maya language appear elsewhere in the corpus of colonial Maya documents, the Chumayel is perhaps unique in its compilation of numerous cosmogonies. This mythography (collection of myths) is composed of some texts clearly redacted from earlier written sources, with others that were perhaps recorded concurrently from oral tradition or perhaps original compositions.

The extant version of this Chumayel mythography was incorporated into a larger corpus of material that became the Book of Chilam Balam of Chumayel in 1782, when it was compiled by Juan José Hoil of the Maya town (*cah*) of Chumayel, Yucatán (Gordon 1993 [1913]:viii). It is unknown whether Hoil himself was the anonymous compiler of these cosmogonic traditions and the one who penned the introductory preface to the mythography. If Hoil was indeed the compiler, then the Chumayel mythography would be a collection of Maya creation myths compiled on the eve of the Spanish Crown's late eighteenth-century Bourbon reforms. However, there is little internal evidence in support of such a late eighteenth-century date.

Rather than the late eighteenth century, a brief look at the sociohistorical context suggests the compilation of the numerous cosmogonies into the Chumayel mythography might already have occurred by the late seventeenth century in colonial Yucatán. First of all, the preservation of cosmogonies in alphabetic form would have been necessary by that point, as confiscation or destruction of cosmogonic accounts written in Maya hieroglyphic script by Catholic clergy would have been under way for more than a century at that time. The approach treating all Maya hieroglyphic documents as necessarily "idolatrous" began with the activities of Diego de Landa and like-minded missionaries, and by 1571 the prosecution of Indian *idolatría* was placed under the jurisdiction of the Provisorato de los Indios (Greenleaf 1965). Historian John Chuchiak has uncovered ecclesiastical documentation of the seizure of hieroglyphic texts under the jurisdiction of the Provisorato in the Yucatán peninsula occurring as late as the early eighteenth century (Chuchiak 2004). One example of Colonial era seizures is the 1610 report of Fr. Pedro Gonzalez de Molina in Champoton, in which the friar states:

> We have taken from these witches [*bruxos*] a book of their antiquities written in characters that when interpreted we believe describes another creation of the world . . . and it is their bible which we are now translating with the aid of several older Indians in order to finish understanding what it contains. (AGN Inq. vol. 290, exp. 2, folio 71; Chuchiak 2004:175)

When not destroyed outright, confiscated hieroglyphic texts occasionally were employed for the ultimate purpose of converting the Maya to Christianity. The production of hieroglyphic texts appears to have been finally disrupted with suppression of the calligraphic tradition's pre-Hispanic patrons, the autochthonous priesthood, and an independent indigenous nobility (Landa 1978 [ca. 1566]:12–13). This protracted process that began in the sixteenth century culminated in 1697 with the conquest of the last independent polity on the peninsula, that of the Peten Itzá (Avendaño y Loyola 1997 [1696]; Jones 1998). In the decades just prior to that final conquest, another Franciscan, Diego López de Cogolludo, lamented in the chapter on pre-Hispanic religion from his *Historia de Yucathan* (published in 1688):

> The religious [friars] of this province, in whose care was delivered the conversion of these Indians to our Holy Catholic Faith, with the

> zeal that they had diligently advanced this, not only demolished and burned all the images that were worshiped, but also all the writings in the mode [the Indians] had by which they could record their histories [*memorias*], and all that [the friars] presumed could contain some superstition or pagan rites. For this reason, one cannot discover a single thing from these writings, but even the knowledge of these histories is lost to posterity, because as soon as all of these were discovered, they were put to the flame without taking note of the diversity of the materials. I neither agree with this judgment, nor do I reprimand them, but it seems they could have conserved the worldly histories [*historias temporales*], just as they were conserved in New Spain and in other converted provinces, without having been an impediment to the rise of Christianity. Therefore I can say only little more than that which is written in other histories of the observance of religion in the time of their paganism. [Therefore] it is not known with certainty that the preaching of the gospel had occurred to give light to the people of this America before that of we Spaniards was manifested. (Cogolludo 1867 [1688], 1:304–305; translation mine)

Cogolludo goes on to discuss the reports of how regular clergy in other areas, such as Dominican Bartolomé de las Casas, were better equipped to convert other Indian groups since they could draw parallels between pre-Hispanic and Christian beliefs. The idea that the coming of Christianity may have been prophesied prior to the coming of the Spaniards was current among the Franciscans, so much so that indigenous prophecies of the Chilam Balam are to be found not only in Maya literature but in Franciscan histories of the region, which will be discussed at greater length in the following pages.

Also, as we will see below, whoever compiled the Chumayel mythography writes with explicit concern about the continued veneration of the images of pre-Hispanic deities. John Chuchiak's examination of the idolatry trials reported in the *Relaciónes de Méritos* (Chuchiak 2002) demonstrates a decline in the prosecution of the worship of graven images, which accounted for all of the late sixteenth-century idolatry cases, to about half the idolatry cases of the seventeenth century, to only a mere 13 percent of prosecutions in the eighteenth and early nineteenth centuries. Chuchiak (2002) demonstrates that although cases of *idolatría* continued to be prosecuted throughout the Colonial period, the regional definition of idolatry expanded from the veneration of idols to include various other activities, such as drinking *balché*. Finally, the annals that immediately follow the placement of the Chumayel mythography in the manuscript provide a chronicle of events beginning in the year 1519 and concluding with the year 1692 (ms. pages 63.7–64.6). Thus, in light of sociohistorical context and its place within the manuscript itself, the most likely period for the initial compilation of the various myths into the Chumayel mythography would be the late seventeenth century, by which time the persecution of hieroglyphic documents was nearly complete, the veneration of pre-Hispanic deity images was still relatively common and widespread, and even Christian friars could lament the loss of pre-Hispanic sources about the histories, and even the origin stories, of the Maya people.

THE MYTHOGRAPHER'S PREFACE

The collection of creation myths in the Book of Chilam Balam of Chumayel, written in the Classical Yucatecan language, begins with the following preface:

Ti hach kabet u bel y ocsabal ti ol	*It is essential to believe this way*
Lay u tunil / t u patah ca yum citbil	*that our lord the Father abandoned this stone*
Lay u kamchi	*It blasphemes*
Lay / baalche	*It is a wild animal*
Licil ca tzicic vay con ah tepal uin/cob	*while we revere it here, we who are the sovereign people*
Hach paybentzil u kultabalob	*These [stones] are worshiped with much care*
Hahilob / kuob	*as true ones, as divine ones*
Laobi tunob cumlahic hahal ku	*These stones are seated as the true deity*
Ca yumil ti dios v yumil caan y luum Hahal / ku	*Our Lord who is God, the Lord of heaven and earth, is the true deity*
Bacac ix yax kuobe	*even though, as for these first deities*
Hauay kuob	*they are perishable deities*
Dzoc / v than v kultabalob	*The word of their worship is over*
Kazpahiob t u men v ben/dision v yumil caan	*They were invalidated by the blessing of the Lord of heaven*
Ca dzoci v lohol balcah	*that accomplished the redemption of all the things of the world*
Ca / dzoci v ca put cuxtal	*that accomplished the resurrection*
Hahal ku	*The true deity,*
Hahal dios	*the true God*
Ca u cicithantah caan y luum	*who blessed heaven and earth*
Ti kazpahi a kul maya / vinicexe	*Then your sacred images were invalidated, you Maya people*

Xeth au ol t a kulex lea	*Deliver your heart from these sacred images of yours!*
V kahlay / cab t u kinil	*The World History of the Era*
Lay t u men dziban lae	*This was written for this reason*
T u men ma / kuchuc t u kin v meyah	*because the day of this task has not yet arrived*
Lay hunob lae	*As for these books,*
Picil thanob lae	*these many words*
V tial katabal v chi maya vinicob vay	*are for the Maya people here when inquired*
Y ohelob bix sihanilob	*if they know how they had been born*
Edzlic cab	*and the founding of the world*
Vay ti peten lae.	*here in this peninsula.*

(CHUMAYEL 42.6–21)

This preface provides several important clues to the sociohistorical context that will allow us to best address the subject matter, origin of, and function of the creation myths contained in the Chumayel mythography. First of all, the title given by the anonymous compiler(s) to the mythography is *u kahlay cab tu kinil* 'the World History of the Era' (42.17–18). *Kahlay* is an indigenous genre in Classical Yucatecan–language texts, meaning *memoria* or *memorial* (Ciudad Real 2001:319).

In Classical Yucatecan documents of the Colonial period, *kahlay* is the term indigenous authors sometimes used to refer to their historico-legendary accounts. Examples include both public community *títulos* (primordial titles) such as those produced by members of the prominent Pech patronym group from the towns of Chicxulub and Yaxkukul (in Restall 1998:109) and the clandestine and often arcane *katun* prophecies attributed to the Chilam Balam and other *ah kin*, indigenous calendar priests (Códice Pérez 65.3). *Kahlay* is likely derived etymologically from the word *kah* 'to remember,' which appears on inscribed pre-Hispanic stela from the northern lowland area (Grube 1994:339). Again, writing in the late seventeenth century, Cogolludo (2006 [1688]:275) notes:

> [C]ontaban sus eras y edades, que ponían en sus libros de veinte en veinte años, y por lustros de cuatro en cuatro. . . . Llegando estos lustros a cinco, que ajustan veinte años, llamaban Katún, y ponían una piedra labrada sobre otra labrada, fijada con cal y arena en las paredes de sus templos y casas de sacerdotes, como se ve hoy en los edificios que se ha dicho, y en algunas paredes antiguas de nuestro convento de Mérida, sobre que hay unas cedulas. En un pueblo llamado Tixualahtun, que quiere decir lugar, donde se pone una piedra labrada

> sobre otra, dicen que estaba el archivo, recurso de todos acaecimientos, como en España lo es el de Simancas.
>
> They [the Maya] counted their eras and ages, which they put in books of twenty years subdivided into periods of four years. . . . Counting five of these periods, they make up twenty years, called a *katun*. And they place a piece of carved stone atop another stone, fixed with lime and sand in the walls of their temples and the houses of their priests, like one sees today in the buildings they have made, and in some of the old walls of our convent of Mérida above where some cells are. In a town named Tixualahtun, the name of the place meaning 'where carved stone is placed one over another,' they say there was the archive [containing] the records of all occurrences, as in Spain [the archive] is in Simancas.

Both barkpaper books and inscribed monuments were the sources of history for the Maya, and memory of this historical function continued long into the Colonial period even as the documents were seized and destroyed and knowledge of the logosyllabic writing system was increasingly lost. With the advances in recent decades in the decipherment of the ancient Maya's logosyllabic writing system (V. Bricker 1995; Houston 2000; Vail 2006; Wichmann 2006), hieroglyphic texts dating from the Classic period now paint a vivid picture of the ancient city-states (Martin and Grube 2000). With the content of the ancient texts increasingly accessible to modern scholars, it has been argued that the genre of *katun* "prophecies" (also referred to in colonial Maya documents as *kahlay*) in the Books of Chilam Balam have antecedents in Late Classic period monumental inscriptions (Lacadena 2006).

But in the study of Classical Yucatecan creation myths, it is not sufficient to consider simply the pre-Hispanic antecedents; the meaning of the genre of *kahlay* is itself subject to dialogical processes, always present, although acutely so in colonial documents in indigenous languages. The Pech accounts mentioned earlier that refer to themselves as *kahlay* toward the beginning of that document go on to state "from now on then this is the history [*ytoria*] of don Pedro Pech and don Martín Pech" (in Restall 1998:123). Therefore, the Maya historical genre of *kahlay* is used to refer to accounts of past events that in colonial Spanish historiography might be expressed, as they are in the earlier quote from López de Cogolludo, as *memorias* or *historias*, as well as related terms like *relaciones* or *crónicas*. The Classical Yucatecan texts under discussion here are most closely akin to Spanish *historias*, accounts presenting and interpreting the chronological relationship of events on the grandest scale of time and causality (Adorno 1982). Upon further examination, it is evident the preface shares some similarities with primordial titles, such as the Pech documents, just as the author(s) of the preface orient(s) these creation accounts within the scheme of European Christian salvation, or eschatological, history. In this second sense of *historia* we see that the Chumayel mythography is not simply a *kahlay* but *u kahlay cab t u kinil* 'the World History of the Era' before Christianity arrived in the Peten, the land of the speakers of Yucatecan Mayan languages. Therefore, the Chumayel mythography is simultaneously local and universal in scope, both within the pre-Hispanic tradition of Maya historical reckoning and coming to grips with the new era ushered in by Christian colonialism. As Mignolo (2003:204–207) notes, although alphabetic writing and Renaissance genres were tools of European colonization, these same tools were appropriated by native authors in creating alternative histories thoroughly hybrid in character. These tensions and contradictions encountered between indigenous American and European historiographies have led scholars working in other New World regions to refer to colonial indigenous language histories as "chronicles of the impossible" (Salomon 1982).

THE CHILAM BALAM LEGEND

With the demise of the Classic Maya city-states and the ultimate conquest of the various Postclassic Maya *cah* by the Spaniards, autochthonous intellectual institutions came under attack. Christian missionaries promoted a world religion whose exclusivist position toward local cosmologies and metaphysics was quite unlike what the Maya had ever experienced, and the subsequent destruction of books and suppression of the indigenous priesthood who were the literati of Postclassic Maya society served to obliterate many of their intellectual achievements. Nonetheless, the activity of some authors, copyists, and translators in Maya communities persevered, their collected works attributed to the Chilam Balam, the Prophet Jaguar. One such *kahlay* from the town of Maní begins:

U than hahal ku t u natahob chilam	*The word of the true God in the prophecies of the Chilan*
I. Lai u kahlail uchci u yemel hunnab ku	*This is the history of the descent of the Sole Deity*
Oxlahun ti ku	*the Thirteen Who is Deity*
Hun pic ti ku	*the Innumerable Who is Deity*
T u thanob ah kinob chilam balam yetel ah xupan nauat	*in the words of day-keepers Chilam Balam and Xupan Nauat*

Yetel bin ah na puc tun ah kin yetel ah kin naahau pech yetel ah kin ah kauil chel	*and according to Na Puc Tun the day-keeper, the day-keeper Naahau Pech and the day-keeper Kauil Chel*
Ti bin hun molob y icnal ah nacom balam chilam lae	*when they came together in the presence of Nacom Balam the chilan*
Ca bin uch than y okol uy otoch chilam lae	*Thus would the word occur at the house of this chilan*
Ca tzol u thanil almah xicin tiob.	*Thus the word of the* soul *shall arrive to them.*

(CÓDICE PÉREZ 65.1–8)

As the excerpt above suggests, texts produced in the voice of the Chilam Balam simultaneously claimed the authority of pre-Hispanic priests or day-keepers (*ah kinob*) and a rereading of ancient deity complexes as expressions of the "sole" God (*hunab ku*) and the evangelical message of the Christians (*u thanil almah*, borrowing the Spanish word *alma* for "soul"). Spanish colonial interpretations of pre-Hispanic Maya religion promoted the emergence of the legend of the Chilam Balam and other indigenous prophets who supposedly foretold the coming of Europeans and Christianity. This legend was an early feature of Spanish sources on the Maya Yucatán, with variants of the legend circulating at least by the 1560s. Around that time, Friar Diego de Landa (1978 [ca. 1566]:19) wrote:

> In the district of Maní, in the province of Tutul-xiu, an Indian named Ah Cambal, filling the office of Chilan, that is one who has charge of giving out the responses of the demon, told publicly that they would soon be ruled by a foreign race who would preach a God and the virtue of a wood which in their tongue he called *vahom che*, meaning a tree lifted up, and of great power against the demons.

Another similar account was provided in 1579 by Landa's sometime Maya aide, Gaspar Antoinio Chi. A son of nobility from the Xiu patronym group (*chibal*), Chi provides the first known reference to the name of the Chilam Balam in the *Relacion histórico-geográfica* for the town (*cah*) of Maní (Garza 1983, 1:69; English translation in Restall 1998:149–150). Maya-language prophecies attributed to the Chilam Balam and his companions were even published, with Spanish translations, in the Franciscan Bernardo de Lizana's 1633 publication *Historia de Yucatán: Devocionario de Nuestra Señora de Izamal y conquista espiritual*. The Chilam Balam legend was such a prolific area of missionary discourse that by the mid- to late sixteenth century, the Franciscan historian Diego López de Cogolludo devoted a chapter of his *Historia de Yucathan* (published 1688) to a discussion of the various written sources on the legend available to him at the time (Cogolludo 2006 [1688]:293–298).

Whether or not a real Chilam Balam existed, the legend of the Chilam Balam provided a framework by which the literate Maya could reconcile their allegiance to the economically and politically dominant religion of Christianity with the preservation of knowledge of the pagan past. As evidenced by Friar Diego de Landa's campaign against idolatry, European (and later creole) clergy were often quick to seize or destroy indigenous books as works of the devil (Landa 1978 [ca. 1566]:82). However, their attitudes toward indigenous prophecies perceived as reifying their Christian mission could be positive on occasion. The early seventeenth-century extirpator of idolatry, Doctor Pedro Sánchez de Aguilar, who himself seized hieroglyphic and alphabetic Maya books, relates another version of the Chilam Balam legend. In his account (Sánchez de Aguilar 1987 [1639]:95), the prophet (called here the Chilan Cambal) is set not in Maní but far to the east in the ancient pilgrimage center of the island of Cozumel:

> A pagan priest called Chilan Cambal took notice of this cross [that Cortes placed on the island of Cozumel] and composed a poem [*poesia*] in his language that I have read many times, which said that the new people they had just conquered had venerated the cross. . . . Our own thought is that these Indians erected this cross, and they took the poem [*poesia*] of Chilan Cambal for prophecy [*profecia*]. And this is the truth: I investigated it by knowing their language and through the correspondence that I obtained of the old Indians, the first neophytes that went on pilgrimage to the Temple of Cozumel and there saw the cross.

Here, the account by the secular clergyman provides interesting insight into the Spanish side of the reception and transmission of the Chilam Balam legend. In an intriguing rhetorical move, Aguilar has moved the words of the *chilan* from the category of *profecia* to that of *poesia*, or "poetry." In this way, he provides a defense for the study of pre-Hispanic America just as this move provided humanistic scholars with a defense for the study of ancient Greek and Roman works in Europe. During the Renaissance, the adoption of the concept of *poeta theologus* meant that, even though ancient Greco-Roman authors were pagans, it did not necessarily follow that their writings were false inspirations of the Devil as opposed to the truth of the prophets of the Judeo-Christian God (Witt 1977). Popular almanacs of astronomical, astrological, and medical lore such as the various *Reportorios de los Tiempos* (Zamorano 1585; Li 1999 [1492]) made frequent citations to Classical authors and figures (almost a necessity, given the subject matter). Interestingly, these *reportorios* were among the European works most regularly referenced and incorporated by the Maya into the Books of Chilam

Balam (V. Bricker and Miram 2002:xvi–xvii, 8). By moving the *chilan* from the role of prophet to poet, Aguilar makes it acceptable for Spanish and creole scholars to find sacral truth within pagan Maya sources. This attitude did not extend to the indigenous people themselves, from whom Aguilar continued to seize both barkpaper hieroglyphic codices and *cartapacios* (handwritten copybooks) in alphabetic script as part of his extirpation of idolatry.

Aguilar's account leads us to reflect on several issues related to both transmission and performance of texts (presumably including mythological ones) in the Books of Chilam Balam, information that will be helpful in interpreting these Classical Yucatecan texts. First, Aguilar asserts he had *read* many times the account of the Chilan Cambal. This raises the issue of composition and transmission of Chilam Balam traditions; to what kind of written source is Aguilar, writing in 1613, referring? As mentioned above, Aguilar is known to have seized both pre-Hispanic books in the Maya logosyllabic ("hieroglyphic") script and copybooks in alphabetic script (Chuchiak 2004). Second, Aguilar's assertion that the works are *poesia* highlights that even upon being recorded through the medium of alphabetic writing, the works were recognized as being *performed* in some sense. Additional statements by Sánchez de Aguilar about the performance of creation myths contained in the Books of Chilam Balam (see following) suggest a form of "recitation literacy" that likely has its roots in pre-Hispanic times (Houston and Stuart 1992; D. Tedlock 1992a).

AUTHORIAL VOICE AND THE MYTHOGRAPHY'S SOCIAL FUNCTIONS

Early in the otherwise anonymous preface above, there is a reference to the authorial voice, to *con ah tepal uinicob* 'we, the sovereign people.' *Ah tepal* is a pre-Hispanic title near the pinnacle of the Late Postclassic Maya political hierarchy alongside the title *halach uinic*. In the Colonial period, *ah tepal* was usually reserved for the Spanish Crown, the *Rey ah tepal* (e.g., see the Pech account in Restall 1998:113). It is followed by references to the addressees of the mythography: "you Maya people" (*maya vinicex*). It may seem odd to the reader that the compilers (or compiler) of these Maya mythic texts do not directly refer to themselves as Maya, but one should not take this as indicating that the compilers are Spanish clerics or another group that Yucatec speakers would refer to as *dzulob* 'foreigners.' As Matthew Restall (2004) has pointed out, not all indigenous Yucatecans at different points in the Colonial period recognized themselves by the term "Maya." This is not to say that a "Maya" ethnic identity was never overtly present among certain groups (Knowlton 2008, 2010) but that indigenous elites during the Colonial period often identified and distinguished themselves more in terms of town (*cah*), patronym group (*chibal*), or as belonging to the noble class (*almehen*) than by any broadly shared ethnic consciousness (Restall 1997, 1998, 2001). For example, conquest accounts written by nobles of the Pech *chibal* also distinguish themselves from the "Maya people," who the Pech urged to convert to Christianity, as in Naum Pech's 1541 sermon to the Maya people (Restall 1998:121). Instead, we should view this contrast between *ah tepal uinicob* 'we sovereign people' and *maya vinicex* 'you Maya people' as an indication that the compiler(s) belonged to the indigenous noble class, similar to those who sought to position themselves as "Maya conquistadors" through primordial titles with the goal of reaffirming their noble rights and prior occupancy of the peninsula (Restall 1998). At the same time, however, the author does not mention his/their particular *chibal*, and the fact that his/their location is described as *uay ti peten lea* 'here in this peninsula' rather than in any individual *cah* suggests that this *kahlay* is being compiled from a perspective that is pan-peninsular and pan-indigenous relative to what we find in the sort of primordial titles discussed previously.

Whether we are dealing with one anonymous compiler or many, for convenience during this study I will refer to the authorial voice of this preface as the Chumayel mythographer. From the beginning of the preface, what the Chumayel mythographer seeks to address is a point of "essential belief" that apparently both "we sovereign people" and the "Maya people" have missed: that the *hahal ku* 'true deity' Dios had abandoned the "stones" and "perishable deities" previously venerated by "you Maya people" (*maya uinicex*). The mythographer characterizes these "stones" or *hauay kuob* 'perishable deities,' meaning the pre-Hispanic deities, as *baalche* 'wild animals.' On one level, this symbolic attribution draws upon the practice of associating pre-Hispanic deities with devils and demons and the connection between malevolent supernaturals and dangerous animals in European Christian demonology.[1] Furthermore, *baalche* is the Yucatecan Maya word to denote creatures of the forest, of the *kax*. The symbolic distinction between town and forest had very real religious implications from the late sixteenth through seventeenth centuries in Yucatán, in which the Maya of settled communities of the northwestern part of the peninsula assisted the military and ecclesiastical efforts to establish control over the independent and runaway *ah chun kaxob* 'forest dwellers' of the Maya communities of the interior (Chuchiak 2005).

The Chumayel mythographer insists that such deities were "invalidated" upon completion of the high mark of the Christian view of history, the redemption of the world through the sacrificial death and resurrection of Christ. In European Christian historiography, the event of the resurrection of Christ inaugurated the eschatological phase of history. This interpretation of history is loosely based on sermons and epistles in the New Testament (first century AD), which state that the Judeo-Christian God "overlooked" the veneration of divine images of stone (by Greeks) and astral beings such as angels (by ancient Judeans) until the event of Resurrection, which then set eschatological history in motion (Acts 17:29–31; Hebrews 1:1–4).

The authorial self of the mythography's preface is double-voiced: it exhorts "you Maya people" to abandon the worship of the *hauay kuob* 'perishable deities' that have been invalidated with the coming of Christianity and its eschatological history, while at the same time defending both the composers of the old cosmogonies *in illo tempore* and the compiler's (or compilers') own role in the preservation of the ancient lore. This historical detachment is a common discursive strategy among literati in societies in which an evangelizing world religion has recently received elite sponsorship.[2] One can imagine the precarious position of such literati as the repositories of cultural traditions, often indispensable for the legal claims of indigenous elites in the colonial system (Restall 1998), but traditions that must be simultaneously appropriated or repudiated in light of newly enforced religious and cultural norms of the Spaniards.

Yet while some of the language of the mythography's preface is hortatory, the explicit purpose given for the compilation is expository. It is "for the Maya peoples here when inquired / If they know how they had been born / And the founding of the world / Here in this peninsula." The preface indicates that this compilation is conceptualized in terms of a colonial dialogue, occurring *here* in Yucatán; the several cosmogonies are meant to serve as rejoinders to the questions of an unidentified interlocutor. Because we lack the implicit knowledge shared by the Chumayel mythographer's original audience, questions arise in our ignorance of the communicative context: the Maya people were being questioned by whom and to what end? To understand the discursive environment of the Chumayel mythography, we must first look toward the social and historical context of literary production in the Classical Yucatecan language itself.

"AS FOR THESE BOOKS . . ."

Decades after Fray Diego de Landa's infamous burning of twenty-eight Maya hieroglyphic books before the church in Maní in 1562 (Clendinnen 1987), the Spanish religious authorities in Yucatán were again concerned about documents circulating among the indigenous populations. Unlike the "diabolical" manuscripts Landa and others destroyed or confiscated in the mid-sixteenth century and after, these heterodox documents were not the writings of the indigenous priesthood of *ah kinob* in hieroglyphic characters but of the Spanish clergy's own indigenous lay teachers, the *maestros*. Trained by the Franciscans in the Latin alphabet, these Maya literati continued to compose, copy, and edit manuscripts in Maya for Maya purposes. Like most products of educated Indians in New Spain and other colonial societies, the existence of these uncensored autochthonous works raised some alarm. Near the beginning of the seventeenth century a secular clergyman, Doctor Pedro Sánchez de Aguilar, formally reported in his *Informe Contra Los Adoradores de Idolos* (1987 [1639]:115; translation mine):

> It would be very useful for there to be printed books in the language of these Indians that deal with Genesis and the creation of the world; because they have fables, or very dangerous histories. And they have written some of these, and they guard them, and they read them together. And I have one of these copybooks that I confiscated from a schoolmaster, named Cuytun of the town of Sucop, who escaped me. And I was never able to make known to him the origin according to Genesis.

This brief statement tells us something of the maintenance and transmission of cosmogonies in Yucatec Maya communities at the time. Indigenous language cosmogonies were recorded in handwritten manuscripts, or *cartapacios* 'copybooks.' From his repeated reference to them in the plural, it is clear that Aguilar was aware of not just one but several creation myths current at the time and circulating in these copybooks. The manuscripts containing these cosmogonies were read aloud, clandestinely and communally (*a juntos* in the Spanish original). And the guardians of these cosmogonies, if not their scribes and authors as well, were the Maya *maestros de capilla* 'schoolmasters' trained by the regular clergy.

Although there is no known record of the contents of the Sucop copybook beyond Aguilar's designation as "fables, or very dangerous histories," we can surmise that it contained an eclectic collection of texts such as those in other clandestine Maya community books of the period, the Books of Chilam Balam. Within Mayanist studies, the Books of Chilam Balam for decades have been routinely cited as evidence of the persistence of Maya paganism or "Christo-paganism" in the colonial era. Given the title of Aguilar's report, one would assume at first glance that this is a statement concerned with the clandestine persistence of pre-Hispanic beliefs (in this case, about an entrenched pagan cosmogony) among the Maya.

And certainly the persistence of "idolatry" and how to extirpate it are concerns of Aguilar's report. But for a moment, let us consider what we know of the "pagan" content of the Books of Chilam Balam, as well as these books' relationship to the larger corpus of literature present in Yucatán at the time. We will then return to both Aguilar's statement and the preface to the Chumayel mythography.

Certainly, the Maya *maestros de capilla* (schoolmasters) and *maestro cantores* (choirmasters) did not always cooperate with the colonial system. In the independent indigenous communities in the interior forests that served as safe havens from imposition of colonial dominance in the north, some of these refugees were Maya educated by the clergy for local roles of Christian religious leadership, just like the compilers of the Books of Chilam Balam. Cogolludo (quoted in Jones 1989:128–129) reports of an expedition by Ambrosio de Argüeles in the years 1595–1601, which discovered that

> [a]mong those infidels there were a large number of baptized fugitives, who in order to live with the freedom that the others permitted them had gone over to them. Many knew how to read and write, and even speak Spanish from having been sacristans and cantores in the towns of this province, which caused them great fear because they were the more guilty.

However, as is evident in the preface, the compiler of the indigenous cosmogonies in the Chumayel mythography exhorted against the practice of venerating pre-Hispanic divine images, or *idolatría* as the Spanish clergy would call it. So, on the surface at least (and since these were clandestine books explicitly directed at a Maya audience, there seems little reason to suspect dissimulation), the Chumayel mythographer's intention is not the promotion of a nativist back-to-paganism movement against Christianity. In fact, the preface of the mythography places the relevance of the compilation squarely within the framework of "orthodox" European Christian salvation history.

Furthermore, one should note that a great many of the texts collected in the handwritten manuscripts known as the Books of Chilam Balam are from European and Spanish Mexican sources. These sources often were translated and/or adapted into the Yucatec language, although sometimes they were copied directly as Spanish. These sources include, among other things, popular almanacs (called *reportorios*), missals, medical and apothecary books, and even excerpts from grammars of the Yucatecan Maya language produced by non-Maya clergy (V. Bricker and Miram 2002:86–87). Again, the content of this literature, although often of the popular type, appears to have been relatively unproblematic in terms of Spanish-imposed orthodoxy and certainly not deserving of the epithet "idolatry" in a majority of cases.

Finally, and perhaps most surprisingly, the collection of materials in Maya copybooks from Spanish sources is not limited to materials of overtly Spanish provenance but includes the copying of the supposed pre-Hispanic Maya-language prophecies of the Chilam Balam and other pre-Hispanic *ah kinob* 'day-keepers' or divinatory calendar priests from Franciscan sources published in the early seventeenth century.

The complex relationship between Franciscan and Maya literary production during this period becomes evident if we compare the publication of Maya-language prophecies and Spanish translation (pages 61–64) in Bernardo de Lizana's 1633 *Historia de Yucatán: Devocionario de Nuestra Señora de Izamal y Conquista Espiritual* with the version of these same prophecies appearing on the final pages (104–107) of the Book of Chilam Balam of Chumayel (Gordon 1993 [1913]). When we compare Lizana's publication with those appearing on the concluding pages of the Chumayel, it is clear that Lizana is the source of the Chumayel version rather than vice versa. Line numbers begin on the second half of the Chumayel page 104, just where the material paralleling the 1633 publication (whose lines are also numbered) begins. The introduction to the section on page 104, line 12, is the Spanish phrase *La interpretaçión historias de yucatan*. This line not only directly cites the 1633 title of Lizana's publication but it also includes the phrase *la interpretaçión*, which refers to the Spanish translation appearing in Lizana's work, a translation not reproduced in the Chumayel. Paradoxically, we have ostensibly pre-Hispanic Maya prophecy copied into a Maya community book from a published book in Spanish concerning the "spiritual conquest" of Yucatán by the Franciscan clergy!

All this suggests a much more complex social situation of Maya literary production in a climate of Church censorship than just the suppression of *idolatría* and the "hunting down of mélanges," as Gruzinski (2002: chapter 12) refers to the antisyncretic activities of the era. It is important to note that during the sixteenth and seventeenth centuries, not only the Maya but even European authors and the missionaries to the Americas were subject to this censorship. In the period of the European Counter-Reformation, books arriving in New Spain required the approval of the Holy Office of the Inquisition for fear that the Protestant heresies would cross the Atlantic and infect the minds of those inhabitants of the colonies newly converted to the faith. Export lists from this period (Kropfinger–von Kügelgen 1973) provide a valuable tool for assessing what European works might have been available to the Maya during the period when the Books of Chilam Balam were composed and compiled.

There is also the question of the limits imposed upon doctrinal works produced by the regular clergy in the vernacular languages of New Spain. Since a major point of contention between Catholics and Protestants revolved around whether the individual Christian was competent to interpret the Scriptures independent of Church tradition, the translation of biblical texts and individual terms of significant theological depth from Latin into any vernacular became a delicate issue. In a letter dated January 19, 1578, Diego de Landa, by then bishop of Yucatán, assures representatives of the Holy Office in Mexico that no part of the Sacred Scriptures had been translated into Yucatecan Maya (Acuña 2001:176). Acuña, however, points out that Maya translations of biblical passages do occur as examples in a Maya dictionary from the same time, the *Calepino Maya de Motul* (Ciudad Real 2001), and that such vernacular translations did exist in the handwritten sermons of the Franciscan evangelists that served as the sources of later collections published in Yucatec Maya (Acuña 2001:170).

Confirmation of Acuña's hypothesis is to be found in the document known as the Morley Manuscript, a colonial Yucatecan Maya manuscript currently in the collections of the library of the Laboratory of Anthropology in the Museum of Indian Arts and Culture in Santa Fe, New Mexico. A transcription and annotated translation of this rare manuscript, neglected by scholars for decades, have recently been completed by Gretchen Whalen (Whalen 2003a). Like the Books of Chilam Balam, this is a leather-bound handwritten copybook, originally consisting of 346 numbered manuscript pages. Although one expert analysis determined that the extant copy dates to the eighteenth century (Whalen 2003b), there is internal philological and historical evidence to suggest the copy derives, at least in part, from a late sixteenth-century original consistent with the date 1576 present in the manuscript (Knowlton 2008).[3] A sort of "missing link" between the Books of Chilam Balam and Christian doctrinal works produced by the Franciscans, the Morley Manuscript contains both versions of sermons later edited for Fray Juan Coronel's 1620 Yucatec Maya–language publication *Discursos Predicables*, as well as Maya-language cosmogonic and cosmological texts based on European sources that were never published but were later copied into the clandestine Books of Chilam Balam of Kaua and of Chan Kan (Knowlton 2008). As such, the Morley Manuscript is a significant source for understanding the relationship between Maya and Franciscan literary production in colonial Yucatán.

In the introduction to the 1620 publication of the *Discursos Predicables*, Coronel (in Bolles 2001; translation mine) makes several statements that help shed light on the status of handwritten religious manuscripts in Yucatec during the period:

> [C]on mi trabajo he recogido, y recopilado de los padres antiguos avian escrito, enmendando algunas cosas que en este tiempo ya no se vsan, y corrigiendo lo que no estaba verdadero, para aliuiar el trabajo a los ministros por ser les de mucho auer los de trasladar por mano de Indios.
>
> [W]ith my work I have gathered and recopied from what the old *padres* had written, emending some things that at this time are no longer used, and correcting that which was not true, to alleviate the work of the ministers because there are many that have been translated by the hand of Indians.

And also:

> Muchas son las causas Christiano lector, que me han mouido a recopilar y enmendar estos tratados, como son. Que doctrina tan buena y espiritual (que religiosos doctos con diuino espiritu y zelo del bien de las almas tradugeron en esta lengua con que tanto fructo se ha echo en ellas) no andubiesen en cartapacios manuscriptos, donde se hallauan muchas mentiras sin poner las letras que se requeria para la buena intelligencia y pronunciacion de la lengua.
>
> Christian reader, there are many reasons that moved me to compile and emend these works as they are. A doctrine so good and uplifting to the spirit (that the learned religious [friars] with divine spirit and zeal for the well-being of souls translated in this [Maya] tongue with which so much fruit has been borne among us) should not circulate in handwritten copybooks [*cartapacios manuscritos*] where one finds many lies, without putting it in print, which is required for it to be well understood and for its pronunciation in the tongue.

Again what is reinforced here is the potential danger from the perspective of the colonizing missionaries of work left too much in the hands of Indian translators, as well as the circulation of copybooks that, unlike printed works subject to censorship by the Inquisition, contain *muchas mentiras* 'many lies.' Furthermore, lest we accept uncritically Coronel's frequent assertion that the principal concern in composing his work is simply to make the doctrine more intelligible to the *indios* or *naturales*, we should note that while sections of the handwritten Morley Manuscript incorporate Maya translations of biblical passages, passages of scripture and from the Church Fathers in Coronel's *Discursos* are given instead in Latin throughout that publication.

In its composition, the Morley Manuscript is in many ways analogous to the Books of Chilam Balam, even containing some texts that would later be copied into some of these clandestine works (Knowlton 2008). In other ways, it is something of a Franciscan equivalent of a Book of Chilam Balam, a copybook of handwritten sermons in the Classical Yucatecan Maya language, containing both materials sufficiently orthodox to be publishable (as evidenced by the presence of previous versions of some texts that would appear in the 1620 *Discursos*) and other cosmological materials the Inquisitors would apparently seek to censor as heterodox.

So, returning to the earlier statement by the secular clergyman and extirpator of idolatry Sanchez de Aguilar, recall that his request to his superiors was that there be *libros impresos* 'printed books' in the language of the Indians dealing with Genesis and the creation of the world. Subject to Inquisitional censorship, such printed books would not contain the "fables or very dangerous histories" of the vernacular copybooks currently in circulation among the Franciscan-educated Maya schoolmasters. Aguilar did get his wish in the publication of Fray Coronel's *Discursos*, the first thirty-four pages of which are devoted to Genesis commentaries in Maya, with all actual quotations of Scripture remaining in Latin as the Holy Office mandated. Nonetheless, the late dates of the extant copies of the Books of Chilam Balam and the Morley Manuscript bear witness that the *cartapacios* of both Maya histories and Franciscan sermons remained in circulation for centuries. The danger of these copybooks was not simply that of "idolatry," but that, as unregulated literature, they were potential sources of Christian heresy so feared by the embattled Roman Church in Europe at the time. The Inquisition could bar the import of certain books into the Americas from Europe or enforce their concerns during the process of publication in New Spain, but the copybooks of Maya *maestros* and the clergy's handwritten collections of Christian sermons in Maya were alike in their inaccessibility to the censors.

Rather than the monologic ideal of the censors and the catechists, the Chumayel mythographer provides his explicitly Maya audience, in preparation for their inquest, with *hunob lae picil thanob lae* 'these books, these many words.' For its compiler(s), knowledge of the mythic origins of the world and human beings was not bound by what Bakhtin (1981:271) calls the "centripetal forces in sociolinguistic and ideological life" that informed the poetics of the Church, which reduced all truth to a Latin monologue.

Given the close relationships between them in the early years of Spanish colonialism, it should perhaps be of little surprise that a principal site on the dialogical frontier of colonial Yucatán is the cross-fertilizing corpus of Maya and Franciscan copybooks. Supervision of the content of works on the creation of the world in the Maya vernacular, as Aguilar envisioned, did not inoculate the language of these texts against dialogizing processes of historical reproduction. In an analysis of the social uses of writing among literate Kaqchikel Maya during the Colonial period, Robert Hill (1992) interprets several indigenous language documents as case studies of nativism, adaptation, and resistance. In a similar vein, the motivations for the compilation provided by the Chumayel mythographer involve the preservation of indigenous knowledge while adapting it to the realities of European Christian political and military dominance. Compared to the elite authors of primordial titles, the Chumayel mythographer is innovative in addressing the claims of not just a single family or town but of *maya uinicob* 'Maya people' of the entire *peten* 'peninsula' through an account of their origins, a form of resistance transcending familial or regional rivalries. Therefore, to understand the words and worlds of Classical Yucatecan Maya creation myths, this intersection of the pre-Hispanic literary tradition, the transmission and censorship of missionary doctrine, and the needs of the Maya people from the perspective of the local literate elite must all be taken into account. It is with this in mind that I provide an interpretation of the myths that follow.

NOTES

1. For example, the Morley Manuscript (ms. page 234) and its cognate text in Coronel's *Discursos Predicables* quote the New Testament book of 2 Peter as it likens the devil (*cisin* in Maya) to a lion (*cooh*). Medieval and Renaissance demonology is replete with such examples (Russell 1986), as was its transference and expression throughout New Spain (Cervantes 1994:13–15).

2. For example, note the discursive strategies employed in describing pre-Christian Germanic rites in the Anglo-Saxon epic of *Beowulf* (Heaney 2000:xvi) or in the Christian prologue to the Norse myths of the *Prose Edda* (Sturluson 2005).

3. The basis for dating the extant copy to the eighteenth-century date resulted from the analysis of drawings of watermarks provided to the expert and on the orthographic conventions of the manuscript (Whalen 2003a). However, the fact that the document is hand-printed in *letras de molde* might not be conclusive in the case of documents by indigenous authors, who since the mid-sixteenth century would sometimes compose in a printed style. In 1559, Las Casas reported being shown by a Franciscan an alphabetic book handwritten by an Indian in such a style that Las Casas initially mistook it for a printed book (Las Casas 1967 [1559], 1:327; see also Gruzinski 2002:61).

CHAPTER FOUR

Creation and Apocalypse: The Katun 11 Ahau Myth

This chapter examines the first creation myth contained in this Chumayel mythography, a *kahlay* 'history' of the destruction and re-creation of the world in Katun 11 Ahau. This myth is particularly interesting because it is attested to by redactions in two other Books of Chilam Balam, that of the town of Tizimín, and that of the town of Maní (contained in the Códice Pérez). By interrogating the similarities and differences that exist between the surviving examples of this creation narrative, we can gain insight into the history of its composition. Then, by examining the main characters and themes of the narrative itself, we can explore both the Postclassic world view in which it is rooted and the process by which Maya scribes engaged pre-Hispanic mythic themes in dialogue with their experiences living in a colonial world.

COMPARATIVE ANALYSIS OF THE EXTANT REDACTIONS

Alternate redactions of this myth of the destruction and subsequent re-creation of the world in Katun 11 Ahau appear in three extant texts:

1. Book of Chilam Balam of Chumayel: page 42, line 22, through page 48, line 8.
2. Book of Chilam Balam of Tizimín: folio 14v, line 26, through folio 15v, line 23.
3. The Códice Pérez (sometimes referred to as the Chilam Balam of Maní): page 117, line 16, through page 120, line 10.

All three versions are closely related, but they are not identical in length, content, or artistic elaboration, indicating a history of editorial redaction. Upon constructing a line-by-line cross-reference of all material shared by two or more of these texts (the appendix), a few aspects of the history of the myth's composition emerge.

Comparison of all three extant versions of this cosmogony reveals that they derive from at least two previously existing texts, texts no longer extant independent of their daughter texts. I will call the first of these hypothetical sources *u kahlay hay cabal* 'History of the Destruction of the World' (contained in C42.23–43.28 / T14v.26–15r.16 / P117.16–118.17). The "History of the Destruction of the World" details the defeat of Oxlahun Ti Ku by Bolon Ti Ku, the birth of Lady Quetzal–Lady Lovely Cotinga, the theft of maize by Bolon Dzacab into the heavens, the subsequent destruction of the world in a flood, and finally the establishment of world trees and their respective bird deities in the five cardinal directions by the Bacabs.

The second text I will refer to as *u cuch nicte ahau* 'The Burden of the Flower King,' based on a phrase that occurs in line C46.11 / T15r.28–29 / P119.4. The extant versions of this narrative are contained in C45.21–47.2 / T15r.17–15v.5 / P118.18–119.19. This text details the descent of Bolon Dzacab for his *ca put sihil* 'second birth' ceremony and the sprouting of a multitude of personified flowers, indicative of both the active fertility and ephemeral beauty of the world.

Together, these two source texts compose the bulk of what material is shared among all three redactions of the extant Katun 11 Ahau creation myth. Although the Tizimín and Pérez are the versions most similar to each other, each redaction diverges from the other in ways that suggest none is a direct copy of any other. Rather, all three appear to be drawing on yet another earlier source or sources no longer extant. Although extant Chilam Balam manuscripts date from the eighteenth or early nineteenth century, they are the results of copying, redacting, and recopying of manuscripts that date much earlier. In the case of the Katun 11 Ahau creation myth, there is both philological evidence internal to the Classical Yucatecan texts themselves and supplemental evidence about Maya myth traditions from Spanish sources that suggest that the *alphabetic* source text of this myth was in existence by the sixteenth century.[1]

Although only speculation, several lines of evidence converge that suggest that an educated son of Maya nobility, Gaspar Antonio Chi, was a source for the flood narrative of the "History of the Destruction of the World" that appears in the Books of Chilam Balam of Chumayel, Tizimín, and the Códice Pérez. First of all, Chi is a likely source for Friar Landa's (1978 [ca. 1566]:60) knowledge of this mythological episode. Second, after leaving the employ of Franciscans such as Landa, Chi served as *maestro cantor* and *maestro de capilla* in Tizimín in the northeast before returning in 1572 as governor of his native community of Maní (Restall 1998:146), the latter being the town from which Juan Pio Pérez copied his redaction of the myth. The most divergent redaction, the Chumayel, could easily have been transmitted later in the absence of Chi, given the proximity of Chumayel to Maní. In any event, whether or not Gaspar Antonio Chi was involved in the origin of the alphabetic version of the "History of the Destruction of the World," the content of this colonial-era myth indicates it was clearly composed in dialogue with Postclassic Maya traditions, such as those recorded by scribes and priests in logosyllabic (or "hieroglyphic") script of the pre-Hispanic barkpaper codices.

NARRATIVE CONTENT OF THE KATUN 11 AHAU CREATION MYTH

Despite the differences among redactions in the Chumayel, Tizimín, and Pérez manuscripts, an overall theme evident in this narrative is the destruction and the subsequent reordering and flowering of the world. This creative process parallels the lowland Maya practice of swidden or "slash-and-burn" cultivation, in which destruction is necessary to ensure a productive soil in order to grow the crops on which all human life depends. Following the Chumayel redaction of the narrative, the myth opens with:

Ti peten	*On the Peten*
Ychil buluc ahau	*during the katun Eleven Ahau*
Tij ca hoki ah mu[s]en cab	*when the Ah Musen Cab emerged*
Kaxic u uichob oxlahun ti ku	*Oxlahun Ti Ku blindfolds them*
Ma yx y oheltahobi v kaba halili v cic y v mehenobe	*Neither his older sister nor his children knew his name any longer*
Y alahob t i	*They spoke to him*
Ma ix chacanhij v uich ti ob xan	*but his face was not revealed to them either*
Tuchi yx ca dzoci vy ahalcabe	*So when it finished dawning*
Ma yx y oheltahob binil vlebal	*they knew not that it would come to pass*

4.1. Ancient Maya bee-keeping ceremony framed cosmologically by glyphs of the four cardinal directions. Madrid Codex, page 106a (reproduced by permission of the Museo de América, Madrid).

Ca ix chuci oxlahun ti ku tumenel bolon ti Ku.	*that Oxlahun Ti Ku was caught by Bolon Ti Ku.*

(CHUMAYEL 42.22–28)

The Chumayel version introduces the myth by setting us in place and time, along with an anchoring event. The place is the *peten*, the land of the Maya in the Yucatán peninsula. It is important to note that the Chumayel mythographer begins by grounding the events of creation not in Central Mexican Tollan or Mesopotamian Eden but in the world of the lowland Maya themselves. Mythic time likewise is measured in the system of historical reckoning using *katun* periods typical of the *kahlay* 'history' genre as it exists in the Books of Chilam Balam.

As *katun* dates repeat after a series of thirteen, it is necessary to distinguish this particular Katun 11 Ahau date in some way. This is accomplished here by anchoring it to another event. This event is the emergence of Ah Musen Cab, identified by Roys (1967:64) as the bee deity of the same name reported by ethnographers working in modern Yucatec Maya communities (Figure 4.1). Stingless bees (*Melipona beecheii*) were important sources of honey and wax for candles in pre-Hispanic times (Vail 2001:84–85) and their beehives the subject of numerous rituals in the hieroglyphic

Madrid Codex that have been analyzed by Gabrielle Vail (1994) and Mary Ciaramella (2002).

Why is a bee god associated with the creation of the world? On the poetic level, the relationship is expressed through the Maya delight for puns, as the word for "bee" and "honey" in Yucatec (*cab*) is homophonous with the word for "world, town, or region," which is also *cab* (Ciudad Real 2001:94). The same logograph is used in the ancient script to represent both concepts. On the practical level, the pollinating activities of bees are an important part of traditional Maya agriculture, with hives being moved to different areas to take advantage of plants' flowering cycles (Vail 2001:85). By invoking the emergence of Ah Musen Cab, the myth-teller anticipates the pollination of the world, the flowering of life that will succeed the devastation about to be related.

Following the initial grounding in place and time, the text introduces the protagonist Oxlahun Ti Ku ("Thirteen As God"). Oxlahun Ku appears by name on page 101 of the Madrid Codex, represented iconographically by the figure scholars call God C (Figure 4.2), which is itself the anthropomorphized form of the concept of divinity and sacredness (Ringle 1988; Taube 1992:27–31). This may help explain Oxlahun Ti Ku's explicit association with Hunab Ku, the Sole Deity referred to in texts attributed to the Chilam Balam, like the one previously discussed from Códice Pérez, page 65 (see Chapter 3). God C is known to stand in place of other deities in the iconography of Postclassic Maya codices, most notably the rain god Chac (Love 1994:44; Vail 2000b:130–131). Whether Oxlahun Ti Ku and Bolon Ti Ku are treated as individual deities or composites for groups of deities varies from text to text, although Oxlahun Ti Ku in the text presently under discussion is treated as a singular discrete being.

The myth goes on to relate in poetic language the conflict and abuse of Oxlahun Ti Ku by Bolon Ti Ku:

Ca emi kak	*When fire descended*
Ca emi tab	*When tumplines descended*
Ca emi tunich y che	*When stone and wood descended*
Ca tali v baxal che y tunich	*When his stick and stone came*[2]
Ca ix chuci oxlahun ti ku	*Then Oxlahun Ti Ku was caught*
y ca ix paxi u pol	*and then his head was wounded*
Ca ix lahi v uich	*Then they put out his eyes*
Ca ix tubabi	*Then he was spat upon*
Ca ix cuchpachhi xan	*Then he was knocked down flat, too*
Ca ix colabi v cangel y v holsabac.	*Then his archangel was tugged and shall be removed.*

(CHUMAYEL 42.28–43.3)

4.2. God C named as Oxlahun Ku, Postclassic version of Oxlahun Ti Ku. Madrid Codex, page 101c (reproduced by permission of the Museo de América, Madrid).

This abuse concludes with the "tugging" of Oxlahun Ti Ku's "cangel" and anticipates its "removal" from its station in the cosmos. The word *cangel* is the Mayanization of the Spanish word *arcangel* 'archangel' (Victoria

Bricker, personal communication, 2003), following the same phonological processes colonial Maya scribes used to incorporate other Spanish loanwords from Spanish to Yucatec.[3] In the European iconography the Spanish introduced among the Maya, European angels were associated with the winds of the different directions, which Maya immediately considered parallels to the pre-Hispanic deities of the cardinal directions (Miram and Bricker 1996; V. Bricker and Miram 2002). I argue that in the present case, the "cangel" is a manifestation of the Chacs, the pre-Hispanic rain gods of the four color-directions. This identification is confirmed intertextually elsewhere in the Chumayel manuscript where it relates in language very similar to that in the 11 Ahau myth, as shown here:

Tii ca colabi v cangel chac xib chace	*That was when the archangel of Red Man Chac was tugged*
Sac xib chac colabi u cangel	*As for White Man Chac, his archangel was tugged*
U cangel ix ek yuuan chac colabi xan.	*And the archangel of Black Yuuan Chac was tugged too.*

(CHUMAYEL 3.16–18)

The archangel of Oxlahun Ti Ku is the rain god aspect of the divinity. Therefore, the removal of Oxlahun Ti Ku's archangel is the removal of a rain god from its station in the heavens. By building an anticipation of the archangel's removal from its regulatory duty, the myth-teller is heightening the audience's anticipation of the coming apocalyptic deluge that will result.

The verb used to refer to the "tugging" of Oxlahun Ti Ku's archangel is *cóol*, with a long, high tone not distinguished in the colonial orthography. This is a near homonym with *còol* 'to clear a milpa,' the ubiquitous activity of Yucatec Maya farmers past and present. Delighting in this play on words, the myth-teller now shifts attention from events in the heavens to events on the earth, and the subsistence activities that depend on both, by introducing the engendering of Lady Quetzal.

Ca cħabi yx kukil yx yaxun	*Then Lady Quetzal, Lady Lovely Cotinga was engendered*
ɏ ca cħabi ybnel [ꝑ]uyem viil	*And then a bundle of shelled edible beans was engendered*
ɏ v pucsikal [ꝑ]uyem sicil	*And her heart was shelled piepan squash seeds*
ɏ [ꝑ]uyem toꝑ	*and shelled round squash seeds*
ɏ [ꝑ]uyem buul.	*and shelled black beans.*

(CHUMAYEL 43.3–5)

4.3. Yucatec Maya *maestro cantor* working in his milpa. Xocén, Yucatán, 1999 (photograph by author).

Lady Quetzal–Lady Lovely Cotinga is a divine personage whose name also forms part of the title of the young princess Uchuch Q'uq' Uchuch Raxon in the K'iche' Achi dance drama, the *Rabinal Achi* (for a discussion of the K'iche' character, see D. Tedlock 2003:13). The name Lady Quetzal suggests the green plumage of the Resplendent Quetzal (*Pharomachrus mocinno*), the color green-blue (Yucatec: *yax*) being suggestive of vegetation as well. In the Yucatec myth Lady Quetzel is herself a bundle made up of some principal Maya crops one would encounter in a milpa. In this way the myth-teller reminds us, as the reference to the Bee God at the beginning of the myth also signaled, that the creation of the world is the creation of a milpa (Figure 4.3). The world, like a milpa, is the product first of violent clearing that results in a flourishing rebirth of all things. The seeds of the staple crops within her, Lady Quetzal–Lovely Cotinga embodies the potential sources of life and nourishment in the coming world.

V tepah ynah yax bolon dzacab	*Yax Bolon Dzacab wrapped the seed corn*
Ca bini t uy oxlahun tas caan	*Then went to the thirteenth plane of the sky*
Ca yx tun culhij v madzil	*So then the maize husk resided there*
y v ni v baclili vay y okol cabe	*and only the tip of the corncob was here on the surface of the earth*
Ca tun bin u pucsikal t u menel oxlahun ti ku	*So then her heart is gone missing because of Oxlahun Ti Ku*
Ma ix y oltahob binci v pucsikal viil lae	*Neither did they know that he had made off with this heart bundle*
Ca ix hu[t]lahi	*And then it collapsed*
Ixma yumob y ah numyaob	*Without the lords or the lowly*
Ixma ychamob	*without spouses*
Cuxanob ix ti minan u pucsikalob	*That's how they lived without their hearts*
Ca yx mucchahij	*and so were submerged*
T u men v yam sus	*by waves of sand*
T u yam kaknab.	*and waves of sea.*

(CHUMAYEL 43.6–14)

The story of the theft of maize was a common, if variable, theme in Postclassic Mesoamerican mythology, with Central Mexican versions in the *Leyenda de los Soles* (Bierhorst 1992:146–147), as well as in the cosmogony on page 43 of the Borgia Codex (Boone 2007:202–204). Among the Yucatec Maya, the protagonist of this episode is Bolon Dzacab, whose name means "something perpetual" (Ciudad Real 2001:89). Bolon Dzacab is the deity who oversees the New Year ceremonies beginning on the day named Kan (Landa 1978 [ca. 1566]:62–63) and who appears in the Dresden New Year's pages as God K. Known to the Classic Maya as Kauil, God K (Bolon Dzacab) is sometimes depicted carrying large bundles of foodstuffs (Figure 4.4). Another *kahlay* text in the Book of Chilam Balam of Tizimín (13v) states that *Bolon Dzacab uah, Bolon Dzacab haa, y al Ix Kuk, y al Ix Yaxum* 'Bolon Dzacab bread, Bolon Dzacab water is the child of Lady Quetzal, the child of Lady Lovely Cotinga.' So the appearance of Bolon Dzacab is the birth of the everlasting sustenance of the earth from the cornucopia corpus of Lady Quetzal.

But the sustenance does not remain on the earth. With the seed corn stolen away to the sky, the cornucopia collapses. The peoples of this era of creation can only live on without *pucsikalob* 'cores,' a word that can refer to maize kernels as well as the actual physical hearts of human beings and other animals. The absence of "hearts" in these first peoples is coupled in the text with the lack of recognition of class divisions and marriage partners, an "unnatural" state resulting in their extermination by "natural" catastrophe. This Yucatec Maya account recalls the bloodless "wooden people" of the K'iche' (Quiche) Maya *Popol Vuh* who were also destroyed in a flood before the present creation of human beings from maize (D. Tedlock 1985; Christenson 2003a; see also Thompson 1970:282).

Hun vadz hail	*One fetching of rain*
Hu[n] lom haail	*One lancing of rain*
Tij ca uchi col cangelili	*Back then when only the Milpa Archangel arrived*
Ti homocnac canal	*it was tempestuous above*
Homocnac ix ti cab.	*and tempestuous below.*
	(CHUMAYEL 43.14–16)

The imagery of the destruction by flood of the "heartless," maizeless peoples is worth reflecting upon. The text here describes the great deluge as *hun uadz hail, hu[n] lom haail* 'one fetching of rain, one lancing of rain.' *Uadz* is the numeral classifier used to count trips to and from a well for water (V. Bricker, Po'ot, and Dzul de Po'ot 1998:297), while *lom*, the noun for "point of a lance or dart" (Ciudad Real 2001:367), has in this case been derived as a numeral classifier as well. Together, these verbal images match the painted depiction of the overturned water jar and spear-thrower lances carried by deities in the very well-known "flood scene" of the Dresden Codex on page 74 (Figure 4.5). Although the date and the tabular context of the Dresden Codex account are different, and therefore the scene is

4.4. God K, or Kauil, the Classic Maya form of Bolon Dzacab. Unprovenanced painted capstone (drawing by Elissa Ferguson).

4.5. The "apocalyptic" flood scene of the Lower Water Table. Dresden Codex, page 74 (Förstemann 1880).

not a *direct* equivalent to the present myth, we do have a clear example of shared imagery between pre-Hispanic iconography and colonial alphabetic texts. This intertextuality transcends the distinction between "writing" and "painting" that speakers of many European languages make but that is *not* marked in many Mayan languages.

Valic can tul ti ku	*Four stand as gods*
Can tul ti bacab	*four as Bacabs*
Lay hayesob	*They caused their [the core-less people's] destruction*
Tuchij tun ca dzoci hay cabil	*And then when the destruction of the world was finished*
Lay cahcunah uchebal ca tzolic kan xib yui	*They settled this [land] so that Kan Xib Yui puts it in order*
Ca ualhi sac imix che ti xaman	*Then the White Imix Tree stands in the North*
Ca ix ualhi y ocmal caan	*and stood as the pillar of the sky*
V chicul hay cabal	*The sign of the destruction of the world*
Lay sac imix che valic cuchic	*This White Imix Tree stands there supporting it*
Ca yx ualhi ek ymix che	*Then the Black Imix Tree stood*
Cu [lic] ek tan pidzoy	*[where] the Black-Bellied Pidzoy resides*
Ca yx ualhij kan ymix che	*Then stood the Yellow Imix Tree*
V chicul hay cabal	*The sign of the destruction of the world*
Culic kan tan pidzoy	*The Yellow-Bellied Pidzoy resides*
Cumlic ix kan xib yui	*and Kan Xib Yui sits*
Yx kan oyal mut	*The Yellow Caller Bird*
Ca ix ualhij yax imix che t u chumuc	*Then the Blue-Green Imix Tree stood in the center*
U kahlay hay cabal	*The History of the Destruction of the World*
Culic uatal.	*It is erected.*

(CHUMAYEL 43.16–27)

Here we have the reestablishment of the world by the Bacabs. According to Landa, the Bacabs not only sustain the heavens after the world-destroying deluge but also "signalize the misfortune or blessings which are to happen in the year" corresponding to each of the four Mayapán year-bearer dates [Kan, Muluc, Ix, Cauac] (Landa 1978 [ca. 1566]:60–61). The colored world

4.6. Postclassic depiction of the deity Kan Xib Chac ("Yellow Man Chac"). Dresden Codex, page 29c (Förstemann 1880).

trees set up during this myth are each called *v chicul hay cabal* 'the sign of the destruction of the world' and the central blue-green tree, *u kahlay hay cabal* 'the History of the Destruction of the World.' Like an inscribed stela, the central tree stands as an embodiment of memory of a past age.

In this section, the myth-teller emphasizes the placement of the trees following the deluge by Kan Xib Yui ("Yellow Man Yui"). Kan Xib Yui may be the same being as Kan Xib Chac, who is mentioned by Landa (1978 [ca. 1566]:61) as the patron of years beginning on the day Kan and who also appears by name in almanacs in the Dresden Codex (Figure 4.6). The prominent roles of this Kan Bacab and Bolon Dzacab within the narrative identify the destruction and re-creation of the world not only as occurring in a year beginning on the Maya day Kan but also with the concept of "ripeness" the day name itself elicits, as *kan* also refers to ripe fruit (Ciudad Real 2001:325). This is the theme on which all three redactions elaborate in the "Burden of the Flower King." This theme is picked up again in the Chumayel account after diverging for several manuscript pages to include a unique account of an event of considerable cosmogonic significance to the Maya that is not present in either the Tizimín or the Pérez redactions of the myth.

THE VENUS PASSAGE

The text below begins on the line at which the Chumayel (ms. page 43.27–28) significantly diverges from the Tizimín (folios 15r.15–16) and the Códice Pérez (ms. page 118.16–17) versions of the Katun 11 Ahau creation myth. At this point, a unique account of the first dawn begins:

Cumtal u cah u lac	*The ceramic idol sits down*
Canah ual katun	*above the page [relating the] katun*
Ah pay kab ah pay oc t u yum	*The guide of the hand, the precursor to the foot of the lord*
Cumtal u cah chacpil tec t u lakin cab	*Rosiness settles there in the eastern region*
Ah pay oc t u yum	*The precursor to the foot of the lord*
Cumtal u cah sacpil te t u xaman cab	*Grayness settles there in the northern region*
Ah pay oc t u yum	*The precursor to the foot of the lord*
Cumtal u cah lahun chan	*Lahun Chan sits down*
Ah pay kab t u yum	*The guide of the hand of the lord*
[hex u uol cab valic]	________________

Cumtal u cah kanpil tee	*Light yellow settles there*
Ah pay kab t u yum.	*The guide of the hand of the lord.*

(CHUMAYEL 43.27–44.3)

From this passage, we can discern a couple of important aspects of the composition of this text. First of all, the redactor of the surviving version found in the Chumayel is clearly working from a previous, probably alphabetic, version. This is discernable because in the manuscript itself (see Gordon 1993 [1913]:44) the redactor crosses out the line *hex u uol cab valic*, which, as we shall see, should appear one manuscript line further down. This suggests the scribe lost track of where he was in the text as he was transcribing it from another manuscript, only to catch his mistake briefly thereafter. Therefore, the redactor of the extant version we have is likely not the author of the text, and therefore it was composed (and redacted an uncertain number of times) at some point prior to its transcription in the mythography contained in the Book of Chilam Balam of Chumayel.

Second, the Chumayel first diverges from the Tizimín and the Pérez by inserting the line *canah ual katun*. From context, I am reading *canah* as *canal* meaning "above," although I should note that the verb *caan-ah* 'rose' appears in both colonial dictionaries and hieroglyphic sources (Dresden 68a), in the latter appearing in reference to the heliacal rise of an astronomical body (Mars, in the case presented in V. Bricker 1997:136). *Ual* refers to the leaf or folio of a book (Ciudad Real 2001:569), and thus I take *ual katun* to be a reference to the manuscript page from which the Katun 11 Ahau creation myth was being transcribed.

The thing that either "sits above" or perhaps "rose" is *u lac*, which according to the sixteenth-century Motul Dictionary (Ciudad Real 2001:350) can refer to a ceramic plate or to an "idol" made of ceramic. The redactor of the Pérez version (ms. page 118.16–17) clearly interpreted *u lac* to refer to "his/her/its plate" since he redacts the final cognate line as *Lai licil u cumtal u lac u luch u pop u dzam katunob t uy ahaulil mta* ["This plate, the cup, the mat, the throne of the katuns sits in its reign, *mta*"].

But it is not at all clear that the redactor of the Chumayel shares this interpretation. The additional material, as well as the explicit reference to the page itself, suggests this redactor is interpreting *u lac* as referring to something that appears at the top of the page he is working from. Continuing on, we see he applies to *u lac* the paired title *ah pay kab ah pay oc t u yum*. According to the Motul Dictionary, *ah pay* refers to a "guide or precursor" (Ciudad Real 2001:51). Consulting Miram and Miram's (1988) concordance, this particular phrase is unique to the Chumayel in the known corpus of Books of Chilam Balam. Ralph Roys in his translation of the

Chumayel (1967:101) glosses this as "messengers of their lord," although in the Maya text the term does not appear in the plural but is rather yet another example of a couplet, so favored in Maya poetics. As *u lac* takes on this paired epithet, I believe it is possible the redactor of the Chumayel account who originally composed these lines is referring to the depiction of an anthropomorphic supernatural being appearing at the top of the *katun* page (*ual katun*) he is transcribing from. Since depictions of Maya gods are rare if nonexistent in the known alphabetic Books of Chilam Balam, this suggests the following account may be inspired by direct reference to, if not a transcription or oral elaboration from, an illuminated codex.

So what do we make of this *ah pay*, and who is the "lord" (*yum*) being referred to? Since Roys's research, scholars have been aware that one of the deities of the Venus Table of the Postclassic Maya Dresden Codex, with the Ch'olan Maya name Lahun Chan, appears in this text (Roys 1967:100–101). It is Lahun Chan who takes the *ah pay* title in the Chumayel text. This strongly suggests that the *ah pay* is in fact Venus, and the *yum* 'lord' is the Sun. But the common title for Venus in both the codices and later colonial sources is *chac ek* 'great [or red] star.' Why this unusual title if in fact Venus is meant? Venus in the *Popol Vuh*, also known in that text as the "Great Star," goes by the title Icoquih, variously translated by Dennis Tedlock as "daybringer" (1985:335) or "sun carrier" (1996:357) and by Allen Christenson (2003a:218n569) as "Accompanies/Bears/Passes Before the Sun." Therefore, the semantic equivalent of *ah pay* 'guide, precursor' appears elsewhere in Maya creation mythology as a title for Venus.

Having argued that the title *ah pay kab, ah pay oc* refers to Venus, let us consider the structure and content of this passage in light of what we know of pre-Hispanic Maya Venus texts, in particular the Venus Table in the Dresden Codex (ms. pages 24, 46–50). In the Chumayel, the link between the colors and directions is made explicitly in the first two instances, with colors explicitly mentioned in three out of four lines. The deity Lahun Chan substitutes where the color black and the direction west otherwise would occur in the text. The colors appearing in the text are described as light or dim (*-pil*) equivalents of the standard directional colors, presumably because the Sun has not yet risen and Venus alone provides light. In contrast, the Dresden Venus passages do not include color terms, just as the Chumayel passage lacks dates. Despite these differences, the pre-Hispanic passages and the Chumayel overlap in their division into four stanzas and the presence of directional colors, gods' names, and Venus titles.

To make full sense of the Venus passage, we also need to account for the two variants of the *ah pay* title that occurs in the Chumayel text, the *ah pay <u>kab</u> t u yum* (literally, "guide of the hand of the lord") and *ah pay* *oc t u yum* (literally, "precursor to the foot of the lord"). Unfortunately, since the Chumayel account of Venus lacks the mathematics and calendrical information of the Dresden Table, associations between the text and the movement of Venus in the night sky are far more speculative in the Chumayel than in the Dresden. However, for argument's sake let us suppose that the directions in the Chumayel text in fact correspond with the directions in the Dresden and their corresponding place in the Venus cycle related there. If we map the pre-Hispanic directional correspondences (as they are represented in the Dresden Venus Table) onto the Chumayel text, we arrive at the follow associations:

Rosiness, East	Heliacal rise	Ah pay oc 'foot'
Grayness, North	Last visibility before superior conjunction	Ah pay oc 'foot'
Lahun Chan [Black, West]	First appearance in western sky	Ah pay kab 'hand'
Light yellow [South]	Last appearance before inferior conjunction	Ah pay kab 'hand'

This reading of the Chumayel passage would suggest that to precede the "foot" of the Sun is to act as Morning Star, marching out ahead along the celestial footpath of the solar lord. For Venus to guide the "hand" of the solar lord is to serve as Evening Star. Interestingly, note that there are two references each to "hand" and to "foot" in the passage, accounting for all four limbs to form the image of a complete anthropomorphic being, in this case the divine Sun, which thereafter makes its appearance in the narrative.

THE FIRST DAWN AND THE HIDDEN NAME OF ITZAM CAB AIN

The limbs making up the body of the Sun god now in place, the text picks back up at the line the redactor of the extant manuscript had previously inserted too early, only to mark it out:

Hex v uol cab valic ah vuc chek nale	*However, throughout the world Seven-Limbed-Maize stands*
Tali t u uuc tas cab	*It came to the seven divisions of the world*
Ca emi v chekeb te u pach Ytzam Kab Ain	*so that it descended to copulate with Itzam [C]ab Ain*
Tij ca emi t u muk u xuk luum can	*So then it descended to its task as the cornerstone of earth and sky*

Ximbal v cahob t u can cib	*Walking to the four candles*
T u can tas	*to the four divisions*
Ti ek ma sasil cab	*When the world was black and without light*
Ti hun minan kin	*When there was not one day*
Ti hun minan akab	*When there was not one night*
Ti hun minan v	*When there was not one month*
Ah ubahob	*They sensed [it]*
Ti yx tan vy ahal cab	*and then it was dawning*
Ca tun ahi cab +	*So then it dawned! +*
Valaci to y ahal cab	*In the time after the dawn*
Oxlahum pic dzac t u uuc	*thirteen multitudes plus seven*
V xocan y ahal cab.	*counted the dawn.*

(CHUMAYEL 44.3–12)

At the beginning of this passage we are introduced to Ah Vuc Chek Nal ("Seven-Limbed Maize") who arrives in the seven *tas* of the *cab* 'world' to fertilize the earth caiman Itzam Cab Ain. The word *tas* is often translated as "layer" and is the most common term appearing in reference to the divisions of the cosmos in Classical Yucatecan Maya texts. However, the number of "layers" of different parts of the Yucatecan cosmos is not entirely consistent from text to text or even necessarily transparent within texts. The source of some of these inconsistencies is more apparent than others; texts with cosmologies grounded in the Postclassic Maya worldview like the Katun 11 Ahau creation myth make reference to the *oxlahun tas caan* 'thirteen *tas* sky' (Chumayel ms. page 43.7). In contrast, the descriptions of the universe in the Ptolemaic-Christian mold found in the Books of Chilam Balam of Kaua (ms. page 148.13–14), of Chan Kan (ms. page 30.3), and the Morley Manuscript (ms. page 180.10) refer to only eleven *tas*. Although "layer" would be an appropriate translation of *tas* for the enveloping series of concentric spheres composing the earth-centered Ptolemaic-Christian cosmos, it may be problematic to think of the Maya *tas* we encounter in the present text in such a fashion. Eric Thompson (1970:195) proposed the following model of the Maya cosmos found in the Books of Chilam Balam:

> There were thirteen "layers" of heaven and nine of the underworld. Although the Maya spoke of the thirteen *taz* ("layers") of the heavens, *taz* covering such things as blankets spread out one above the other, in fact, the thirteen celestial layers were arranged as six steps ascending from the eastern horizon to the seventh, the zenith, whence six more steps led down to the western horizon. Similarly, four more steps led

> down from the western horizon to the nadir of the underworld, when four more steps ascended to the eastern horizon. Thus there were really only seven celestial and five infernal layers. The sun followed this sort of stepped rhomboid on his daily journey across the sky and his nightly traverse of the underworld to return to the point of departure each dawn. There is some inconclusive evidence that the Maya divided the day into thirteen "hours" and the night into nine "hours," corresponding to the numbers of steps or layers.

There are admittedly some problems with Thompson's application of Eduard Seler's (1996, 5:3–23) stepped model of Central Mexican cosmology to account for the Maya sources. For example, the colonial Maya incantation texts of the *Ritual of the Bacabs* speak of Metnal (the name of the Postclassic Maya underworld) as being composed of ten *tas* (Arzápalo Marín 1987:420), an even number rather than an odd one as Thompson's model demands. Nonetheless, Thompson makes an important point by suggesting that the term *tas* refers not simply to vertical but also to horizontal divisions of the cosmos of Classical Yucatecan creation myths. For this reason, perhaps the translation of *tas* as "plane" or "division" is preferable to "layer" as it does not necessarily imply a simple vertically stacked cosmos.

Considering *tas* as potentially both vertical and horizontal helps us account for an apparent contradiction in the text above: that the *cab* 'world' is first referred to as consisting of the seven *tas* but then is referred to as having four. The people of this creation (*ah ubahob*; literally, "hearers" or "sensors"), in the absence of the light of the Sun or moon to see, walk to the four "candles" in the four *tas*. Not considering *tas* to mean strictly vertical or stacking layers enables us to identify these four *tas* as the four color-directions previously mentioned in the text, the only lighted portions of the pre-dawn cosmos due to Venus's previous appearances as Morning and Evening Star.

Having addressed occurrences in the heavens, the narrative returns to the earth, where the Yucatecan version of the Mesoamerican earth monster, the crocodilian Itzam Cab Ain, resides. Crocodiles or caimans have loomed large in epigraphers' attempts to interpret aspects of pre-Hispanic mythology (Taube 1989a; Stuart 2005:70–76; Velásquez Garcia 2006). At this point in the myth a maize being, Ah Vuc Chek Nal, descends to copulate with Itzam Cab Ain. The significance of this action could easily be overlooked, as little is said of Itzam Cab Ain in the Chumayel manuscript. However, in the Tizimín and Pérez manuscripts, their versions of the Katun 11 Ahau creation text are preceded by an account of events involving Oxlahun Ti Ku, Bolon Ti Ku, and Itzam Cab Ain during the immediately previous epoch, that of Katun 13 Ahau:

Ca tali uy ahal cab ti oxlahun ku tumen bolon ti ku	*Then the dawn of Oxlahun Ku came because of Bolon Ti Ku*
Ti ca sihi cħabi	*when he was born, engendered*
Ca sihi Ytzam Cab Ain	*Then Itzam Cab Ain was born*
Xoteb u kin balcah	*that he may signal the day for the whole world*
Ca haulahi caan	*Then the sky was turned face up*
Ca nocpahi peten	*Then the land was turned face down*
Ca ix hoꝑi u hum oxlahun ti ku	*And then Oxlahun Ti Ku's din began*
Ca uchi noh haicabil	*Then the great destruction of the world arrived*
Ca liki noh Ytzam Cab Ain	*Then great Ytzam Cab Ain ascended*
Dzocebal u than u uudz katun lai hun ye ciil	*that this deluge may complete the word of the katun series*
Bin dzocecebal u than katun	*that the word of the katun might be complete*
Ma ix y oltah bolon ti ku i	*But Bolon Ti Ku did not desire it*
Ca ix xoti u cal Ytzam Cab Ain	*And then Ytzam Cab Ain's throat was cut*
Ca u cħaah u petenil u pach	*So he sprinkled the island, its back*
Lai ah uoh puc u kabae	*This is its name: Calligrapher Hill*
Ma ix u toh pultah u kaba tiob	*Neither did he really confess to them its name*
Ti kaxan tun u uich ualac y ahaulil lae.	*He had bound the eyes then of this current reign.*

(TIZIMÍN 14V.16–25)

The portion of the Katun 13 Ahau text above begins with the origin of the Oxlahun Ku, who is/are said to "dawn" by the work of Bolon Ti Ku. The presence or absence of the plural suffix *-ob* in the different manuscript redactions informs us that the Tizmín's myth-teller conceived of Bolon Ti Ku as a singular entity for the purposes of his text, and the teller of the Pérez thought of it as a plurality of deities for his. Note in both cases the pairing here of both female (*sih*) and male (*cħab*) creation verbs to refer to the birth of Oxlahun Ti Ku, recalling the possible male and female associations of the Classic Maya diphrase *cħab akabil* 'genesis and darkness' (see Chapter 2). It is also noteworthy that Bolon Ti Ku is/are prior to and elder(s) to Oxlahun Ti Ku, a clue that upon future research may give insight into the relationship between these two enigmatic deities (and their possible Classic period counterparts).

Itzam Cab Ain is born next in the narrative, after Oxlahun Ti Ku. Itzam Cab Ain's intention to destroy the world with a deluge seems to be motivated by calendrical divination. *Xot* 'to cut' is the principal verb used here, with *xot u kin* (literally, "cut the day") referring to "determine or mark the day," "desire the death (of someone)," or "judge" (Ciudad Real 2001:592–593).

With this verdict, heaven and earth are turned upside down as Oxlahun Ti Ku makes a bunch of racket (*hum*), like that accompanying the "tempestuous (*homocnac* or *humucnac*) sky and earth," that we have already seen occurs during the later Katun 11 Ahau deluge. Itzam Cab Ain "ascends" (*lik*) to fulfill the *katun* prophecy with its own deluge, a great *haicabil* 'destruction of the world.' That Itzam Cab Ain goes up in order to bring a flood down suggests its likely placement in the sky at this point in the narrative. This observation is significant, as it provides the hitherto lacking textual support that the celestial saurian appearing in the skyband of the flood scene on Dresden Codex page 74 (Figure 4.5) may represent a previous incarnation of the earth caiman well attested to elsewhere in Maya texts and iconography.

The teller of the Códice Pérez redaction (ms. page 117) clarifies that these prophetic events are occurring after 18 × 400, or 7,200 days, the equivalent one complete *katun* (20 × 360). Like prophecy throughout the Books of Chilam Balam, its fulfillment is described using the subjunctive, as is typical of the genre (in this case the subjunctive referential intransitive verb suffix *-ebal*). So we are left with some doubt as to the success of Itzam Cab Ain's attempt to kill off life in the world, which may explain why we are later told there is yet another world-destroying flood immediately following, during Katun 11 Ahau. This doubt is compounded when we are told Bolon Ti Ku does not want the Katun 13 Ahau deluge to happen and apparently turns the tables on the celestial saurian. Itzam Cab Ain, who was going to judge (*xoteb u kin*) the world, finds his own throat cut (*xoti u cal*), utilizing a pun no Maya storyteller could have resisted. The passive form of the verb here, however, leaves implicit who actually did the cutting.

Apparently by sprinkling the saurian's blood, Bolon Ti Ku paints/writes on the *petenil* 'island' now stated to be Itzam Cab Ain's back, now called *ah uoh puc*. *Ah uoh* means "he who paints or writes," a synonym for the scribal title *ah dzib*. Furthermore, *puc* is listed in the Motul Dictionary (Ciudad Real 2001:500) as a near synonym for *vitz* and means "hill or mountain" (and the source of the name of the hilly Puuc region of the Yucatán peninsula). Trickster that he is, Bolon Ti Ku does not fess up (*toh pul*: "to tell the truth before a judge") as to who the mountain really is, and so his subversion of Itzam Cab Ain's attempt to fulfill the katun prophecy is said to have "bound the eyes of the current reign."

This final reference to Itzam Cab Ain as Ah Uoh Puc confirms textually that Itzam Cab Ain of the Books of Chilam Balam is in fact analogous to the *dzibal pat ain* 'painted back caiman' who is decapitated in the eighth-century AD mythological text of the Palenque Temple XIX Platform (Stuart 2005:70–76; Velásquez Garcia 2006), the caiman with glyphs on its back depicted on the Postclassic Dresden Codex 4b–5b, and the Colonial period Maya ritual related in the 1579 *Relación de la Ciudad de Mérida* (Garza 1983, 1:72; see also Taube 1989a). Epigraphers had earlier suggested all of these identifications, but textual confirmation was less secure given the problems with the then-available translations of the Katun 13 Ahau text.[4] Furthermore, the naming of Itzam Cab Ain as a mountain also recalls the maker-of-mountains Zipacna (Nahuatl: Cipactli 'Crocodile') who is himself turned to stone within a mountain in the K'iche' *Popol Vuh* after being tricked by the Hero Twins (D. Tedlock 1985:98). Aztec mythology recorded in the *Historia de los Mexicanos por sus pinturas* (in Garibay 1965:26) also relates that the land is made from Cipactli, who is said to be painted as the earth god. The weight of these correspondences suggests that this episode of Classical Yucatecan creation mythology was composed in dialogue with Maya traditions of considerable antiquity and was also a part of the network of intellectual interchange that existed within the Postclassic Mesoamerican world system.

Also worth noting is that elsewhere in the Chumayel manuscript, Ah Uoh Puc is a title of Hun Yuuan Chac, a personage listed among the various *cangel* and Xib Chac of the four directions, mentioned earlier in this chapter. The manifestations of Hun Yuuan Chac are described as having glyphs written on their throats, feet, and hands and are said to be the *thupilob* 'younger brothers' of the Chacs of the other color-directions (Chumayel ms. page 3). In contemporary Yucatec Maya ritual discourse, the class of spirits called *thup* is positioned in the center of quadripartite space and, according to ethnographic accounts, is considered to be the most powerful (Hanks 2000:225, 240). As the force of destruction in the previous epoch, the body of Itzam Cab Ain is now the *petenil* itself, carrying the title of a rain god and the site of a procreative act that foreshadows the return of life and abundance with the descent of the deity Bolon Dzacab.

THE "BURDEN OF THE FLOWER KING"

Following the account of the first dawn and the subsequent reign of Bolon Ti Ku, the Chumayel, Tizimín, and Pérez texts converge once more to form our second hypothetical source text for the Katun 11 Ahau myth, the "Burden of the Flower King." In this myth, we learn that Bolon Dzacab, who in the "History of the Destruction of the World" ascended into the sky with the seed corn, now descends for his rebirth ceremony.

Tij / ca emi u than bolon dzacab	*So then the word of Bolon Dzacab descended*
. . .	. . .
Ca emi ti caanil	*Then he descended from the heavens*
Kan ix / u kinil kaxci u cuch	*and Kan is the day his burden had been tied*
Tij ca emi haa	*Then when the rain descended*
Tali tan y ol caan vchebal u ca put sihil	*he came before Heart of Sky for his rebirth*
Bolon haaban y otoch	*Bolon haaban is his house*
Y et emcij bo/lon mayel	*and nine fragrances had descended*
Ꜧahuc u chi v ni y ak	*Sweet was his mouth, his nose, his tongue*
Ꜧahuchi u dzomel	*His mind is sweetened*
Ti ca emi can tul chaac	*Then when the four Chacs descended*
Vay acaat lae	*Here is Acat*
Lay u cabilob nicte lae.	*These are the flower nectars.*
	(CHUMAYEL 45.22–23, 45.25–31)

At the point where the Chumayel, Tizimín, and Códice Pérez versions of the myth begin to correspond once again, we are explicitly informed the New Year date is Kan, which is exactly what one would expect given that Bolon Dzacab and Kan Xib are patrons of Kan years. Furthermore, in Classical Yucatecan, *kan* refers to "ripe fruit" and Bolon Dzacab now returns from the heavens to be "sweetened" through the *ca put sihil* 'second birth' ritual that Friar Landa (1978 [ca. 1566]:42–45) likened to a kind of "baptism." What Friar Landa was observing was a rite of passage from childhood to adulthood, explicitly linked to the beginning of licensed sexuality among segments of Postclassic Maya society (and therefore the beginning of the creation of new human beings).

At this point, there is an important discrepancy between the various versions that should be mentioned here. The line *vay acaat lae* 'here is Acat' in the Chumayel seems to suggest the redactor has a visual cue he is referencing, perhaps even an illustration from the *ual katun* or sheet of paper dedicated to the history of the *katun* previously mentioned. According to Cogolludo (2006 [1688]:291), "there were also idols of those that tattooed and pierced the bodies [*labraban los cuerpos*] of the Indians, saying they converted them into flowers, called *Acat*." Historian Chuchiak (2000:302) notes that at least one colonial document mentions this deity, a legal case against one Juan de Sosa in 1676, a Spaniard accused of having pierced his nose and made offerings to the deity Ah Cat. Therefore, the redactor may be referencing an illustration of this deity contained in a previous source manuscript that was not reproduced in the extant *cartapacio*.

This fascinating reference to the patron of Maya body artists present in the Chumayel text is absent in the Tizimín manuscript and its cognate line in the Códice Pérez. In turn, these manuscripts relate an equally fascinating episode in its place:

ca emi ca tul chac uayab sodz	*then two Red Sorcerer Bats descended*
lai dzudze u cabilob nicte	*they shall suck the flower nectars*

(TIZIMÍN 15R.21–22)

The role of the bat in myths of the birth of flowers is found in highland Mexican sources such as the illustrated cosmogony on page 44 of Borgia Codex and an alphabetical annotation in the Codex Magliabechiano. Elizabeth Boone (2007:204) summarizes the latter example as follows:

> A bat is born from the semen of Quetzalcoatl. The bat then goes to Xochiquetzal while she is sleeping and bites a piece out of her vulva. When the gods wash the piece of flesh, only malodorous flowers come from the water; but when the bat takes the flesh to Mictlantecuhtli (the lord of the underworld), who washes it, only fragrant flowers emerge.

The role of the bat in the Tizimín and Pérez versions not only illustrates one possible connection between the traditions of Central Mexico and the Maya lowlands but may also help put in context the reference to Bolon Dzacab as being *ku mitnal* 'god of the underworld' found later in all three redactions of the myth. Following his descent from the sky to attain sexual maturity and rebirth, it is this chthonic aspect of Bolon Dzacab (like the Aztecs' Mictlantecuhtli) that enables new life to flower from the earth beneath. In keeping with what we know from other sources about these characters, the appearance of Acat (or, alternately, the Sorcerer Bats) is then followed by the numerous *nicteob*, or flowering plants. Ethnobotanical studies among contemporary Maya speakers have demonstrated that *nicte* refers specifically to species or varieties of the *Plumeria* tree, or frangipani (Hofling and Tesucún 1997; V. Bricker, Po'ot, and Dzul de Po'ot 1998). Writing in the sixteenth century, Landa (1978 [ca. 1566]:102) relates:

> There is also a kind of tree they call *nicte*, that bears many white roses, and others half yellow, and yet others half purplish; these are fresh and odorous, and of them they fashion handsome garlands, and lectuaries when they so desire.

However, many of the names listed in the text do not have known one-to-one correspondences in Colonial period sources rich in ethnobotanical references, such as the Book of Chilam Balam of Kaua (Bricker and Miram 2002:477–485). Those in the Katun 11 Ahau text whose names are readily identifiable, in whole or in part, are *cacau* or cacao; *kom*, a kind of flower described by Landa (1978 [ca. 1566]:102); and *ix laul*, the Yucatán laurel, none of which are *Plumeria*. Of course, the authors of Classical Yucatecan sources simply might not have categorized plants the way we do: cacao, like *Plumeria*, is also a flowering tree, as well as one of considerable economic, culinary, and religious importance to the pre-Hispanic Maya (Martin 2006; McNeil 2006). Although *nic* and *lol* serve as generic terms for "flower" today, the sixteenth-century Motul Dictionary defines *nicte* as a "rose or flower, not denoting of what tree, shrub, or grass" as well as "dishonesty, sin of the flesh, and the transgressions of women" (Ciudad Real 2001:435). In light of this discrepancy between colonial and contemporary sources, I will defer here to the usage of *nicte* as a generic taxonomic category of "flower" along with the symbolic meanings as it appears in this earliest dictionary source. However, I suspect future studies of colonial Maya plant nomenclature will resolve the issue in favor of the more specific meaning of *Plumeria* found among contemporary Maya communities or, alternately, a broader category of flowering trees.

Tij ca hokij yx chac hoch kom t i	*Then when Ix Red Hoch Kom[5] sprouted from it*
y yx / sac hoch kom t i	*and Ix White Hoch Kom from it*
y yx ek hoch kom	*and Ix Black Hoch Kom*
y yx / kan hoch kom	*and Ix Yellow Hoch Kom*
y yx haunal	*and Ix Ha U Nal*
y yx huk nab	*and Ix Huk Nab*
Y et hokci tun yx hoyal nicte	*And then Ix Hoyal Flower had sprouted*
y yx ho / nix te	*and Ix Ho Nix Te*
y yx ni nicħ cacau	*and Ix Ni Nicħ Cacao*
y yx chauil / tok	*and Ix Chauil Tok*
y yx bac nicte	*and Ix Bac Flower*
y yx macuil xuchite	*and Ix Macuil Xochitl*
Yx hobon y ol nicte	*Ix Hobon Yol Flower*
y yx laul nicte	*and Ix Yucatán Laurel Flower*
y / kouol y octah nicte	*and Kouol Yoctah Flower*
Lay hokob nicte	*These flowers sprout*
Laob / ix ah co mayelob	*and these virile pollens*

Lay v naa nicte	*This is the flower mother*
Ca ho/kiob	*Then they sprouted:*
Y udzub ah kin	*the day-keepers bouquet*
Y udzub ahau	*the king's bouquet*
Y u/dzub holcan	*the warrior's bouquet*
Lay u cuch nicte ahau	*This is the burden of the flower king*
Ca emi	*Then he descended*
Minan ix u yanal	*and there is nothing else*
Lay uile c u than	*"This is hunger" it is said*
Ma ix uah u cuchma	*and he has not carried food*
Tij tun ca hoki / yx haulah nicte	*So then when Ix Ha U Lah Flower sprouted*
Ocsic u keban bolon / ti ku	*Bolon Ti Ku caused his sin to enter her*
Ox te ix ti hab u kin	*"And three years he reigns"*
Ca y alah / cuchij	*so he said back then*
Ma ix kuchi	*But he did not arrive*
Cħab naci ku mit/nali bolon dzacab	*that he might engender there the underworld deity Bolon Dzacab*
Ca emi t u chun nicte p̧ilim te	*Then Ppi[z]lim Te[c] descended to the base of the flower there*
Yax bac dzunun ix v uayinah	*and First Scattering Hummingbird dreamed*
Ca emi	*Then he descended*
Ca u dzudzah / u cabil bolon y al nicte t u ychil tun	*and he sucked the nectar within the fruit of Bolon Yal Flower then*
Ca cħaycham/nij yx hoyal nicte	*So Ix Ho Yal Flower took a husband*
Ca tun hoki u pucsikal nicte lae	*And then the core of this flower sprouted*
V ximbantes u ba	*They might visit each other*
Can hek ix u lac nicte lae	*And four branches are his plate of flowers*
Ti yx culan ah kin xocbiltun chumuc	*And then the day-keeper Xocbiltun was seated in the middle*
Tij ca / uchi u huhu y ol oxlahun ti ku	*back when Oxlahun Ti Ku wandered as a vagabond*
Ma yx y oheltah.	*and he did not notice it.*

(CHUMAYEL 46.1–23)

The sexual symbolism continued in the narrative of the flowers continues the link between rites of coming of age, the beginning of licensed sexual activity (noted in regard to the *ca put sihil* ceremony), and the metaphorical meanings of *nicte* discussed previously. Also of interest in this section is the appearance of the Central Mexican god of music and dancing, Macuil Xochitl (Roys 1967:104), whose Nahuatl name means "Five Flower," a meaning shared by the name of the Maya god Ho Nicil, who appears in the pre-Hispanic Madrid Codex (Vail 2000a:39–41). Also appearing is the deity of music, song, and poetry Xocbiltun, who Cogolludo (2006 [1688]:190; see also Roys 1967:105) identifies as another name for the god Pizlimtec, also named here in the text. I believe this alternate name, Pizlimtec, is a Mayanization of yet another Central Mexican deity name, that of the Piltzintecuhtli. Together these images evoke the flowery paradise of color and song along the path of the sun, as documented among Uto-Aztecan speakers by Jane Hill (1992) and more recently for the ancient Maya by Karl Taube (2004).

As we have now seen, episodes of the Katun 11 Ahau creation myth unambiguously ground the mythic narrative in the actual ritual practices of the Postclassic Yucatec Maya and the cosmologies of the broader Postclassic Mesoamerican world system. Although the events, characters, and motifs of each of the redactions are thoroughly grounded in a Postclassic Maya cosmology, each of the manuscripts concludes with a prophecy related to Christianity. The Tizimín and Pérez versions are the most closely related, both texts sharing the same apocalyptic conclusion after the point they and the Chumayel redaction diverge (at C47.2 / T15v.6 / P119.19). However, the Chumayel redaction inserts (from yet another source?) the most elaborate and explicitly apocalyptic conclusion of any of the redactions:

Hex ca bin dzocnac / v than katun lae	*And thus the word of this katun may be accomplished*
Ca tun u dzab d[io]s	*and then it was given by Dios*
Y uchul hun / yeciil t u ca ten	*a deluge occurs for the second time*
Lay hay cabile	*This is the destruction of the world*
Lay tun c u / dzocole	*Then this ends*
Ca tun emec ca yumil ti jesucris/to	*that Our Lord who is Jesus Christ may then descend*
Y okol komil josapat t u xax cah je/rusalem	*upon the valley of Jehoshaphat beside the town of Jerusalem*
Vchic u lohicoon t u cilich kikel	*It occurred that he redeems us by his holy blood*
Lay ix / bin emec ti noh muyal	*and he may be going to descend from a great cloud*
V dzab u tohol canil	*The payment of heaven is given*

Hah / v mansah ti sinan ti crus che cuchie	*In truth he transferred it when he was stretched out on the cross-tree back then*
Tij tun / y emel ti noh v cuchil	*Then when he descends to his great burden*
Ti noh ix u tepal xan	*and to his great reign too*
Hahal d[io]s lay hahal ku	*Being true God, this true deity*
Lay sihes caan ỵ luum	*he caused heaven and earth to be born*
ỵ y okol cab t u lacal	*along with everything upon the world*
La yx bin emec	*And he may descend*
Tax / cuntic y okol cab xan	*to pacify those upon the earth too*
T uy utzil ỵ v lobtacil	*for the good ones and the bad ones*
Y ah dzoy sahulob ah nunob.	*The barbarians fear their conqueror.*

(CHUMAYEL 47.27–48.8)

What sense does it make to conclude an essentially pre-Hispanic Maya myth with a prophecy of the Second Coming of Christ? Since the Books of Chilam Balam were clandestine works, subject to seizure by colonial authorities just as hieroglyphic books were (Chuchiak 2004; Sánchez de Aguilar 1987 [1639]:115), the reason for inclusion of this Christian apocalypse at the end certainly was not a display of piety to ward off overzealous priests. I propose that the Christian apocalypse made sense to colonial Maya scribes within the context of an otherwise Postclassic mythic narrative itself. To understand the composition and artistry of this Classical Yucatecan creation myth requires an exegesis not only of Postclassic Maya cosmology or colonial Maya cosmology but of the relevance of Postclassic mythology for Maya scribes coming to grips with the colonial world.

INFLUENCE OF THE *FIFTEEN SIGNS* TEXTS ON MAYA COSMOLOGY

An important source of the transmission of European Christian apocalyptic lore to the Maya was the popular list of the *Fifteen Signs before Doomsday* (Heist 1952). At least two different versions of this European text circulated in Classical Yucatecan Maya–language versions during the Colonial period, one appearing on pages 9r–10r of the Book of Chilam Balam of Tusik (Barrera Vásquez 1944) and another on pages 101–105 in the Morley Manuscript, the latter a Yucatec-language manuscript dating to perhaps as early as the late sixteenth century (Whalen 2003a).

The lexicon of the *Fifteen Signs* is of significance for understanding something of the colonial dialogue that produced the Maya creation myth under discussion. Given that "the word in language is half someone else's"

(Bakhtin 1981:293), I argue that it is significant, not simply coincidental, that the language of the apocalyptic *Fifteen Signs before Doomsday* in the Yucatec-language Morley Manuscript also serves as lexical choices in all three versions of the "History of the Destruction of the World."

The Morley text is a list of the "signs" (*chicul* in the Maya-language text) that will occur at the "destruction of the world" (*haay cabil*) (Morley 101.3–5). The language for the popular signs of the Euro-Christian apocalypse is the same as that employed repeatedly to describe each of the great trees that the Bacabs set up at the four cardinal directions as *u chicul hay cabal* 'the sign of the destruction of the world' in all three versions of *u kahlay hay cabal* 'the History of the Destruction of the World.' Recall also that Friar Landa, in recounting the tradition of the Flood, noted that the Bacabs themselves were signs and omens and that they each "signalize the misfortunes or blessings which are to happen in the year belonging to" them (Landa 1978 [ca. 1566]:60–61).

In keeping with Maya versions of the popular *Fifteen Signs*, the redactor of the Chumayel version of the myth also relates that Dios, the newly introduced Christian God, will again destroy the world by a deluge (Chumayel 47.28–29), just as the first of the *Fifteen Signs* states, *binil likebal kaknab* 'the sea shall rise' (Morley 101.9; see also Tusik 9r.4).

A further parallel can be found in that the *ca put sihil* 'rebirth' coming-of-age rites described by Landa (1978 [ca. 1566]:45) ended in a feast called the *em ku* 'descent of the god.' This ritual and its mythological accompaniment are the descent (*em*) of Bolon Dzacab in the "Burden of the Flower King." This is then paralleled in the Chumayel text where it states that following the future apocalyptic flood, Jesus Christ *y emel ti noh u cuchil / ti noh ix u tepal xan* 'descends to his great burden / and to his great reign too' (Chumayel 48.4–5). The birth of this new cosmos will involve the "pacification" of "barbarians" or *ah nunob*, the title applied to the Itzá from ancient times. This prophesied conquest of the pagan Itzá parallels the destruction of the "heartless" people in the previous Katun 11 Ahau flood.

CONCLUSION

As we have seen, there are several points of comparison that the Yucatec Maya redactors of the myth of the destruction and re-creation of the world drew upon to reconcile Postclassic Maya traditions with those of the politically dominant Christian world view of the Colonial period. The world trees, birds, and Bacabs were the signs of the destruction of the previous world, just as the *Fifteen Signs*, or *chicul*, propagated in Yucatec translations of colonial Christian literature were. Bolon Dzacab, born of Lady Quetzal, ascends into the heavens and then descends to the earth and underworld to restore the New World emerging after the Old World's destruction, just as the Franciscans would later teach the Yucatec Maya that Christ descended into the underworld, ascended to heaven, and then would descend yet again following another great deluge to renew the world. Thus, the Postclassic Maya myths grounded in the experience of milpa farming and the rituals of New Year and coming of age were reinterpreted by educated Maya in dialogue with the Euro-Christian written traditions of apocalyptic expectation following the Conquest.

NOTES

1. There are archaic elements in language that suggest the extant redactions are drawing on early colonial sources. For example, the Tizimín redaction uses archaic forms such as *manan* 'it is not,' the form characteristic of Yucatec manuscripts from the sixteenth century until shortly after 1620, in contrast to the form *minan*, which gradually displaced it. The Chumayel redaction uses the declarative paradigm for intransitive verbs, a feature of early colonial Yucatecan Maya discourse.

2. We lack for Classical Yucatecan Maya the rich compilations of metaphors and interpretations extant for Classical Nahuatl. Notable sixteenth-century collections by Fray Bernardino de Sahagún and by Fray Andrés de Olmos associate the metaphorical falling of sticks and stones with oppression, toil, and pestilence (Sullivan and Knab 1994:222, 228), and such a meaning appears to be shared here by the Maya.

3. For example, see the case of deletion of consonant clusters and preference for consonant initial words at play in *quisision*, the Mayanization of *inquisición* (V. Bricker 2000:95).

4. Compare Edmonson (1982:39–41) and Craine and Reindorp (1979:117–118) for examples of divergent translations of cognate texts in the Tizimín and Pérez.

5. For more on the use of gender markers such as *(i)x* in the folkbiological taxonomy of Yucatecan languages, see Lois 1998.

C H A P T E R   F I V E

Theogony, Cosmology, and Language in the Ritual of the Angels

Munro Edmonson wrote in the introduction to his translation of the Book of Chilam Balam of Tizimín (1982:xiv):

> Students of the Books of Chilam Balam will have noted the really extraordinary discrepancies between one translator and the next. . . . I cannot but agree with Barrera that these are texts of quite unusual difficulty. The *Popol Vuh* is a model of explicitness and clarity by comparison. All scholars who wrestle with colonial texts in the Indian languages of Middle America must cope with archaism and homonymy—multiplied by textual, orthographic, and lexicographic inadequacies. But these texts are purposely obscure. They are not intended to make sense to outsiders—and they don't.

Perhaps the single best example of what Edmonson observed is the text he dubbed the Sevenfold Creation (Edmonson 1986) and that Ralph Roys (1967) had earlier called the Ritual of the Angels. Perhaps no myth in the Classical Yucatecan corpus is so filled with contradictions, contradictions born of the colonial situation of the Maya scribes who engendered it. The Maya language of the text is in high form, composed of frequent parallelisms, couplets, and triplets, but is at the same time full of opaque references and perhaps intentionally incomprehensible lines mixing Maya, Spanish, Latin, Nahuatl, and "nonsense" language that Roys (1967:108) refers to as "abracadabra." The supernatural beings who populate its cosmology range from entities known from Classic period Maya hieroglyphic texts of the first millennium AD to the angels and celestials disseminated through the Christian Mass, Maya-language doctrinal texts, and the Greco-Roman-inspired astrological lore of Spanish popular almanacs introduced since the sixteenth century. Cosmic in scope and arcane in language, the myth's topic, the apotheosis of Divine Maize, addressed the regular concern of every Maya, commoner and noble, whose life was tied to the life of the fields. While elaborating on a version of the earth-centered Ptolemaic-Christian cosmos imposed by the institutions of the invading Europeans, the historical scope of the myth concludes in a prophetic voice critiquing the inhumane treatment of the indigenous nobility following their Christianization.

In this chapter, I do not pretend to provide a comprehensive interpretation of such a complex work. What I wish to accomplish here is to first contextualize the myth known as the Ritual of the Angels by noting its self-identified genre and determining its possible performative context. Next, I illuminate prominent mythological characters within the text's cosmic mélange by taking what is left implicit for its original audience and making these elements explicit through highlighting intertextual connections. Finally, I reflect on one aspect of the internal organization of the myth, the reported speech attributed to a Divine Maize being. By focusing on divine reported speech, I am able to foreground how the relationship between language and cosmology in this myth is in some ways similar and in other ways distinct from other known examples of creation mythology in both Maya and Judeo-Christian traditions.

SYNOPSIS OF THE RITUAL OF THE ANGELS

The text Roys called the Ritual of the Angels begins with a prologue (48.9–48.16) establishing the narrative scene as *ti minan caan y luum* 'when there was no heaven and earth.' The initial geography of the events occurs in the midst of the *homlah cabil* 'submerged earth,' presumably submerged after a great flood like that related in the Katun 11 Ahau myth. The "Three Cornered Stone," perhaps related to both the "First Three Stone Place" of pre-Hispanic Maya cosmogonies (Looper 1995) and the European iconography of the Trinity, is associated by the myth-teller with the Christian concept of "grace" and emerges as the instrument "forming" (Yucatec: *pat*) the "divinity of the Sovereign." (This double-voiced usage of Christian doctrinal terminology will be discussed in what follows.) Rather than the precise cycles of the calendrical-astronomical tables contained in pre-Hispanic Maya codices, time in this myth is organized into "seven *tuns*, seven *katuns*," an uncharacteristic imprecision that suggests a succession of seven vaguely defined epochs prior to the creation, more akin to the Judeo-Christian *yom* 'days' than Maya mythological timekeeping. The deity sums these epochs (ms. page 48.21), each characterized by a "word" of the deity and the birth and naming of an angel (ms. pages 48.16–49.26). Here and throughout, the words of the deity switch between linguistic codes, various mixtures of Maya, Spanish, and Latin. The deity complains that there is no one to reply to his speech during the creation, an element of narrative tradition that the author/redactor indicates he considers somewhat dubious through the inclusion of the particle *uil* 'perhaps' in the quotative clause (49.23–24).

The dawn occurs upon the completion of these several *bacam* 'birth vigils' (49.29–50.1) during the seventh *katun*, the same epoch said to have witnessed the destruction of the other, presumably pre-Hispanic, deities (*tex kuexe* 'you who are deities') who serve as a mute audience to the deity's monologues (49.22; 50.3). This resonates with similar statements about the invalidation of the pre-Hispanic deities in the preface to the Chumayel mythography (see Chapter 3). In an allusion to the New Testament book of Revelation, the deity's "new word of the first seal," that he is the "beginning" and will be the end, is buried (50.5–8). Dios Citbil 'God the Father' asserts the "united" nature of the persons of the deity in a mixed Maya, Latin, and Spanish monologue (50.2, 8–12). Afterward, numerous celestial and cosmological elements of pre-Hispanic Maya or Ptolemaic-Christian provenance are born and established in the cosmos: the Five Winds, the Three Stones, the Pauahtuns, the Empyrean and Crystalline Heavens, the Four Angels of the Winds, and the planets.

Following this creation, a battle is waged in the sky in which the *Op* bird assembles much tribute. Not all details of this celestial rebel are provided, as the author asserts twice, *tech au ohel sihil u cah* 'you know the birth of its nature' (53.7–8; 53.10), followed by its titles: "the Very First" and "the Slave in Heaven." This period is characterized by further linguistic diversity, with Nahuatl, Spanish, and even pan-Mayan "gibberish" words interjected into Maya narrative.[1]

The result of the battle is that the "first Pope" places heavenly *corporales* 'bodies' in *ojales* (ms. page 53.19–20) in fulfillment of the "word" or prophecy of an angel. Narrative voice then shifts to the future and subjunctive future of prophecy (beginning 53.22), signaling that this war in Heaven foreshadows the destruction of kingdoms in the age of Katun 13 Ahau. Following the arrival of Christianity with the Spanish invasion in AD 1539, the new Maya Christian nobility are treated "like wild animals" (54.7–8). This section concludes upon its attribution to *chilam balam, profeta*.

After a break in the manuscript, the narrative is supplemented by a brief text accompanying an illustration of unidentified historical provenance (for attempts at deciphering the symbols and ciphers of that page, see Mediz Bolio 1930:64–65; Edmonson 1986:243; Velásquez Garcia 2007). The text on the page reports the names of the different *dzic* 'sides' of God, including different epithets of Dios in Latin and Spanish. The four Pauahtuns, or pre-Hispanic sky-bearing deities, are also juxtaposed with European names, three being those of winds and the fourth, that of the Yellow Pauahtun, with Moses. The section concludes with the revelation of the transgressions of the angels against Dios.

COSMOGONIC TRADITIONS IN REJOINDER

Of all the cosmogonic traditions composing the Chumayel mythography, this narrative draws on perhaps the most diverse source materials. As we shall see, given the scope of materials cited, its colonial author must have been conversant in the cosmogonic lore originating historically on both sides of the Atlantic.

Dominus vobiscum u lahci u thanob u kail	"Dominus vobiscum" *had finished the words of its song*
Ti minan caan y̤ luum	*when there was no heaven and earth*
Tij ca sih tan homlah cabil	*When it was born in the midst of the submerged world then*
Ti minan caan / y̤ luum	*when there was no heaven and earth*
Ox amay tun grasia uchci	*The Three Cornered Stone Grace had come to pass*
U patci v / kuil ah tepale	*It had formed the divinity of the Sovereign*
Ti minan caan cuchie	*when there was no heaven back then*
Ti ca / sihi vuc te tun vuc ꝑel katun	*So when seven tuns, seven katuns were born*
C̄huyan t uy ol / yk vuc te tete	*The seven elect were suspended from the heart of the wind*
Ci bin	*so it is said*
Ca pecni	*Then [the bell] sounded*

Vuc pel ix / v grasiail xan	*and seven are its graces also*
Vuc tul ix v santoil xan.	*and seven are its saints also.*

(CHUMAYEL 48.9–16)

In this introduction, the text begins at the ending, at the conclusion of a "song" (Yucatec: *kay*), or more specifically, a sung mass such as those frequently requested in colonial Maya testaments. That this is in fact a *misa kaybil* 'sung mass' is clear from the benediction *dominus vobiscum* 'the Lord be with you' as well as the reference to the sounding of a bell (*pec*), as occurs during the raising of the consecrated host (*hostia* in Spanish or *oxtia* in some Maya texts). With this phrase, the interpretation of this Maya theogony is perhaps best approached by reference to the *Discursos Sobre Las Misas y Significas* 'Treatise on the Mass and its Meanings,' a Maya-language doctrinal text that is extant in both the Books of Chilam Balam of Kaua (ms. pages 162–165) and of Chan Kan (ms. pages 118–123). The doctrinal text allegorizes parts of the Mass with episodes in the Passion of Christ. The Kaua version states (V. Bricker and Miram 2002:306):

lay u dzooc dominus bobiscum ca y alic padre
ca yumil ti d[io]s nac t uy ahaulil can

[When] the priest says the end of this Dominus Vobiscum,
It is Our Lord who is God who rises to the kingdom of heaven.

The treatise links the phrase *dominus vobiscum* with the apotheosis of Christ. The author of this Maya theogony appears to be aware of this exegesis of the Mass and adapts it to another narrative of apotheosis, the account of the formation (*pat*) of "the divinity of the Sovereign" (*u kuil ah tepal*) (48.12–13). Rather than *ch̄ab* or *sih*, the verbs of creation with male and female associations, *pat* is the verb used for making objects of "clay, wax, or dough" (Ciudad Real 2001:482). As the myth later relates, the name of this sovereign who is being formed, the name of *ca cilich yum citbil* 'our blessed Lord, the Father,' is Sustina Gracia ("Sustaining Grace") (50.18–24), "saint grace" being the title applied to maize by contemporary Maya farmers in Yucatán (Roys 1967:107n3; Burns 1983:39).

Given the association of maize with the divine, an according-to-the-Vatican interpretation of this particular sung mass is unlikely to take us too far into the world of this Maya myth-singer. As Erik Velásquez Garcia (2007) has recently suggested, the early nineteenth-century report by the priest of the Maya town of Yaxcabá, Bartolomé del Granado Baeza, may be of relevance to interpreting this text. In this report, related in 1813, the priest Baeza notes that although the Indians under his supervision "do not seem to retain some of the traditions of their primitive parents, nor do they have knowledge or tradition regarding from whence they came to populate this land" (Baeza 1845 [1813]:174), Baeza is nonetheless aware that "there are many superstitions" (ibid.:168). Among these superstitions, Baeza (170) relates:

> In the Maya language that is used exclusively throughout this entire province, there is a catechism of Christian doctrine approved by the lord bishops. It seems to me that idolatry of the kind by which in other times worship was given to the Devil in diverse figures of clay or of stone is already very rare in the entire bishopric. The thing that endures today is what the Indians call *tich*, which means "obligation" or "sacrifice," and is commonly called the farmers' mass (*misa milpera*), being an imitation of the true mass. (translation mine)

The sacrifices involved in the *tich* described by Baeza include a native turkey, fourteen tortillas (called the *can lahun taz, taz* also being the term used to refer to the layers or planes of Maya cosmology), copal incense, and the native liquor, *balché* (ibid.). Baeza's description of the *tich* or *misa milpera* also provides details that suggest that the Ritual of the Angels, if not a script for similar rites practiced by near-contemporary Maya elsewhere in Yucatán, was certainly composed by an author in dialogue with similar traditions:

> Some of the informants and of the principal culprits and their accomplices have assured me that [the ceremony] begins with invoking the three Divine Persons, and that they recite the Creed, and soaking up the mead [*pitarrilla; balché*] with an aspirgillum, go about sprinkling to the four winds, invoking the four *Pahahtunes* [Pauahtuns], who are the lords or custodians of the rains. . . . A leader, about eighty years old, was urged to declare to me who were these *Pahahtunes*. He told me that the red *Pahahtun*, who is seated in the East [*oriente*], is Santo Domingo; the white one, seated in the North [*septentrion*], is Santo Gabriel; the black one, seated in the West [*occidente*], Santo Diego; and the yellow one (who is also called *Xkanleox*) seated in the South [*mediodia*] is Santa Maria Magdelana. He confessed to me also that it is truly said that the mead is the *yaxhá*, which means "first water" or the first liquor. This is because he has heard it said that it is the first liquor that God [*Dios*] created, and that with this God the Father said the first mass. And having to rise to Heaven [*el Cielo*] with Maria Santísimia, [God] left the said four Saints the care of the rains. (Ibid.)

While in the eyes of Baeza's informants they are practicing a form of Christian ritual, the four Pauahtun are also Maya deities of great antiquity (Figure 5.1). Michael Coe (1973:15) proposed the phonetic reading of the name glyphs identifying God N—long known as such following Schellhas's

5.1. God N, a possible Postclassic depiction of the deity Pauahtun. Madrid Codex, page 104b (reproduced by permission of the Museo de América, Madrid).

(1904) nomenclature—as *pauahtun*, which is often affixed with the number "four" or "five" (see also Taube 1989b:36–37; 1992:92–99). Recently some epigraphers have challenged the accuracy of Coe's decipherment, suggesting that the God N glyph should instead be read **ITZAM** (in Bassie-Sweet 2008:130–140). Writing in the sixteenth century, Friar Landa's informants equated the four colored Pauahtuns with the *bacabs* and *xib chacs* that served as year-bearers and sky-bearers (1978 [ca. 1566]:60–61), the latter role attested to for the *pauahtuns* in pre-Hispanic Maya iconography (Taube 1992:94). In her analysis of the relationships among Maya deities based on the substitution or pairing of their name glyphs in the Postclassic Maya codices, Vail (2000b:129) notes that God N is associated with God E, the maize god Nal, establishing a late pre-Hispanic link between this deity and agricultural fertility.

It is clear from Baeza's early nineteenth-century account that the sky-bearing Pauahtuns found a place in colonial Maya cosmology as the custodians of the rains in four cardinal directions. The Pauahtuns' central role in the *misa milpera* likewise suggests the continuation of their direct connection with maize growth, unsurprising for the custodians of the rain. Nonetheless, the Pauahtuns of Baeza's account do not simply represent a veneer of Christianity on otherwise pagan practice but rather a new form born of the dialogue between pre-Hispanic cosmological discourses with sources of exported European tradition. As Miram and Bricker (1996) convincingly argue, the colonial Pauahtuns in the Ritual of the Angels are the angelic guardians of wind and rain positioned along the four corners of an otherwise spherical Ptolemaic-Christian cosmos (Figure 5.2).

Cangeles yk valic tamuk u čhabtic ek	*These Wind Archangels are posted while he engenders the stars*
Ma sa/sac cab	*There had never been light in the world*
Minan caan y̦ luum	*There was no heaven and earth*
Chac pauahtun	*Red Pauahtun*
Sac pauahtun	*White Pauahtun*
Ek pauahtun	*Black Pauahtun*
Kan Pauahtun	*Yellow Pauahtun*
He yax caan valic dios citbile	*God the Father posted this first heaven*
U machma u tunil	*He has grasped the stone*
U machma u cangel	*He has grasped the Archangel*
U machma u kabalil	*He has grasped the wheel*
Ti čhuyan t u cangeles yk.	*when it was suspended by the Wind Archangels.*

(CHUMAYEL 51.13–21)

As V. Bricker and Miram (2002) and Velásquez Garcia (2007) have demonstrated, materials in the Books of Chilam Balam are alternately

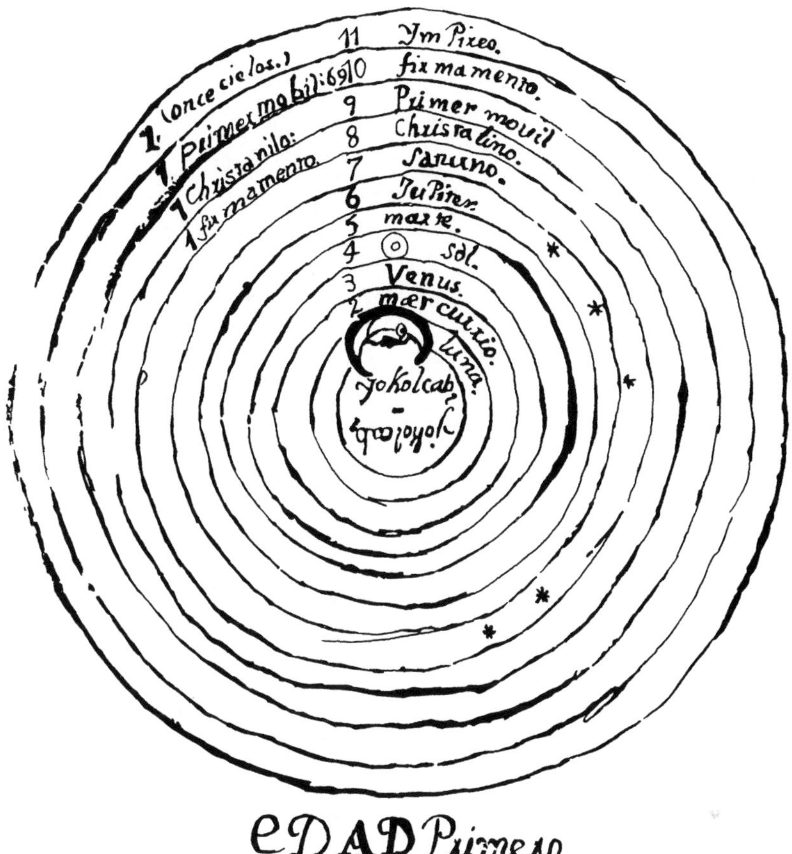

5.2. The celestial spheres of the Ptolemaic-Christian cosmos as depicted in the Maya Book of Chilam Balam of Kaua (V. Bricker and Miram 2002:92; reproduced by permission of the Middle American Research Institute, Tulane University, New Orleans, Louisiana).

derived from or syncretized with the world view of the *Reportorios de los Tiempos*, popular almanacs of European astrological lore (see also Mignolo 2003:206–207). As I argue throughout the remainder of this chapter, the dialogic process that populated these myths with beings like Pauahtun-Wind archangels was not simply uncritical borrowing or capitulation, as the priest Baeza suggests by referring to the *tich* as *un remedo de la verdadera misa* 'an imitation of the true mass,' but a dialogical process in rejoinder to literary sources of both pre-Hispanic Mesoamerican and European cosmologies.

COSMOLOGY AND DEITIES OF THE RITUAL OF THE ANGELS

Despite the many overt references to aspects of Ptolemaic-Christian cosmology throughout the Ritual of the Angels, I believe it is unlikely that the Pauahtuns are the only divine beings of the pre-Hispanic traditions within this Maya rejoinder to the Latin Mass. Velásquez Garcia (2007) has recently argued that the placement of the seven angels of the *katuns* in this mythic narrative is the placement of the seven "planets" of the Ptolemaic cosmos, as inspired by various *reportorios* or Spanish almanacs. I believe there is considerable merit in this proposal, as in some cases the names of the angels and their placement in the order of the Ptolemaic cosmology do clearly match. For example, the name of the angel of the third *katun* or night of creation in the myth, Alba Congel, literally means "Daybreak Archangel," an appropriate term for the Morning Star aspect of Venus, the denizen of the third sphere of the Ptolemaic cosmos. However, it is also worth noting that the placement of seven divine beings in the dark predawn night of creation can be found in a hieroglyphic text a millennium earlier in the Classic period Maya painted ceramic known as the Vase of the Seven Gods (Kerr no. 2796; Coe 1973:109; see also Miller and Martin 2004: 58–62). Although demonstrating a clear chain of transmission from such ancient precedents to colonial accounts would be daunting in a great many cases, I believe it is productive to leave open the possibility that what may appear to be even the most obvious borrowings from European sources may in fact be the colonial product of a dialogic process in rejoinder with indigenous traditions of considerable antiquity.

Another example I wish to point out is the three-star constellation of a turtle of the pre-Hispanic Maya zodiac (H. Bricker and V. Bricker 1992; B. Tedlock 1999), referred to here in the Chumayel manuscript as *ox coc* 'Three Turtle.'

Leon te	*"Stretched out on us there*
Hun tic ca tic ox hun tic	*"One fold, two folds, three and one folds*
Hun tuuc ox hun bakam / v katunil	*"One heap, three and one birth vigils of its katun*
Ox uuc pis vy ahal cab	*"Three and seven counts of the dawn"*
Ca / sihi u lamay tun u lamay akab	*Then the central tun, the central night was born*
Ti minan caan y̱ luum	*when there was no heaven and earth*
Ca than t u men g[rasi]a citbil t u ba t u hunal	*So he speaks by the grace of the Father by himself, alone*

Ti ox coc ox akab cuchie	*at Three Turtle, Three Night back then*
Lay u yax than ku	*This is the deity's first word*
Ti minan caan y̦ luum.	*when there was no heaven and earth.*
	(CHUMAYEL 52.23–53.2)

After the forming of the celestial spheres, "Three Turtle" is the location of the deity's "first word." In the Late Postclassic Maya Madrid Codex, the turtle has on its back three stones (Figure 5.3). Freidel, Schele, and Parker (1993) suggest that these three stones are analogous to the "Three Stones of Creation" appearing in several brief references to creation mythology on Classic Maya monumental texts. These "Three Stones of Creation" have themselves been linked by Looper (1995) to another prominent cosmological actor in the Ritual of the Angels, the *ox amay tun gracia*. What are we to make of these references to pre-Hispanic cosmology in the otherwise Ptolemaic-Christian universe laid out in the Ritual of the Angels?

According to the terse references on surviving pre-Hispanic texts, a pair of canoeing deities known to scholars as the Paddler Gods established three stone thrones at the "First Three Stone Place." As hearths in traditional Mesoamerican domiciles consist of three stones (Figure 5.4), scholars have hypothesized that this "First Three Stone Place" may be synonymous with the K'iche' constellation *oxib' xk'ub'* 'Three Hearth Stones' documented ethnographically by Barbara Tedlock (1992:181–182; see also D. Tedlock 1985:261n85). As for the reference to the *ox amay tun gracia* in this Chumayel myth text, Looper (1995) suggests glossing this as "three stelae," following Barbara MacLeod's reading of *amay tun* as the compound word *amaytun* in the compilation of Yucatec Maya dictionaries *Diccionario Maya Cordemex* (Looper 1995:24–25). However, we must be cautious in our use of such compilations. The definition of *amaytun* in the *Cordemex* dictionary as "stela" is itself derived from don Juan Pío Pérez's nineteenth-century "Diccionario de la Lengua Maya" (Barrera Vásquez et al. 1995:15). In contrast, the much earlier sixteenth-century *Calepino Maya de Motul* lists *amay* as simply "esquina o cantero" (Ciudad Real 2001:63). Maya grammar requires a numeral classifier to follow the numeral, so it is unlikely one should read *amay tun* as a compound word. Instead, an argument consistent with Maya grammar and utilizing early Colonial rather than Independence period dictionary sources would be that the phrase *ox amay tun* refers to a "three-cornered" stone, as Roys (1967:107) originally suggested.

Let us consider for a moment what is meant by this "three-cornered" stone; what would the Maya hearing this text have been seeing, whether

5.3. Postclassic depiction of celestial Turtle constellation with three stones on its back. Madrid Codex, page 71a (reproduced by permission of the Museo de América, Madrid).

5.4. Traditional Mesoamerican three-stone hearth. Xocén, Yucatán, 1999 (photograph by author).

before them in ritual or in their minds' eye? A "three-cornered" stone is a triangular stone. Figure 5.5 is a detail from the frontispiece of an early seventeenth-century book on angels, incorporating many of the popular iconographic elements of Christian cosmology popular during colonial times that circulated, and in some cases still circulate, in the Maya area.[2] Visually following the base of the frontispiece image up the ladder from the *Electi* 'Elect' (the *tete* in the Maya text of the Chumayel manuscript), one encounters this diagram of the heavens populated by the Angelic Orders, some of which are named in the Chumayel narrative. Besides the *angeli*, these include the *Archangeli* (written as *aucangel* in the Chumayel) and the *Virtutes* (written as *virtutus*), both of which are listed as examples of *v kaba yk* 'the wind's name' (ms. page 50.15–17), as well as the *Throni* (written as *tronas*; ms. page 52.14). In the center of these nine celestials, the Trinity is represented by a triangle, itself composed of three triangles, with Latin names of the Father, the Son, and the Holy Spirit in each corner. The concluding lines of the myth provide further support for this interpretation:

5.5. Detail from frontispiece of *The Hierarchie of the Blessed Angells* (Heywood 1635; reproduced by permission of the Huntington Library, San Marino, California).

He ix u ca kaba dios / citbil	*And this is his second name, God the Father*
Ca tali u / yanhal t u perso/nase	*that came into the possession of persons*
Sihanili / balcah y̧ luume	*The things of the world and the earth are given birth there*
Lay tun u kaba / lae	*This then is his name*
Sosue u ca / dzice	*Joshua is the second side*
T uy ox dzice	*of his three sides*
U ca kaba e	*His second name*
Ox uch / ox tenhi lae	*Three of old, three times*
Mesister latin tun	Mesister latin *then*
Dei romanse	Dei [in] romanse

Chac pauahtun	*Red Pauahtun*
Ut coru sis	*Ut coru cold*
Sac Pauahtun	*White Pauahtun*
Cora calbo	*Cora calbo*
Ek pauahtun	*Black Pauahtun*
Colru si pro vento	*Colru si pro vento*
Kan pauahtun	*Yellow Pauahtun*
Moses	*Moses*
No vis no va	*No vis no va*
Mesias u kaba / dios	*Mesias is the name of God*
Ti ma sihic / caan y luum	*when heaven and earth had not been born*
Lay mexias xpoe / u kaba	*This is his name, Messiah Christ*
Ca tun v / sihsah angelob	*And then he gave birth to the angels*
Heuac chacannili	*Nonetheless revealed there*
Ti dios / binili	*to God it goes there*
Sipic / angelobe	*The angels transgressed*
Tan / has tze	*Facing misery and imperfection*
U ca dzic u kaba / dios	*The name of God is his second side*
Lay manuel / v dzaci u kaba	*This name Emanuel was added*
T uy ox dzic u ka/bae	*to the three sides of his name*
Lay tun / heremias / u kabae	*Then this is his name, Jeremiah*
Ti minan caan y luume.	*when there was no heaven and earth.*
	(CHUMAYEL 56)

The emphasis on each different *kaba* 'name' and *dzic* 'side' of Dios we encounter throughout the Chumayel narrative, combined with the substantial material on *angelil* 'angels,' supports the interpretation of the *ox amay tun grasia* 'Three-Cornered Stone Grace' as a reference to such a popular illustration of the divine Trinity. This interpretation also corresponds well with Baeza's (1845 [1813]:170) account that the *tich* or *misa milpera* involved the invocation of the *tres Divinas Personas* 'three Divine Persons.' The juxtaposition of clearly pre-Hispanic cosmological motifs with European Christian cosmological motifs suggests a subtle syncrisis throughout the double-voiced discourse that characterizes the Ritual of the Angels.

In addition to the identification of the Christian Trinity with the pre-Hispanic "Three Stones" established at creation, there are numerous lines of evidence within the Chumayel theogony that suggest the apotheosis of the Christian *dios* in this narrative is simultaneously the apotheosis of the Maya maize god. Among the many agricultural references in the narrative, *mehen dios* 'the Son of God' is referred to as the *yax le dios* 'first (or green) leaf of God' (51.4–7). Prior to his apotheosis, the deity refers to himself repeatedly as *baca[l] mac* 'the Corncob Man.'[3] *Bacal* is the term for a corncob devoid of the kernels. The term *bacal mac* itself may be a verbal play on the doctrine of the Incarnation, in which God became a human being, or a *bakel mac bacel mac* 'man of flesh, man of bone.' This divinity of *dios* is *patah* 'formed' or 'molded,' a verb that can refer to the processing of maize dough (one of the original substances of the human body in the K'iche' *Popol Vuh*) or earth (the original substance of the human body in Judeo-Christian tradition). After this *dios* receives its divinity in the seventh *katun*, the name "Corncob Man" no longer appears, being replaced by the name *Sustina Grasia* 'Sustaining Grace,' a reference to the feeding, "sustaining" role of the maize plant, called *gracia* or *santo gracia* among contemporary Yucatec Maya (Roys 1967:107n3; Burns 1983:39). Here again we uncover examples of a double-voiced use of language capable of simultaneously expressing "heterodox" Maya and "orthodox" European understandings of divinity.

What, then, do we make of the references to "grace" in the names of both the Three-Cornered Stone and that of the narrative's newly apotheosized deity? In Christian doctrinal texts in Classical Yucatecan Maya, *gracia* is referred to as the source of *cuxtal* 'life' and *toh olal* 'health' (Morley ms. pages 205, 209–210). *Gracia* is also likened to *tostonesob* (half *pesos*) to explain its function as spiritual currency (Morley ms. page 265). The most vivid example of *gracia* as spiritual currency is the *gracia* inherent in the sacrificial blood of Christ, by which *u mansah* 'he transferred' *u tohol canil* 'the payment of heaven' through the Crucifixion (Chumayel 48.2–3). Divine blood sacrifice had independent parallels in pre-Hispanic Maya culture, and some scholars have argued that the iconography of the hieroglyph for the word *kul* 'divine' appearing in the name collocations of many divine kings represents spilt blood droplets (Stuart 1984). In the Ritual of the Angels, the names of the stones associated with newly deified *Sustina Grasia* suggest cutting, piercing objects with points or claws whose color is red, presumably red with blood (Chumayel 50.23–29), just as the Maya used stone implements to let their own blood in sacrifice. The Maya may have found in the missionaries' discourses on *gracia* a parallel to their own ancient ritual metaphysics, sometimes expressed in the diphrastic kenning *c̆hab akab* 'genesis, darkness.' Similar to discourses of *gracia* in colonial and contemporary Maya communities, the ancient ritual discourses of *c̆hab akab* (discussed in Chapter 2) developed their own culture-specific associations with sacrificial bloodletting, fertility, theogony, exchange, and (as we will discuss in Chapter 6) health.

A Bakhtinian reading of the Ritual of the Angels as double-voiced discourse is productive here, in which "Dominus Vobiscum" may symbolize when "Our Lord who is God who rises to the kingdom of heaven" (V. Bricker and Miram 2002:306) while simultaneously recalling the ascent of maize-related deities, like Bolon Dzacab, who stole away the seed corn to the sky (Chapter 4). Thus, in contrast with the explicit syncrisis of different points of view on the same object expressed in the Maya-Spanish heteroglossia of colonial cosmological texts such as the Genesis commentary of the Morley Manuscript (Knowlton 2008), we may have an implicit syncrisis evident in the double-voiced application of Christian doctrinal discourse.

Of course, the double-voicedness of a narrative is inferred from the shared cultural understandings of its audience. As the quote from Edmonson (1982) that began this chapter reminds us, we are neither the intended audience nor is this text meant to be clear. But by recourse to intertextuality, to the language and content shared between these Classical Yucatecan myths and contemporaneous religious texts and ritual practices, we come much further toward a coherent understanding of such a beautiful yet elusive mythology.

CODE SWITCHING AND CREATION

Beyond the intertextual references to the Catholic Mass and related indigenous documents, the Ritual of the Angels also explicitly displays the use of multiple voices, these being instances of reported speech and code switching, discourse features internal to the text that can also be amenable to interpretation. Theogonies (narratives of the births of deities) emerging from colonial situations raise interesting problems in their negotiation of the concept of divinity. Through this double-voiced narrative of origins, the monologic characteristics of Spanish Christian monotheism are recognized, problematized, and perhaps even satirized in the reported speech of the deity. In this way, the polyglossic reality of life in colonial Yucatán is foreshadowed in the divine speech prior to the creation of the universe itself, "when there was no heaven and earth."

For example, in the preface to the myth discussed earlier, note how the author refers to the Ritual of the Angels as if it were a tradition derived from the reports of others, *ci bin* (Chumayel 48.15). It is interesting that, although at the end of this theogony the narrative is attributed to the Chilam Balam (54.14), it is identified here as a reported tradition. This suggests that, at the very least, the scribe penning the Ritual of the Angels presents himself *not* as the Chilam Balam but as one conducting a self-conscious redaction of the prophetic traditions attributed to the Chilam Balam and other sources. This problem of the authorial self in a dialogic text, such as we necessarily encounter when dealing with a colonial and syncretic text, is described by Bakhtin:

> This interaction, this dialogic tension between two languages and two belief systems, permits authorial intentions to be realized in such a way that we can acutely sense their presence at every point in the work. The author is not to be found in the language of the narrator . . . but rather, the author utilizes now one language, now another, in order to avoid giving himself up wholly to either of them; he makes use of this verbal give-and-take, this dialogue of languages at every point in his work, in order that he himself might remain as it were neutral with regard to language, a third party in a quarrel between two people (although he might be a *biased* third party). (Bakhtin 1981:314)

As will become even more apparent as we go along, the author/redactor of the Ritual of the Angels effectively utilizes the multiple dialogic tensions that characterize the "languages" of colonial Yucatán: the social, the cosmological, and the linguistic. Perhaps more than any other narrative discussed in this study, the Ritual of the Angels emerges from these multiple tensions seething with these contradictions, contradictions that must have weighed heavily on a Maya author educated in both pre-Hispanic and Spanish Christian traditions.

Amax / yiclo	*Amaxyiclo (?)*
Uchci v sihil	*Its birth came to pass*
Ti hun tun g[rasi]a	*in the first tun of grace*
Hun picib / g[rasi]a	*The first multitude of grace*
Uchci u picil akab	*It came to pass in the multitude of nights*
Ti minan d[io]s cuchie	*when there was no God back then*
Mayto v kamab v d[io]sil cuchie	*Mayto (?) he received his Godhood back then*
Tijli yan / ychil g[rasi]a	*Still there in grace*
T u ba t u hunal ychil akbil	*by itself, alone in the darkness*
Ti mi/nan caan y luum	*when there was no heaven and earth*
Ca buki t u dzoc katun	*Then he summed the end of the katun*
Ti ma u chac sihil ti hun te katun	*Before he could be born in one katun*
Yanij / v tuyij	*There was just a pinch of it*
Adeu ti para mij	*"Adeu ti para mij"*
Uchci v kuil.	*His divinity came to pass.*

(CHUMAYEL 48.16–23)

The narrative structure of the Ritual of the Angels is arranged in relation to numerous instances of reported speech, including divine speech. The narrative voice, and the reported speech of the deity in particular, switches codes among Maya, Latin, Spanish, and Nahuatl numerous times throughout the text.[4] Code switching, and the social and cultural significance of this phenomenon, have been investigated by anthropologists and linguists in various societies around the world for several decades now (Blom and Gumperz 1972; Heller 1988; Myers-Scotten 1993). Instances of code switching in the context of a colonial Maya theogony are intriguing for several reasons. It was the policy of the Counter-Reformation Church that "divine words," such as Sacred Scripture, be rendered in Latin. The Mass, the necessary Church ritual for the newly converted Maya, was also given in Latin on the rare occasion a priest was available. Also, as I have discussed elsewhere in regard to the redactional history of a Maya-language Genesis commentary (Knowlton 2008), there is evidence suggesting that Maya scribes penning the Books of Chilam Balam were not inclined to ascribe equal status to the Spanish linguistic code once colonial caste divisions solidified social distinctions between the two groups. This was evident in the tendency to move from unmarked juxtaposition of Maya and Spanish terms for elements of Ptolemaic-Christian cosmology in the earliest redaction, to a marking of the Spanish code as the words of the "foreigners," and finally to the removal of Spanish terms through their translation into Maya in later redactions. As Bakhtin (1981:295) notes: "Consciousness finds itself inevitably facing the necessity of *having to choose a language*. With each literary-verbal performance, consciousness must actively orient itself amidst heteroglossia, it must move in and occupy a position for itself within it, it chooses, in other words, a 'language.'" Here, we will examine the contexts in the narrative where such choices among languages are made on the clause level (thus excluding instances of proper names or isolated doctrinal terms discussed elsewhere). By examining contextual patterns in the switch from one linguistic code to another in the Ritual of the Angels, we may perceive something of the social relationships and cultural meanings of the colonial Maya through the situational uses of different languages.

Ca / ca lukij	*Then it left*
Ca ix xibni t u ca picib tun g[rasi]a	*and then it spread out in the second multitude of tuns of grace*
Ca ku/chi t u ca ꝑel katun	*that arrived in the second katun*
Alpilcon v kaba / v angelil	*Alpilcon is the name of the angel*
Sihci lukul	*Once it had been born, it leaves*

T u cibah v ca / ꝑel g[rasi]a	*It bestowed its second grace*
T u ca ꝑel v picil akab	*in the second multitude of nights*
Ti mamac ya/nac cuchie	*before anyone had existed back then*
Ca u kamah v kuil	*Then he received his divinity*
T u ba t u / hunal	*by himself, alone*
Ca tali v lukul	*Then it came and it leaves*
O firmar	*"O firmar"*
Ci ix v than	*And thus he speaks*
Ca u kamah v kuil	*Then he received his divinity*
T u ba t u hunal.	*by himself, alone.*

(CHUMAYEL 48.23–49.2)

As mentioned earlier, the narrative begins with the Latin benediction that concludes the Mass, although the Mass's singer who uttered the benediction is left unidentified. Beyond proper names and those loanwords (*grasia, santo, angel*) incorporated into the Maya linguistic code (indicated by their taking of the *-il* suffix), the next instance of code switching in the text occurs with divine speech. The words uttered by the deity in the first and second epochs before creation are brief, imperfect utterances mostly deriving from Romance languages (*adeu ti para mij* and *o firmar*; Chumayel 48.23, 49.1; see also Edmonson 1986:229–230). Both of these Romance phrases appear in discursive contexts where Dios is not yet fully apotheosized. The small amount of "divinity" (*kuil*) Dios has received in the first two epochs simply "leaves" (48.24, 49.2–3).

Ca lukij	*Then it left*
Ca / bini t uy ox picib tun g[rasi]a	*Then it went to its third multitude of tuns of grace*
Alba congel v kaba y an/gelili	Alba Congel *is the name of its angel there*
Lay vy ox ꝑel g[rasi]a	*This is its third grace*
Xicen t u can picib tun / g[rasi]a	*"I may go to the fourth multitude of tuns of grace*
V can ꝑel uil akab	*"Its fourth moonlit night"*
Atea ohe lay u ka/ba y angelili	Atea Ohe, *this is the name of its angel there*
Sihil v cibah v can ꝑel g[rasi]a	*The birth bestowed the fourth grace*
Ca ho/ꝑi u thanic v ba t u hunal	*Then he began speaking to himself, alone*
Bee kue ah tepa/le	*Thus this Deity, this Sovereign:*
Ma baca[l] macen t in hunal baca[l]	*"Am I not the corncob man, the sole corncob?"*

C u than / t u banil	*Thus he speaks a great deal*
T u kuil ychil g[rasi]a	*to his divinity within grace*
Xicen to	*"I may go afterward"*
Ci u than.	*thus he speaks.*

(CHUMAYEL 49.2–9)

By the third and fourth epochs, however, Dios makes his first utterances in Maya, each time surmising that his "godhood" may arrive in the following epoch (*xicen*: literally, "I may go"; 49.4–5, 49.9).

Ca bini t u picib tun g[rasi]a	*Then he went to the multitude of tuns in grace*
T u ho picib akab	*in the fifth multitudes of nights*
Sihil v cibah v ho pel g[rasi]a	*The birth bestowed the fifth grace*
T u ho ꝑel katun	*in the fifth katun*
Caa / ualhi u thanob u kuil	*Then the words of deity stood*
Ca sihi y angelili[l]	*Then its angel was born*
De/sipta u kaba y angelili	Desipta *is the name of its angel there*
Ca ualhi	*when it stood*
Xicen it / baca[l] macen vile	*"Perhaps the dregs may go to me, as I am the corncob man?*
Kuen baca[l]	*"I am the divine corncob*
Ah tepaleni / baca[l]	*"I am the Sovereign corncob there"*
Ca ix u than v kuil	*And this is the word of divinity*
T u ba t u hunal	*by himself, alone*
an in nite deis in	"An in nite deis in"
C u than	*thus he speaks*
Ca u kamah u / kuil	*Then he received his divinity*
T u ba t u hunal.	*by himself, alone.*

(CHUMAYEL 49.10–17)

In the fifth epoch, the Dios now asserts his divinity (*kuen*) and sovereignty (*ah tepalen*) (49.14) in Maya and then switches to make a similar assertion in Latin (Chumayel 49.16; Edmonson 1986:231). This switch to Latin signals the consummation of his apotheosis: "thus he speaks / Then he received his divinity / by himself, alone" (Chumayel 49.16–17).

Ca bini t u uac picib / tun g[rasi]a	*Then he went to the sixth multitude of tuns of grace*
T u uac ꝑel u ꝑisil akab	*of the sixth midnight*
T u uac te katun	*of the sixth katun*
Kuex ah tepalexe	*"You deities, you Sovereigns*
Nucex yn than	*"You all reply to my word*

Ma baca[l] / mac yan ti hunali	*"No corncob man exists alone there"*
Baca[l] sihil u cibah vuc / ꝑel g[rasi]a	*The corncob's birth bestowed the seventh grace*
Conlamil v kaba y angelil	Conlamil *is the name of its angel*
Ten / kul u ba ku	*"I who am the sacred image of the deity itself*
Tex kuexe	*"You who are deities*
Nucex yn than	*"You all answer my word*
Ma baca[l] mac	*"No corncob man*
Yan mamac nucic yn than	*"There is nobody to answer my word"*
Ci uil u than.	*Thus he speaks perhaps.*

(CHUMAYEL 49.17–24)

Upon receiving divinity *tu ba tu hunal* 'by himself alone,' Dios begins demanding that the *tex kuex* 'you who are [other] deities' respond to him, as "no corncob man exists alone there" (49.19–20). But the deity's invitation to dialogue is met with silence. In a monologic monotheism grounded in the doctrine of the self-sufficient creative power of the unique Divine Word, like that found in the Judeo-Christian theological traditions, the Creator, despite his repeated requests, requires no respondents. Dios finally concludes that "there is nobody to answer my word" (49.23) upon the arrival of the seventh epoch.

Ti ualic tamuk v sihsic vuc te / g[rasi]a	*When he stands in the midst giving birth to the seventh grace*
Cilmac ti y ol sihi	*Born with joy in its heart*
Ci vuc te katun vuc / ꝑel sasil	*The sweet seventh katun, the seventh light*
Vuc ꝑel ix u ꝑisil akab vuc picib	*and the seventh midnight of the seven multitudes*
A biento boca yento	A biento boca yento
De la sipil na	De la *Sin House*
Defente / note	Defente note
Sustina g[rasi]a	Sustina Grasia
Trese mili y no cargo / bende	Trese mili y no cargo bende
Yx hun tic ca tic ox hun tic	*And one fold, two folds, three and one folds*
Ox hun bacam v katunil	*The katun's three and one birth vigils*
Ox uuc pic	*Three and seven multitudes*
Ca ti ah cab ti d[io]s citbil	*Then when the world wakes to God the Father*

T u ba t u hunal	*by himself, alone*
T u tunil ox amay tun g[rasi]a	*in the tun of the Three-Cornered Stone Grace*
Ahci cab ti d[io]s citbil	*God the Father dawned*
+ v kaba v pectzil	*+ is his widely known name*
Vnidad y + d[io]s citbil	Unidad *with God the Father*
Lay u kaba henabilex	*This is the name that demolished you all*
V katunilex	*The katun of you all*
Ox dza / cab hun yaban vaan.	*Three generations, one of great stature.*

(CHUMAYEL 49.24–50.4)

The narrative language introducing the seventh epoch (49.25–31) exhibits a structure that recurs elsewhere in the text. There is the declaration of the time period in Maya (49.25–26), a switch to a (principally) non-Maya linguistic code (49.27–29), followed by a return to Maya for the purpose of counting (49.30), which results in a cosmogonic event, in this case, the Dawn of Dios Citbil 'God the Father' (49.31). The same pattern occurs in a later section (52.13–26), in which the "central" or seventh *tun* petitions in mixed Latin and Spanish (52.14–23) that shares with the previous example an almost identical concluding phrase (49.28–29; 52.22–23). This is likewise followed by a counting of "folds" and "birth vigils" as before (52.23–25). To complement the "dawn" that resulted from the previous example (49.31), we have the birth of *akab* 'night' (52.25–26).

The apotheosis of Dios and the creation of dawn and night in the narrative of the Ritual of the Angels result from a juxtaposition of Maya and non-Maya linguistic codes. Assertions of his divinity first in Maya and then in (somewhat garbled) Latin by Dios directly precede his apotheosis (49.14–17). Likewise, the emergence of dawn and of night involves Maya and non-Maya linguistic codes in their creative activity. As during the consecration of the host in the Catholic Mass (to which this narrative explicitly likens itself), words have the power to transform the very substance of things, to re-create otherwise mundane matter into divine substance. But unlike the monolingual Latin Mass, an account of creation in colonial Yucatán requires recognition of the polyglossic reality of social and cultural life. The author/redactor of the Ritual of the Angels expressed that only when Maya and Romance languages were juxtaposed, were syncretized in Bakhtin's sense, could creation occur. Such a metaphysics of language is consistent with both colonial experience and the ancient Maya metaphysical principles of complementary dualism (see Chapter 2). Furthermore, this view of language has repercussions for Maya-Spanish dialogues on the nature of divinity itself.

POLYGLOSSIA, MONOLINGUALISM, AND COLONIAL MONOTHEISM

Understanding the Maya author's colonial concept of the divine also requires accounting for the linguistic aspects of the deity. In this case, the narrative represents the deity as multilingual not only before the colonial encounter but even before the creation of the universe itself. Therefore, attention should be paid to the contexts of the deity's choice between linguistic codes. This divine polyglossia is also notable given the theory of language embedded in the theology of the Roman Church at the time; in the New Testament, the deity himself was identified with the "WORD" (Greek: *logos*), and as a result the Church father Saint Augustine would later develop a theory of language in which linguistic diversity was a defect of humankind's fallen nature resulting from its original disobedience to God (Janowitz 1993). Variations of this monologic philosophy of language dominated both Western theologies and Western linguistics until well into the twentieth century (Bakhtin 1981:271). Dennis Tedlock has argued that the creation *through dialogue* in many American Indian creation myths is not only an example of an alternative philosophy of language (D. Tedlock 1979) but, in the case of the colonial K'iche' Maya language text the *Popol Vuh*, it may represent an explicit rejection of the missionaries' concept of the singular Logos (D. Tedlock 1986). Numerous lines of evidence within the Ritual of the Angels and elsewhere suggest that the colonial Maya of Yucatán, like their K'iche' cousins, while accepting Christianity, rejected a monologic monotheism.

As stated earlier, roughly the first half of the narrative is organized into seven epochs in the apotheosis of the deity (expressed in Maya as *u kamah u kuil tu ba tu hunal* 'he received his divinity by himself, alone'), a process finally culminating in the dawn. Along the way, seven *angelil* 'angels' and *grasiail* 'graces' are born, paralleling the establishment of seven deities at creation recounted in pre-Hispanic Maya hieroglyphic texts like the Vase of the Seven Gods. In Classical Yucatecan Maya texts, the deity's creative activity may be expressed by the verb *sih* 'to be born' or, more rarely, *ch̄ab* 'to engender.' This concept of creative power is analogous to the gendered complementary dualism of *ch̄ab akab* 'genesis, darkness' (see Chapter 2). Like Classic Maya kings engaged in autosacrifice, the colonial deity contains within "himself" both masculine and feminine creative principles. This is evident not only in the different verbs for creation used in the cosmogonic narratives but in the paired appellations of Dios in Classical Yucatecan: *ah ch̄abtah ah sihsah* 'the genitor, the birth-giver' (Morley ms. page 151.15).

Other evidence for a colonial Maya theology rooted in the autochthonous metaphysics of complementary dualism is to be found in the poetic couplet *tu ba tu hunal* 'by himself, alone.' Variations of this phrase appear throughout the *Discursos Predicables* in reference to the oneness of God, and this phrase is ubiquitous in the Ritual of the Angels, where it is always used in reference to Dios. Contrary to claims by Edmonson (1993:70) that this phrase can refer to the ontology of humans as well as divinity, the use of *tu ba tu hunal* in Classical Yucatecan Maya texts is almost exclusive to the deity.[5] What is so significant about this phrase, of course, is the manner in which monotheism can be appropriately expressed in a Maya cosmogonic narrative: in a couplet. The metaphysics of complementary dualism appearing in the diphrastic kennings of pre-Hispanic hieroglyphic texts demands even the absolute oneness of the Christian Dios be expressed as a pair.

Within the Ritual of the Angels, the reported speech of the deity delineating the narrative structure of the seven epochs is in many cases concluded by the standard quotative phrase *ci u than* 'thus he speaks.' However, in the seventh and final instance prior to the dawn, the deity's assertion that "there is nobody to answer my word" (49.23) is expressed with skepticism: *ci <u>uil</u> u than* 'thus he speaks <u>perhaps</u>' (49.24). Only in this case is the tradition of reported speech of the deity presented as less than certain, signaling doubt about the veracity of such a strong statement of monologic monotheism.

One should not confuse the Maya predilection for expressing many things, including deity, in pairs as suggesting that their concept of deity consisted of pre-Hispanic polytheism with only the veneer of Christianity layered on top. This is clear when one observes the language in which the Ritual of the Angels expresses the doctrine of the Trinity, that aspect of Euro-Christian theology most amiable to polytheistic reinterpretation. As many European clergy would insist, the author/redactor of the Ritual of the Angels does utilize Spanish or Latin to assert the *unidad* of the deity's *personas* (50.2, 50.8–10). When discourse on the Trinity is expressed in Maya terminology, as in the postscript discussion of the names of the multiple *dzic* 'sides' of Dios (56L.1–56R.19), it is using the same Trinitarian language as the 1620 Maya-language publication of the Franciscan *Discursos Predicables* (folio 11r).

The author of the Ritual of the Angels does not reject Christian monotheism but does reject, on autochthonous metaphysical grounds, the "singular universal Logos" of Spanish Christian theology. In fact, it is quite possible that the repeated references to monotheism in the form of a couplet pair and the vain, almost comical attempts of the deity to get the other deities to engage in dialogue (*tex kuexe nucex yn than* 'you who are deities, reply to my word!'; 49.22) are actually satirizing the monologic model of Spanish Christian monotheism.

Although colonial compositions, it is in their critical discourse of other cultures in colonial texts like the Ritual of the Angels that indigenous world views often appear in the starkest relief. As Dennis Tedlock (1999:166) has observed regarding Native American renditions of Christian creation myths:

> [Creation] stories like this one have long been treated as instances of European influence on passive New World others, when in fact these others have actively and even radically reformulated what they heard from European sources. What needs attention now, from the descendents of the invaders, is the cultural critique implied by a discourse that neither ignores European ideas nor accepts them in their original forms.

In this area, the Ritual of the Angels shares the subtle critical attitude toward Spanish Christianity also documented for the colonial K'iche' *Popol Vuh* (D. Tedlock 1986).

THE PROPHETIC CRITIQUE OF COLONIALISM

By concluding its creation narrative with the Chilam Balam's prophecy of the abuses to be suffered with the arrival of Spanish Christianity, the critique of the Ritual of the Angels goes even further, indicting the European colonial enterprise based on the contradictions between discourse and social structure. The Ritual of the Angels relates the coming of Christianity and the success of the conquistadors to the year AD 1539, falling in the final years of Katun 13 Ahau. This is attributed with *numsah ya ti y al u mehenob, v christianomaon tan, tun u mansicoon bay balcheobe* 'causing torment for the nobles; it has christianized us publicly, then it makes us go around like wild animals' (Chumayel ms. page 54.6–8). In the context of colonial Yucatán, the contradiction between the noble Maya being "christianized" but treated like "animals" has both moral and political connotations. Ontologically speaking, to be a "Christian" was in principle to be a "true" person, not an "Other" within the Spanish colonial system. To assert that Maya Christians, especially the local nobility, were treated as the exact opposite of real people, as "wild animals," is to indict the evangelizing rationale undergirding the colonial system with extreme hypocrisy. Elsewhere in the chronicles of the Book of Chilam Balam of Chumayel (78.11–18), we find the account:

Oxlahun ahau u katunil v / hedzcob cah mayapan
Maya uinic u kabaob /
Vaxac ahau paxci u cabobi
Ca uecchai ti / peten tulacal
Vac katuni paxciob
Ca haui u maya kabaob
Buluc ahau u kaba u / katunil
Hauci maya kabaob maya uinicob
Christiano u kabaob tulacal
V cuch cabal / tzoma Sanc Pedro y Rey ah tepale.

Thirteen Ahau is the katun they settled the town of Mayapan
"Maya people" they were called
Eight Ahau the lands were depopulated
And they were all scattered throughout the peninsula
This Six Ahau they were scattered
Then ceased the Maya names
Eleven Ahau is the name of the katun
The Maya people ceased the Maya names
"Christian" they were all called
The subjects of angry Saint Peter and the Sovereign King.

Politically, to be a Christian in colonial Yucatán was to be subject to the Pope (the successor of Saint Peter) and the Spanish *rey*. It is interesting, however, that amid the indictments of the colonial system, the author of the Ritual of the Angels dates the coming of Christianity and the conquistadors in Katun 13 Ahau, as opposed to Katun 11 Ahau, as it is elsewhere. Perhaps the author wishes to tweak the chronology so as to link the beginning of the abusive colonial regime in the "Short Count" of the *katun* cycles with the beginning of the Maya people and the founding of Mayapán. Just as the dominance of Mayapán came and went, so will the new society with its new names and categories of persons. By chronicling Christianity and colonialism within a cyclical, rather than linear, eschatological history, the author places in the mouth of the Prophet Jaguar the implicit prophecy of another revolution to come.

THE FALL OF THE ANGELS

Thus far in the analysis I have neglected discussing in any detail one of the most prominent cast of characters in the narrative, the *angel(es)ob* 'angels' that are born amid Dios and the "graces" in each epoch, and whose *sip* 'transgression' comes at the conclusion of the narrative. A great deal of lore surrounded *angelob* in colonial Yucatán, as preserved in the Maya-language

Christian doctrinal literature extant in the Morley Manuscript, in the *Discursos Predicables*, as well as in documents of early modern European astrology incorporated in the Book of Chilam Balam of Kaua and elsewhere (V. Bricker and Miram 2002). An account of God's creation of the *angelob* is the topic of an entire section of a Genesis commentary appearing at the beginning of the *Discursos Predicables* (ms. pages 10r–14r). All versions of the Genesis commentary shared by the Morley (178.6–9), Kaua (147.3–5), and Chan Kan (27.13–15) manuscripts address this topic, relating that Dios filled the sky (*caan*) with an "innumerable" (*pictanil*) number of *angelesob*.

Unlike the angel lore of contemporary popular Christianity, the angel lore of early modern Europe and colonial Yucatán was primarily cosmological, astronomical, and astrological in character. The Morley Manuscript (279.1) describes the *angelob* as *canil uinicob u balcheob caanob ekob* 'heavenly people, the wild animals of the heavens, the stars.' Angels were conceived of as literally *caanil* 'celestials' that populate the sky, with their own peculiar position in the cosmos, and as responsible for astronomical and meteorological phenomena. As described in the Ritual of the Angels in the Chumayel (51.21), four angels are responsible for the winds (Miram and Bricker 1996). The three versions of the Genesis commentary in the Morley (180.20–181.2), Kaua (148.22–24), and Chan Kan (30.15–31.2) manuscripts report that there is an angel responsible for all movement in the outermost layer of the Ptolemaic cosmos called the Prime Mover, or *yax chun sut* in Maya.

Angels were integral to the practice of astrology, medical or otherwise. Specific angels are associated with the seven Ptolemaic planets and their respective days of the week, and illustrations in the Book of Chilam Balam of Kaua depict angels bearing the twelve European zodiacal constellations (ms. pages 74, 76, 78, 80, 82, 84, 87, 90, 92, 94, 96, 98). Following the Morley Manuscript's definition of the *angelob* to include the "wild animals of the sky," we find they are also responsible for specific diseases, illustrated and described in the Book of Chilam Balam of Kaua (ms. pages 5–6; V. Bricker and Miram 2002:97–99). It is therefore likely that most if not all of the "angels" and "celestials" mentioned in the Ritual of the Angels have observable astronomical parallels, regardless of on which side of the Atlantic they ultimately originated. Mapping the cosmos as depicted in this cosmogony would be a fascinating and challenging task, but it is beyond the scope of this study. For our present purposes, only one problematic portion of the narrative will be interpreted in relation not to where the *angelob* are located in the heavens but to the lore of how some of them fell to earth to plague humanity.

The final mythological section of the Ritual of the Angels, a precursor to the Chilam Balam's prophecy of the fall of kingdoms in Katun 13 Ahau, is that of a mythological war conducted by Op ("Parrot").[6] Parrot is apparently somewhat successful, as he is said to "strongly guard" (53.6–7) his position and to "stack [cloth]" there (53.8–9), cloth being a principal article received as tribute in both pre-Hispanic and colonial times. Very little regarding Parrot and his battle is explicitly described. He is referred to as *u yax batan* 'the Very First' and *ah mun ti caan* 'the Slave in Heaven' (53.10–11), and it is implied that he is of a *co* 'crazy, lustful' nature. The apparent reason for the omission of details by the author is that he presumes that the audience knows the story; twice the narrative voice states: *tech au ohel sihil u cah* 'you know the birth of his nature' (53.7–8, 53.10). It is reasonable to assume then that we are dealing with a much more detailed and widely known mythological episode, although expressed here in the sparsest of forms. But where in the corpus of literature might we find the sources behind this? How would we recognize them?

Perhaps our best entry into the hypothetical sources of this account of warfare in heaven is in the statement of the episode's resolution: "Then heavenly bodies [*corporales*] were placed in *ojales* [holes?] by the work of the first Pope" (53.19–20). This statement provides several lines of evidence by which to determine the sources of the battle in the heavens. In Catholic belief, the first Pope was the apostle Saint Peter. This tradition is based in part on the New Testament reference of Jesus's mandate to Peter:

> "And I tell you that you are Peter, and on this rock I will build my church, and the gates of Hades will not overcome it. I will give you the keys of the kingdom of heaven; whatever you bind on earth will be bound in heaven, and whatever you loose on earth will be loosed in heaven." (Gospel of Matthew 16.18–19)

Saint Peter, then, is clearly the actor referred to. But what of the heavenly *corporales* placed in "holes"?

Returning to the Ptolemaic-Christian Genesis commentary discussed earlier, the Kaua (153.16–154.7) and Chan Kan (55.14–56.10) redactions share an account of the fall from the heavens of the angels who rebelled with Lucifer against God. In these accounts, while Lucifer himself fell to *metnal tu dzu lum* 'Metnal [the underworld] in the center of the earth,' the rebellious angels went into various plants, winds that cause sickness in people, branches and leaves of trees, and holes in the ground (V. Bricker and Miram 2002:292).[7] The *Discursos Predicables* also have their share of angel lore, including the fall of Lucifer *tu dzu lum lay mitnal u kabae* 'to the center of the earth, Mitnal is the name of this' (ms. page 13v.16–17). While the *Discursos* lacks the detailed discussion of the different things that the fallen angels entered, it does share certain doctrinal terminology with the Chumayel account. In the section of the *Discursos* titled "God's Creation of the Angels," the narrator explicates the distinction between *corporales* 'bodies' of the things of earth and the *spirituales* that were the *cahob* 'natures' of angels (ms. pages 12r–12v). Taken together, it seems likely that the reference in the Chumayel account alludes to the fallen angels who gained *corporales* upon being cast from the celestial spheres and entering the physical world. This would suggest that the conflict in the heavens referred to in the text is indeed the rebellion of the angels against God, a theme explicitly mentioned toward the conclusion of the Ritual of the Angels (56L.23–24 to 56R.11–12).

But what then do we make of Op 'Parrot,' the principal antagonist of this section? One would not expect to find this character, a New World bird, in commentaries ultimately deriving from the biblical tradition. The most prominent occurrence of a Parrot character in colonial Mesoamerican myth comes from the K'iche' *Popol Vuh*, a story with its roots in earlier traditions of the "Principal Bird Deity," depicted in Preclassic and Classic Maya art (Miller and Taube 1993:137–138). In the K'iche' account, Vucub Caquix ("Seven Macaw") magnifies himself by grandiose claims:

> "I am great. My place is now higher than that of the human work, the human design. I am their sun and I am their light, and I am also their months . . . because my eyes are of metal. My teeth just glitter with jewels, and turquoise as well; they stand out blue with stones like the face of the sky." (D. Tedlock 1985:86; see also Christenson 2003a:92–93)

But the arrogant Seven Macaw is brought down (literally) through the machinations of the Hero Twins, Hunahpu and Xbalanque, sons of the sacrificed gods Hun Hunahpu and Vucub Hunahpu. It was discovered that painted vases of lowland Classic Maya civilization depict episodes similar to those in the colonial *Popol Vuh* (Coe 1978), suggesting a wide distribution of an ancestral version of this myth cycle in ancient times. Indeed, although no complete Yucatecan version of the myth appears to exist, there are clues suggesting that some parallels to the K'iche' story were in circulation in colonial Yucatán.

One example is the name of the denizens of the Yucatecan Maya underworld. The most common name for the underworld given in Classical Yucatecan Maya documents is *mitnal* or *metnal*, most likely derived from the Nahuatl name for the realm of the dead, *mictlan* (Kartunnen 1992:147). The underworld and its denizens are known in the *Popol Vuh* as Xibalba, a term that appears in dictionaries of Classical Yucatecan, glossed by the

5.6. Postclassic depiction of the deity Hun Ahau. Madrid Codex, page 39a (reproduced by permission of the Museo de América, Madrid).

early missionaries as *diablo* (Acuña 1993:275; Ciudad Real 2001:587). Diego de Landa reported in the sixteenth century that the deity of the underworld among the colonial Yucatec Maya was Hun Ahau (Landa 1978 [ca. 1566]:58), a direct parallel to the K'iche' deity of the *Popol Vuh*, Hunahpu, or perhaps his father, Hun Hunahpu.[8]

Hun Ahau does appear in the Postclassic Maya Dresden (page 50c) and Madrid (pages 38a–39a) codices, the latter in which Hun Ahau is said to be located *ti caan/chan* 'in the sky' (Figure 5.6), but otherwise little is known of Yucatecan beliefs regarding Hun Ahau. A rare Classical Yucatecan source regarding Hun Ahau is the brief narrative that occurs on manuscript pages 125–129 of the Morley Manuscript. This narrative explicitly identifies Hun Ahau as the Christian Lucifer (125.10, 128.3, 129.4) and provides rough translations of two biblical passages applied by later exegetes to Lucifer,

Ezekiel 28:11–20 and Isaiah 14:12–15 (Whalen 2003a). Although a casual reading would discount these Christianized accounts as being irrelevant for understanding Maya concepts, what is fascinating is the degree to which these "translated" passages about Hun Ahau–Lucifer parallel the account of Seven Macaw in the *Popol Vuh*. A translated portion of Ezekiel's prophecy reads (ms. page 126.2–7; modified after Whalen 2003a):

ceex a buc yan tech cuchie
hulpilan / tu coohtacil tunob
ma ua ti yantac / ti hulan tu uich a nok
tu uich a bucie /
nenil tun houal tun potzil tunij /
ytz uah tuni puc tuni kak tamay tu/ni
bayx u yabal takin xanie.

What about the clothes you had back then,
Embroidered with sumptuous stones?
Were they not there sewn on the face of your garment
On the face of your clothes?
Mirror stone, houal stone, emerald
Ytz uah stone, crystal, garnet
And thus a great amount of gold there also.

And continues (ms. page 127.6–10; modified after Whalen 2003a):

Cech yan chumuc ti lemlemnac u / uich ti tuniobe
Ca liki a pucsikal / ti tzicbail tumen a cichcelemil
Lay / u chun a ppathcij y+ a satcij a miatz / loe
Ca picchintabech yokol cabe.

It is you who were in their midst when the faces of these stones shone forth
Then your heart rose with arrogance because of your beauty
This is the reason that you abandoned and you lost that wisdom of yours
That you were cast out upon the earth.

A portion of the Isaiah passage is rendered (ms. page 128.10–18; modified after Whalen 2003a):

Bin naccen ti caan / cij a than
Ca yn dzab ca yn culcin yn / dzam
Ca yx yn xaccun yn kanchee /
Yokol u sihsah ekilob Dios
Ca yx cul/cen yokol uitz licil u moltanba
Te / tu xaxe te ti xamane
Bin ix nacen / yokol muyal canal

Ca yx baacen ah / canalil
Heklay Dios ah tepal
Cij u than / cech Luzifere cuchie

"I will ascend into heaven," thus you spoke
"Then I place, then I seat my throne
"And then I plant my bench
"Above the stars born of God
"And then I may sit upon the mountain [where] they assemble
"There at the side, there in the north
"And I will ascend above the cloud on high
"And then I may become [like] Him-on-high
"Like God the Sovereign."
So you spoke, you who are Lucifer, back then.

The parallels between the K'iche' account of Seven Macaw's attempt to establish himself in the sky as the false Sun and the Morley Manuscript's account of Hun Ahau–Lucifer's attempt to establish himself in the sky as the false God are compelling. The claims of both are illegitimate, their arrogance in both cases is based on accouterments of precious stones and metals, and both are brought crashing down from the heavens to the earth in response.

But remarkable parallels aside, what exactly is the *historical* relationship, if any, between the myths of Seven Macaw and Hun Ahau–Lucifer? Is the episode of Seven Macaw just one more instance of the response of Maya myth to Christian doctrine (D. Tedlock 1986), in this case the story of the fall of Lucifer? Or has the story of the fall of Lucifer overlaid a myth related in some way to the Seven Macaw story but instead substituting Hun Ahau, given that deity's association with the Maya underworld?

In light of the surviving sources, these parallels may raise more questions than answers. Nonetheless, some of the subtle discrepancies between the Maya version and the "orthodox" biblical version are suggestive. One intriguing difference is in the number of precious stones and metals mentioned and their prominence in each text. Whereas there are nine precious stones plus the mention of gold in the biblical version (Ezekiel 28.13), there are only six precious stones plus gold, or seven objects, mentioned in the Maya rendition (Morley ms. page 126.5–7). Furthermore, although the precious stones are mentioned just once in the biblical text, they are referred to repeatedly in the Maya rendition (126.15–16, 127.6). The number seven and added emphasis on the precious stones may indicate that the "translation" of the biblical text was being reproduced in accordance with expectations of an indigenous audience based on autochthonous myth traditions, perhaps even those related to Seven Macaw in the *Popol Vuh*. That the

Yucatecan story in the Book of Chilam Balam of Chumayel of the celestial war of Parrot includes the fall of the angels suggests that once widespread stories of the Principal Bird Deity and the Hero Twins may have had an interesting "afterlife" in the Christianized religious literature of the colonial era.

CONCLUSION

The rich cosmogony Roys dubbed the Ritual of the Angels provides ample evidence that Maya-Spanish syncretism in colonial Yucatán was hardly passive and uncritical. While accepting Christianity, the colonial Maya of Yucatán found problematic those monologic qualities of Spanish Catholic theology that were compatible with neither their autochthonous metaphysics nor the polyglossic and heteroglossic realities of colonial Yucatán. It is these realities that the author/redactor(s) of the Ritual of the Angels inscribed in the double-voiced discourse of this mythic narrative.

Regarding the cosmological lore surrounding the angels in colonial Yucatán, at present it is possible to suggest from internal evidence that the episode of Parrot and the rebellion of the angels in the Ritual of the Angels is part of a larger myth cycle that was current in Yucatán at the time. It is possible to conclude from comparison with contemporaneous Maya-language Christian doctrinal sources that this myth cycle is a rejoinder to the account of the fall of Lucifer propagated by Christian missionaries who sought to cast indigenous Maya gods as devils. One may go on to speculate, albeit based on more circumstantial evidence, that this text is also a rejoinder to some variant of the myth of the fall of Seven Macaw, the documentation of which we have in one lengthy colonial K'iche' account and scattered references among the vase paintings of the Classic Maya. Although tentative, this may provide yet another example in which Yucatecan myths during the Colonial period were composed in dialogue with both Christian doctrinal works and an earlier stratum of mythology that circulated as part of the ideological connections among different regions in the Postclassic Mesoamerican world system.

NOTES

1. Judith Maxwell (personal communication, 2004) points out that the "nonsense" phrase *apa opa* that appears on Chumayel manuscript page 53.13 has a parallel in the colonial Kaqchikel Maya manuscript known variously as the Memorial de Sololá and the Annales de los Kaqchikeles (Otzoy 1999; ms. page 25.2). In the Kaqchikel narrative, *vaya vaya ela opa* is provided as an "example" of the speech

of another group among whom the ancestors of the Kaqchikel lived for a time. Maxwell speculates that these could be a stereotypical representation of either a specific linguistic group, such as Ch'olan or Xinka, or, since neither phrase bears any obvious referent in other languages, a colonial pan-Mayan representation of linguistic "otherness" in general.

2. For example, in June 2004 I photographed the use of a similar triangle to represent the Christian Trinity in the iconography of a festival in the Kaqchikel Maya town of San Antonio Aguas Calientes, Guatemala.

3. My reading of *baca* in the text as *bacal* 'corncob' is based on the following observations. First, the only reading of *baca* in Yucatec dictionaries ("cosa morena") did not make much sense in context, so I began examining what other options might be possible. The reading *bacal* emerged as a possibility because the word final /l/ is sometimes elided in the manuscript text. For example, *cangel*, the term for "archangel," is at one point spelled *camge* in the text (50.4–5). So there is a precedent within the manuscript text itself for underrepresentation of the /l/. Finally, the term *baca[l] mac* for the deity fades from the narrative text following its apotheosis, to be replaced with the name *Sustina Grasia*. *Sustina* suggests something that physically sustains a person, such as food. Furthermore, although one must tread cautiously when projecting ethnographic data from the present into the past, it is suggestive to recall here that in contemporary Yucatán, Maya refer to maize as *santo gracia* (Burns 1983:39). Therefore, it is this intersection of evidence that convinces me that *baca[l] mac* 'Corncob Man' is the best available reading of the name of the emerging deity in this narrative.

4. Note that the forms used in the instances of Latin, Spanish, and Nahuatl appearing in the Chumayel theogony are often irregular, making translation somewhat difficult. Furthermore, my own ignorance of the Latin language makes such a proposal infeasible. Therefore, I have most often left these words and phrases untranslated. In this instance, I have instead relied on suggestions given by Edmonson (1986:228–246) in his translation of the Book of Chilam Balam of Chumayel. Although I and others (Hanks 1988) share strong objections to many details of Edmonson's translation and reorganization of the Maya text, in many instances I find his suggestions regarding the meaning of the non-Maya portions helpful.

5. One exception to this rule can be found in the Morley version's Genesis commentary (ms. page 181.1–2), where *tu ba tu hunal* is used to refer to the angel responsible for movement in the layer of the Ptolemaic cosmos called the *yax chun sut* 'prime mover.' However, the use of this phrase in reference to any being other than Dios was apparently problematic for the Maya, as its later redaction in the Kaua (ms. pages 148.24–149.1) reduces it first to simply *tu hunal* and finally removes the phrase altogether in the Chan Kan.

6. Both Roys (1967:111) and Edmonson (1986:235–236) translate it as "macaw." However, *moo* refers specifically to macaws, whereas *op* refers to a variety of parrot common in the eastern and southern forests of Yucatán (Barrera Vásquez et al. 1995:607). In the absence of more definitive information, I have opted for the more generic term.

7. Edmonson (1986:241) reads *ojales* as *hojales* 'branches,' which if correct would also correspond with the argument I present here regarding the fallen angels in the Ritual of the Angels.

8. The K'iche' deities Hun Hunahpu and Vucub Hunahpu may be conceived of as underworld deities in their own right. They are *not*, however, underworld deities in the same sense as the Xibalbans, those gods of death and disease. Instead, they are underworld deities in their role as the sacrificed ancestor gods that continued to reside in Xibalba even after their resurrection by their sons, the Hero Twins (D. Tedlock 1985:159). These two K'iche' underworld deities are more akin to the Egyptian god Osiris than to the Christian Lucifer.

CHAPTER SIX

The Creation of the First People and the Origin of Suffering

Ox hun ahau	*On Thirteen Ahau*
U lubul u cuch katun ti ah emalob	*the burden of the katun fell to the people of Emal*
Ba ix hol tun suiua	*And thus ended the tun of Zuyua*
Ba ix ho tzuc chakan	*And thus there are five divisions of the savanna* [chakan]
Ti uil uchom salam kohcheil t u cuch ho tzuc chakan	*when Salam Kohcheil will arrive with the burden of the five divisions of the savanna*
Uchc u numya ah canul uai	*The long-suffering Canul had arrived here*
. . .	. . .
Tix u luksah u picil u cuch uai saclactune	*and removed the overwhelming burden here at Sac Lac Tun*
. . .	. . .
Vuc te u picil u cuch yan uaye	*There are seven multitudes of burdens here*
Uai u dzocol u than katun tulacale	*Here the entire word of the katun is complete*

Vuc te uil hab uaye kintun yabil	*Perhaps seven are the years here of drought*
Vuc te ix ti hab katun yah uaye	*and seven years of war here*
Vuc te ti hab ma ya cimlal	*Seven years of pestilence [*ma ya cimlal*]*
. . .	. . .
Ca uchi noh haicabil	*Then the great destruction of the world arrived*
Ca liki noh Ytzam Cab Ain	*Then great Ytzam Cab Ain ascended*
Dzocebal u than u uudz katun lai hunyeciil	*that this deluge [*hunyeciil*] may complete the word of the katun series*
Bin dzocecebal u than katun	*that the word of the katun might be complete*

(TIZIMÍN 14V.1–10, 20–22)

Origin myths are often discourses on the human condition. These discourses often posit a theory of being (ontology) and construct fundamental degrees of sameness and difference between persons and groups, whether gender, kin, ethnic, or racial distinctions. Origin myths such as these may also address the etiology of selected pan-human phenomena, such as the origin of suffering and death. In Classical Yucatecan Maya literature, historical incidents of suffering may be couched in the mythological activities of gods and legendary travails of ancestors, such as in the "prophecy" for Katun 13 Ahau in the Book of Chilam Balam of Tizimín (ms. page 14v.1–25) and the Códice Pérez (ms. pages 116.19–117.15). Such suffering is part of the human condition via the cycle established in myth-history that is seen to recur in latter epochs bearing the burden of the same position in the katun series.

The account from the Book of Chilam Balam of Tizimín given above begins with the shift in the landscape of katun history away from that legendary place of origins and political legitimacy for Postclassic Mesoamerican peoples, Zuyua.[1] The pronouncement for Katun 13 Ahau goes on to recount the arrival of the ancestors of the Canul patronym group (*chibal*) "here" (*uay*) at Sac Lac Tun, another name for the Postclassic city of Mayapán (Chumayel 79.15–16; Códice Pérez 80.6, 163.20). During Katun 13 Ahau, a succession of seven years of drought, war, and pestilence occurs, which in the narrative juxtaposes with Itzam Cab Ain's aborted attempt to destroy the world (see Chapter 4). Although similar historical annals are barely represented in the few surviving Postclassic Maya codices, the following passage from the *Informe* by the early seventeenth-century extirpator of idolatry, Doctor Pedro Sánchez de Aguilar, confirms that now-lost

Maya hieroglyphic books did indeed contain accounts very similar to the one above:

> Tenian libros de cortezas de arboles con vn betun en blanco, y perpetuo de 10 y 12 varas de largo, que se cogian doblandolos como vn palmo, y en estos pintauan con colores la quenta de sus años, las guerras, pestes, huracanes, inundaciones, hambres, y otros sucessos; y por vno destos libros que quite a vnos Idolatras, vi y supe, que a vna peste llamaron Ma Ya Cimil, y a otra Oc Na Kuchil, que quiere decir muertes repentinas, y tiempos en que los cuerbos se entraron a comer los cadaueres en las casas. Y la inundacion, o huracan llamaron Hunyecil, anegacion de arboles. Tuuieron noticia, que el mundo se auia de acauar, y que auia gloria, e infierno.
>
> They had barkpaper books with a white finish, measuring between ten and twelve *varas* in length, which they kept folded up about a *palmo* in size. And in these they painted with pigments the count of their years, the wars, pestilences, hurricanes, floods, famines, and other occurrences. And from one of these books that I seized from some idolaters, I saw and learned about a pestilence named Ma Ya Cimil and another Oc Na Kuchil, which mean "sudden deaths" and "times in which the buzzards enter to eat the cadavers in the houses." And [there is] the flood, or hurricane they called Hunyecil: "flooding of trees." They had notice that the world would end and there would be heaven and hell. (Sánchez de Aguilar 1987 [1639]:95)

In contrast to these Late Postclassic discourses of suffering in Maya myth-history with their focus on legendary Zuyua, patronym groups, and ancient city-states, the European conquerors attempted to introduce the biblical accounts with their own, supposedly universal mythological ancestors (Adam and Eve) and locations (the Terrestrial Paradise). Spanish claims of the universality of Christian salvation, as well as the authority of a universal Christian monarch as announced in the *Requerimiento*, rested on an origin myth positing the common descent and ontological attributes of all peoples. Common origin entailed original sin and capacity for redemption; original sin entailed a common origin of suffering and death and thus capacity for resurrection. Therefore, the Judeo-Christian origin story was ideologically essential to European colonial agendas, for both military conquest and evangelical endeavors. The challenge of a Christian discourse on the origin of human suffering, however, went beyond debates of the substance and soul of human beings. It also entered into discourses of the etiology of those misfortunes making up the human experience, such as illness and disaster, as well as culture-specific explanations and responses to these events. Certainly famines, plagues, and catastrophes weighed

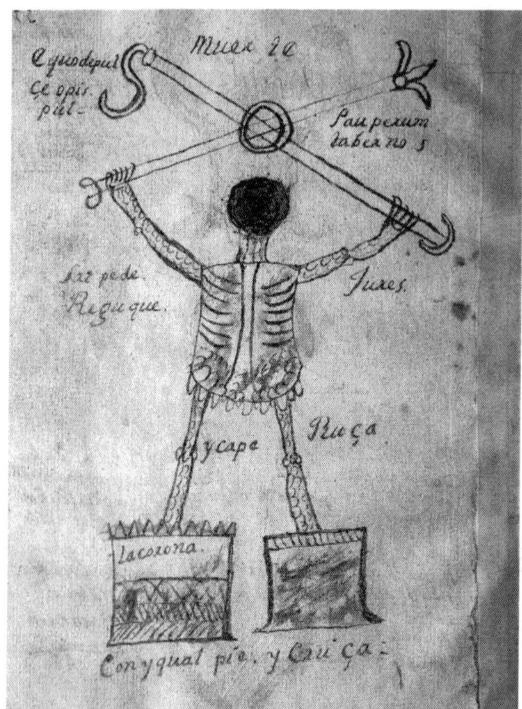

6.1. Colonial period Maya anthropomorphic illustration of Death in the Book of Chilam Balam of Chumayel, page 57 (reproduced by permission of the Princeton University Library, Princeton, New Jersey).

heavily on the Maya of Yucatán during the period that the mythography was likely compiled. The mid-sixteenth through mid-eighteenth centuries were marked periodically by precipitous declines in the Yucatecan Maya population, with a series of epidemics reducing the total population by more than 50 percent in the years between 1648 and 1658 alone (Chuchiak 2006).

The following section of the Chumayel mythography is aptly introduced in the original manuscript by an anthropomorphic illustration of Death (Figure 6.1). The ancient Maya had a skeletal god of death, Schellhas's God A (Figure 6.2), named Xib and Ah Cimil in the hieroglyphic texts (Taube 1992:11–13; Vail 1998, 2000b). However, the image in the Book of Chilam Balam of Chumayel is apparently derived from an as-yet-unidentified European source, perhaps selected by the anonymous Maya mythographer because of its similarity to the pre-Hispanic deity.[2] The figure is captioned with the title *Muerte* 'Death' and various other phrases, including *pauperum tabernos*, *sat pede*, and *reguque tures*. Velásquez Garcia (2007) has recently identified the origin of the phrase in this illustration as the classical Latin poet Horace: *pallida mors aequo pulsat pede paupe-*

6.2. Postclassic Maya depiction of the death deity God A. Dresden Codex, page 5c (Förstemann 1880).

rum tabernas regumque turres 'pale Death strikes with the same foot the huts of the poor and palaces of the rich.'[3]

Titled "A Song of the Itzá" by Roys (1967:114–116) and "The Sins of the Itza" by Edmonson (1986:245–249), the myth begins with an account of the origin of the First People in the Terrestrial Paradise (*parayso*) before introducing a lament for the destruction of the great city of Chichén Itzá, which after its fall remained an important pilgrimage site throughout the Postclassic period (Landa 1978 [ca. 1566]:46). In the process of prefacing this song (*kay*) of the fall of Chichén Itzá with an image of Death and an account of the beginnings of humanity, this anonymous Maya myth-teller composes a rejoinder to ancient Maya and European discourses on the human condition.

THE CREATION OF THE FIRST PEOPLE

Of the texts we have examined, myths of the origin of human beings may be the area of Maya cosmogonic dialogue in which distinctions between form and content in syncretic discourses are completely misleading. As argued here, elements scholars often take to be the most basic aspects of "traditional" Maya cosmology are shown to be objects of indigenous expropriations of Euro-Christian ontological discourses with meanings renegotiated in the context of colonial dialogue.

Let us begin by examining a common element in stories of the origins of the First People, the substance of the human form. For Maya mythologies, by far the best-known account is that of the K'iche' *Popol Vuh* (D. Tedlock 1985, 1996; Colop 1999, 2008; Christenson 2003a, 2003b), in which the bodies of the First People of the present era were made from maize and their blood was made from water. Of course, this single K'iche' account was never the sole authoritative version of Maya belief, although there is often the temptation for scholars from cultures where "religions of the book" are dominant to search for one such Maya "Bible." The diversity that was present, at least as suggested by evidence from the Colonial period, is evident in the following passage from Cogolludo's mid-seventeenth-century *Historia de Yucatan*. After quoting verbatim Sánchez de Aguilar's account of his seizure from a Maya schoolmaster a *cartapacio* containing a heterodox account of the creation of the world (see Chapter 3), Cogolludo (2006 [1688]:284–285) adds:

> [R]ecién venido yo de España, oí decir a un religioso, llamado fray Juan Gutiérrez, y era gran lengua de estos indios, que había visto otro escrito semejante al dicho, y que en él tratando de la formación del primer hombre, se decía, que había sido formado de tierra, y zacate, o pajas delgadas, y que la carne, y huesos se habían hecho de la tierra, y el cabello, barba, y bello, que hay en el cuerpo, era de las pajas, y zacate, con que se había mezclado la tierra.
>
> Being recently arrived from Spain, I heard from a monk named Friar Juan Gutiérrez, who was well versed in the language of these Indians, that he had seen another document similar to that about which [Doctor Pedro Sánchez de Aguilar] spoke. And that regarding the creation of the first man, it said that he was formed of earth and fodder [*zacate*], or thin reeds. Flesh and bones were made from the earth, and the hair, beard, and beauty that is of the body, these were the reeds and fodder with which the earth had been mixed.

The account contained in a Yucatec Maya *cartapacio* as described in Cogolludo differs significantly from the K'iche' *Popol Vuh*, suggesting a diversity of origin stories current throughout the Maya area. It is in this context of the circulation of numerous traditions about the creation of the First People that the following account from the Chumayel mythography must be considered.

FIRST FATHER AND FIRST MOTHER

Damaceno v kaba chakan	*Damascus is the name of the savanna*
Patci ca yax yum ti adan / t u menel dios	*[where] our First Father who is Adam had been formed by the work of God*
He ix u kabae	*And this is his name*

Lay u yax kaba lae	*His is the first name*
Adan	*Adam*
Ca oci / v pixan	*Then his soul entered [his body]*
Ca uacunabi paraysoe	*and he was placed there in Paradise*
Sihanili tun adan	*Adam alone was born there then*
Ca / sihi ca yax naa ti evae	*Then our First Mother who is Eve was born*
Yax cħuplal v naa balcah / t u sinil	*The first maiden, the mother of everything in the world*
Chun thah biin tun	*The original drop of liquid is said to be stone*
Hun thah bin haban	*Another drop of liquid is said to be a shrub*
Ca si/hij ti minan caan cuchie	*So she was born back then when there was no Sky*
He tun citbile sihij t u ba t u hunal ychil akbil	*As for the Father then, he was born by himself, alone, in darkness*
He tunobe hun pai sihciob	*As for these stones, they had been born all at once*
He tun acantune lay / luum lae	*As for the Acantun then, this is the Earth*
Lay ix cħabi	*And it was engendered*
Uchci u patal adan xane	*The forming of Adam had occurred also*
Laytac u mehen	*These are his children*
La ocantacob y icnal acanobe	*They entered in the presence of laments*
Bla hex / u kabatahob	*and perhaps it was these that named them*
Ca patlahobe	*And they were formed one by one*
Layitac v yax chun v ui/nicil	*These were the first beginnings of humanity*
Dios citbil dios mehenbil y̱ / dios espiri santo	*God the Father, God the Son, and God the Holy Spirit*
Lay molcab d[io]s lae	*All together this is God*
Lay sihob / t u tunil	*They were born in this tun*
Chac hilib tun y̱ vy ub tun grasia	*The Red Seeing Stone and the Hearing Stone of Grace*
Lay ber/be u kabae	Verbe *is the name of it*
Josus t in grasia	*Jesus of my Grace*

He tun y ix hun yetae sihi t u tunil ek oyob tun	*As for his Ix Hun Yeta then, she gave birth in the tun of the Black Sprinkler Stone*
Lay berbum tuorum v kabae	*Verbum Tuorum is the name of it*
Ti x co/al tun	*In [I]x Coal Tun*
Ix coaal cab	*Ix Coaal Cab*
+	+
Ti u cħaah v colel cabili	*When she took* U Colel Cab *there*
Ca bin ti cutal ox coc ox caan	*She then goes to sit at Three Turtle, Three Sky*
V coc oxxil caan cuchie	*The Turtle of the third sky back then*
Sac homen cu/lictac cabal	*White cargo already sits below*
Ti y ol sustinal grasia	*at the heart of Sustaining Grace*
Ox/lahun pic u katunil chel	*Thirteen multitudes are the katun of Chel*
An t u tunil.	*which exists in this tun.*

(CHUMAYEL 58.1–22)

In the Chumayel account above, the First Father (Yucatec: *yax yum*) and his children are said to be formed (*pat*). The verb *pat* 'to form' refers to molding earth, clay, or maize dough by hand (Ciudad Real 2001:482–483). The Chumayel account does apply the names of the First People of Judeo-Christian tradition—Adan to the First Father (*yax yum*) and Eva to the First Mother (*yax naa*)—but it is not entirely clear that they are created from earth (*luum*) as in the biblical account, although Classical Yucatecan language accounts in the Morley Manuscript (ms. pages 30, 114, 168–169, 197) do make this explicit assertion.

However, in contrast to the Judeo-Christian tradition, the First Mother is said to be "born" rather than created from Adam and is herself the "mother of everything in the world"—a more expansive, cosmogonic role than imagined in the biblical myth. The medium of First Mother's creative power is *thah*, which refers to a drop of liquor, water, or other such liquid (Barrera Vásquez et al. 1995:831; Ciudad Real 2001:559), of which stones and shrubs are formed. Having no parallel in biblical myth, this creation by First Mother through the medium of liquids recalls various creative roles of female characters in pre-Hispanic iconography, from Teotihuacan's "Great Goddess," who has numerous objects issuing in streams from her hands; to the goddess Chalchiutlicue in the surviving Aztec codices, from whose birth stream issue children and objects; to the ancient Maya goddess Chac Chel, who has streams of water flowing from her loins and armpits (Figure 6.3; see the following discussion). I do not

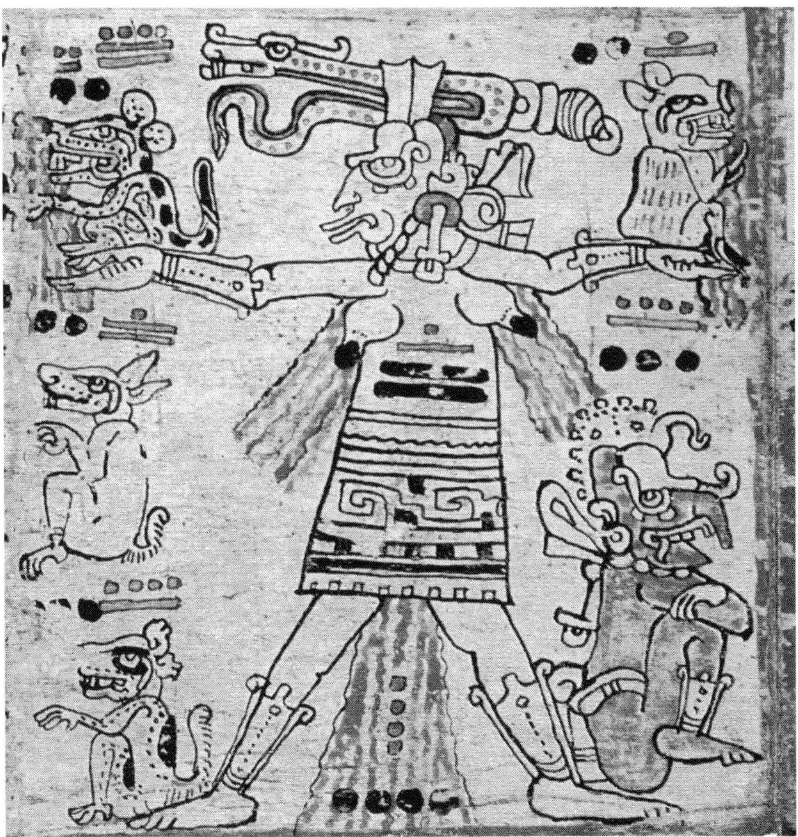

6.3. Goddess O or Chac Chel, Postclassic version of the creator goddess Ix Chel. Madrid Codex, page 30b (reproduced by permission of the Museo de América, Madrid).

mean to assert that the First Mother in this text must be the direct equivalent of one of these pre-Hispanic goddesses but only to note that the symbolism of the Genetrix evoked here in the Chumayel manuscript appears to be composed in dialogue with these pre-Hispanic Mesoamerican traditions of the Female Divine.

Besides the title of *ca yax naa* 'Our First Mother' and the biblical name Eva, several other female appellatives appear throughout the text. As the pantheon of Maya deities was composed not so much of discrete divine entities but as parts of overlapping deity clusters (Vail 2000b), some of the following appellatives may be alternate names, epithets, or multiple aspects of this same First Mother. The first is Ix Hun Yeta, who is also named as the mother of several personified diseases in the manuscript of Maya medical incantations known as the *Ritual of the Bacabs* (Roys 1965:29, 35, 152). There is also the paired appellative Ix Coal Tun, Ix Coaal Cab, which perhaps translates as "Lady Precious Stone, Lady Precious World," preciousness being a fundamental quality of objects such as jade in Mesoamerican world views, itself associated with life-giving breath (Taube 2005).[4]

Some of these female divinities in the myth may have astronomical and cosmological associations, although this requires teasing out the correspondences contained within opaque references in both Maya texts and the somewhat confused reports of Spanish clergy and extirpators. In the present myth text, U Colel Cab, or "The Mistress of the World," ascends to the Turtle constellation.[5] Drawing on the 1697 testimony of Juan Canul held in the Archivo General de la Nación in Mexico City, Chuchiak (2000:278) claims that images of the goddess Ix Kanleox also represented Ix Colel Cab, which suggests these names either are alternating epithets or refer to different aspects of the same goddess complex. The early nineteenth-century report by the priest of the town of Yaxcabá, Baeza (1845 [1813]:170), notes that the goddess X Kanleox was the custodian of the rains and the Pauahtun of the South and was also identified by Baeza's Maya informants with Santa Maria Magdalena. Writing much earlier in the seventeenth century, Cogolludo (2006 [1688]:290) asserts that for the Maya, Ix Kanleox was the consort of the creator deity Itzamna and was the mother of all the other gods.

This reference to Ix Kanleox–Ix Colel Cab as the mother of the other deities is interesting in light of the present myth text, as the various *tunob* 'stones,' or stone idols, associated with aspects of Dios likewise appear to have been borne by the Genetrix "Eva," who is *yax ch̄uplal v naa balcah t u sinil* 'the first maiden, the mother of everything in the world.' In the Morley Manuscript (ms. page 202.9–10), Adam says in reference to Eve that *Uiragois u kaba suhuy bac lae* 'Virgo is the name of this virgin girl.' This association of biblical women with astronomical phenomena was certainly present in New Spain outside Maya communities; a sheet published in 1741 by Mariam de Riveras titled *Purissima Virgo Maria* contains a Latin poem placing the Virgin in the zodiac accompanied by illustrations of the Virgin standing on the crescent moon and crowned with twelve stars, as the face of an anthropomorphic Sun peeks from behind her waist (AGN vol. 904, folio 170).

Such ideas made literal sense in terms of pre-Hispanic Maya cosmology, in which celestial bodies could be conceived of as animals and anthropomorphic beings, whether gods or apotheosized historical personages (Chinchilla 2005, 2006). During the Colonial period, the Yucatec

Maya attempted to find correspondences between their own and the new Christian mythologies, including in relation to astral beings. For example, Cogolludo (2006 [1688]:281) cites a 1545 report by the cleric Francisco Hernández, who relates that the Maya associated the aged pre-Hispanic god of life and creation, Itzamna, with Dios Padre; the Bacab with Dios Hijo; and the goddess Ix Chel with the mother of the Virgin. As for their celestial counterparts, a katun "prophecy" for 9 Ahau on manuscript page 89 of the Chumayel relates, *suhuy cħuplal u kaba v na vuc pel chachac ek* 'the Virgin is the mother of the seven planets.' As noted earlier, in the myth text under discussion, U Colel Cab ascends to the Turtle constellation. The ultimate resolution in the Maya search for astronomical correspondences between pre-Hispanic female divinities and the numerous *suhuy cħuplal* 'virgin maidens' of Spanish Christian cosmology can perhaps be seen in the fact that both contemporary Itzaj- (Hofling and Tesucún 1997:489) and Yucatec-speaking communities (author's fieldnotes; Xocén, Yucatán, July 1999) refer to the three stars of Belt of Orion, once the ancient Mayas' Turtle constellation (V. Bricker and Miram 2002:37), as *las tres Marias* 'the Three Marys.'

The text concludes by referring to the period as the *katun* of Chel, which means "rainbow" and may suggest that the Genetrix in question is Ix Chel, the goddess of childbirth and medicine in Late Postclassic Yucatán (Landa 1978 [1566]:56, 72). *Chel* forms part of the pre-Hispanic name of Schellhas's Goddess O, Chac Chel (Taube 1992:99–105), a divine being associated in the pre-Hispanic codices with identities and activities of the rain god Chac and the god of life and creation Itzamna (Vail 2000b:129). As noted above, Chac Chel is sometimes depicted iconographically with water gushing from her loins and armpits (Figure 6.3), suggesting creation by the First Mother via liquids described in the creation myth above.

So before dismissing this Yucatec account of the creation of the First People as simply a concession to Christian teaching, we should consider the various aspects of the myth that possibly reflect a history of composition in dialogue with both Euro-Christian and Mesoamerican antecedents. For example, the known extant pre-Hispanic hieroglyphic texts that refer to the creation of people state, *patah ah uinic* 'the human being is formed' on the creation date of 4 Ahau 8 Cumku (Dresden Codex pages 62 and 68), utilizing the same verb found in the Chumayel account. These references from the Dresden Codex, which can refer simultaneously to the creation of the twenty-day *uinal* period as well as the (twenty-digited) human body (Schele and Grube 1997:139), do not specify the material utilized in making the First People in pre-Hispanic mythology. The point here is that the language of the Yucatec creation of the First People in the Book of Chilam Balam of Chumayel shares the relevant lexemes with Classic Maya hieroglyphic texts. That fact allows us to presume a dialogue of verbal-ideological systems on a diachronic if not synchronic plane. In terms of shared lexemes, the Chumayel account is, in a way, a step closer to the pre-Hispanic written sources than the most elaborate Maya account of the creation of the First People currently extant, that in the K'iche' *Popol Vuh*. Like the Chumayel, the *Popol Vuh* has its own complex colonial histories of emergent meanings in dialogic relation to both pre-Hispanic and European antecedents. For example, Dennis Tedlock (1986) argues that, far from being an episode translated verbatim from a pre-Hispanic manuscript, the botched attempt by the gods to create a person from earth prior to the creation of a person of maize in the *Popol Vuh* was written as a response to the Genesis account, not in ignorance of it. This account should be read "not as an 'accommodation to' or a 'paraphrase' of the idea of Adam, but as a *negation* of Adam" (D. Tedlock 1986:81; emphasis in original).

Therefore, both Yucatec and K'iche' accounts of the origin of the First People are, to some extent, discourses that posit different dialogic rejoinders to the teachings and interrogations of Spanish clergy and jurists imposed upon them. The interpretation of Maya mythologies is enriched by understanding both pre-Hispanic antecedents and the colonial context of competing discourses in which the surviving texts are composed, for as Bakhtin (1981:284) notes: "one cannot excise the rejoinder from this combined context made up of one's own words and the words of another without losing its sense and tone. It is an organic part of a heteroglot unity."

ON THE SOUL

Continuing our discussion of the ontology of the First People, let us now consider colonial discourses about the soul. The Chumayel text states that the First Father was placed in the Terrestrial Paradise (*paraysoe*) once *oci u pixan* 'his soul entered' his body. It has been argued that in pre-Hispanic times, the indigenous peoples of Mesoamerica believed that the "soul" (*pixan* in Yucatec) consisted of three parts. Furst (1995) has attempted to document the experiential basis of Aztec soul concepts and elsewhere (1998) speculates on how the multiple soul concepts of the Aztecs, the animating *yolia*, *ihiyotl*, and *tonalli* (as well as the alternate physical form of sorcerers known as the *nahualli*), might have informed indigenous interpretations of religious images of the Trinity and Christ. Robert Hill and Ted Fischer (1999) argue from ethnographic analogy and lexical entries in Thomas de Coto's late seventeenth-century Spanish-Kaqchikel Maya *Thesaurus*

Verborum that the traditional Kaqchikel concept of "soul" (*ranima*) is also composed of three parts. They further argue that these three parts of the Kaqchikel *ranima*—the *natub* 'shadow,' *uxla'* 'breath,' and *k'u'x* 'heart'—are comparable to Aztec concepts and, like the Aztec examples, have deep roots in ancient Mesoamerican cosmology. Hill and Fischer are confident enough of the pre-Hispanic origin of this division to conclude, "these data underline the validity of archaeological and ethnohistorical extrapolation based on ethnographic observation" (1999:326).

Nonetheless, given that studies of both Aztec and Kaqchikel Maya ontologies must by necessity upstream from colonial sources, we should tread cautiously before concluding that the integrated three-part Mesoamerican soul concept has deep pre-Hispanic roots. Our ethnohistorical sources for Mesoamerican soul concepts were composed in the context of hotly debated colonial discourses on the ontology of the American Indians themselves (Hanke 1970). Here we examine first the pre-Hispanic evidence and then Classical Yucatecan texts in light of contemporary Spanish colonial discourses. This broader context of colonial discourses of the soul suggests that Mesoamericanists inadequately assessed the extent to which Christian soul concepts were expropriated by indigenous peoples in tandem with the Spanish friars.

First, we should review what is currently known about pre-Hispanic Maya ontology from extant hieroglyphic texts. There are at least two ontological, or soul, concepts Maya epigraphers believe to have identified in the hieroglyphic inscriptions, as well as a third co-essence that is not part of the "soul" proper as it is usually delineated in the studies above. The first is the animate principle *ba*, meaning "self" and "image" in the contexts of some hieroglyphic texts (Houston and Stuart 1998; see also Zender 2004).[6] The second concept is the *sac nich/nic-?* 'white flower(?)' thought to leave or expire as breath with the body at death (Schele 1998:40; Taube 2004). In addition to these two souls is a third "co-essence," *uay*, the spirit familiar of the *kuhul ahau* during the Classic period (Houston and Stuart 1989) and also apparently of sorcerers among the colonial Yucatec Mayas (Ciudad Real 2001:568). The Aztec counterpart of the Maya *uay* is not any of the three souls contained in certain parts of the body but the separate soul concept of the *nahualli* (Furst 1998). Therefore, although our textual evidence for the ancient Maya does refer to beliefs with parallels in the ethnohistorical and ethnographic record, at present it does not neatly correspond to a specifically *three*-part soul concept outlined above for Central Mexican and highland Maya peoples.

Second, it is important to note that the idea of a three-part soul is not restricted to Mesoamerica but had for centuries been the norm among educated peoples in the Old World by the time of the Spanish invasion of the Americas. The Greek philosopher Aristotle (384–322 BC) formulated a three-part concept of the soul in which only human beings had all three souls: vegetal, sensitive, and rational. This theory would be discussed and modified by Arab commentators on Aristotle. Muslim scholars eventually introduced the works of Aristotle along with Ptolemaic astronomy and much of Greek science and philosophy into Spain and Western Europe during the Middle Ages. This occurred first through commentaries by Avicenna (AD 980–1037) and Averroes (AD 1126–1198) and Arabic translations and then by Latin translations of the Arabic or Greek. The works of Aristotle and his Muslim commentators were hotly debated in European theological circles, as Aristotelian philosophy was incorporated into the university curriculum by, among others, Franciscan and Dominican mendicants (Lindberg 1992:216–223).

Christian theology and Aristotelean philosophy would be a major force in determining the legal status of the American Indians, that is, the extent to which the Spanish Christian monarch could legitimately conquer, enslave, and exploit them in the colonial enterprise. The Christian interpretation of the Aristotelian soul concept served as the legal basis for the defense of the Indians by Dominican Bartolomé de las Casas (AD 1474–1566), whose indictments of the encomienda system helped lead the Spanish Crown to enact the New Laws of 1544. This decision was based in part on the judgment that American Indians did in fact have the third, "rational" soul in the Aristotelian sense (las Casas 1967 [1559]; Hanke 1970). As such they were considered to be fully human, made in the image of God with the capacity of responding to Christian evangelism, and therefore could not be abused with absolute impunity by a Christian monarch. Thus the relevance of the friars' mission to the Americas and the legal rights of the American Indians in the Spanish colonial system were together bound to a Christian interpretation of the Aristotelean theory of the tripart soul.[7]

Colonial period dictionaries of Classical Yucatecan gloss numerous words as "soul" or "spirit." In the Motul Dictionary, *pixan* is translated as "alma, que da vida al cuerpo del hombre," while *ol* is translated in the language of scholastic philosophy as "corazon formal, y no el material" (Ciudad Real 2001:460, 495). An interesting entry in the *Bocabulario de Maya Than* employing explicitly Aristotelian soul terminology is *ah cuxtal* 'animal, que tiene anima racional, sensitiba, o bej[et]atiba' (Acuña 1993:99). Beyond dictionary entries, we have the explanation of the concept of the soul following an account of the creation of *yax anom Adan* 'the first *anom* Adam.' Human beings—created from earth and given life (*cuxtal*) by God's breath (*ik*)—are described as follows to the Maya-speaking audience by the author of the Morley Manuscript (page 171; modified after Whalen 2003a):

> lay pixan hach potchicanil u hochbilan Dios
> yokol loe yoklal bay huntulil Dios ti oxtul personae
> bay huntulil Dios huntulil pixan cuxcinnic u cucutil uinice
> ti oxtulob tu ba pixanil u chucile
> heklaobie kaahsah yetel naat yetel olah yan tie.
>
> This soul has truly been made manifest in the image of God
> Because of that, for as there is only one God in three "persons"
> As there is only one God, only one soul gives life to the body of man
> With three selves within it, the spiritual powers
> These which are memory, and understanding, and heart, are in it.

Rather than the singular *ba* 'self' or 'image' of some pre-Hispanic hieroglyphic texts, the soul comprises three selves. The tripart division of the soul reflects the Judeo-Christian cosmogony in which man is made in the image of God (Genesis 1:26). Just as there is a trinity of *personas* 'persons' composing the Christian God *tu ba tu hunal*, the human soul (*pixan*) is likewise composed of *oxtulob tu ba* 'three selves' (see also Morley Manuscript page 29).

We see in this Classical Yucatecan Maya example a parallel with Furst's (1998) hypothesis about the Aztec interpretation of the Christian Trinity in light of their three-part division of the soul turned on its head. Evidence in Classical Yucatecan sources suggests that the language of pre-Hispanic soul concepts was expropriated to construct a three-part concept of the soul in accordance with Spanish Christian doctrine. It may be that this expropriation was restricted to Yucatec Mayas and perhaps does not reflect the different colonial histories of their related ontological categories among the Aztecs or Kaqchikel Mayas. Nonetheless, this should raise a warning for scholars attempting to apply direct ethnographic analogy to the reconstruction of pre-Hispanic soul concepts in the Americas. Certainly, the history of soul concepts in pre-Hispanic and colonial Mesoamerica will continue to be an issue for scholarly discussion for a long time to come. For our present purposes, though, it is enough to note that both the friars' missionary project and the Indians' legal rights in the Spanish colonial system depended on the applicability of a Christian modification of the Aristotelian theory of the three-part soul. There was therefore a substantial motive for both friars and Yucatec Maya people to promote early on a discourse whereby ancient Maya soul concepts were expropriated into the language of Old World philosophy, a discourse that is in fact documented in Classical Yucatecan Maya didactic literature.

ELEGY AND ETHNICITY

In the discourses of Spanish colonial Christianity, to argue that the American Indians shared the same ontology as a European was to argue their common descent from Adam and Eve, *ca yax yum yetel ca yax naa* 'Our First Father and Our First Mother' in the Classical Yucatecan Maya language. The Spanish missionaries did this not only in the royal court of Spain but also in the mission schoolhouses of Yucatán. An interesting passage from the Morley Manuscript is identified and translated by Gretchen Whalen (Whalen 2003a:169.10–170.1, with modifications):

ta xocahi tac helel cech christiano
hijbic sihsabcij yax anom adan ti lume
u yumit tulacal vinicob yanob yokol cab tu sinile
lacech dzulob laac francesob
laac morosob laac judiob laac ekboxob
laac ah mex cuc uincob laac ah maya uincob
huntulili adan yax anom chunpahcij uinicilob loe
bacac ix ua uecaanob ti petenob lae.

You read already now, you who are Christian,
Just how the first *anom* Adam had been born from earth
To father all the people who exist upon the world everywhere
Though they may be the Spaniards [*dzulob*], though French
Though Moors, though Jews, though Blacks
Though Ah Mex Cuc people, though Maya people
It is only Adam, the first *anom*, from whom those people began
Even though they are scattered to these lands.

This text from the Morley Manuscript evidences that colonial Christian discourse sought to undermine New World as well as Old World interpretations of ethnic difference as distinct (sub)human races. The text contrasts groups in terms of nationality, distinguishing *dzulob* 'foreigners' or Spaniards from French, and in terms of race, Moors from Jews from Blacks (the three "others" of European racial classification), finally reducing intra-Yucatecan distinctions between "Ah Mex Cuc people" and Maya people.

These debates provide the backdrop of indigenous ethnic distinctions and Christian discourses of universal humanity in which the text of the *kay* 'song' of the fall of Chichén Itzá appears (Figure 6.4).

Ca pecnahi	*Then [the drum] sounded*
V uil im hunac ceel ahau	*The feast (?) of Hunac Ceel the king*
Kay	*Song:*
Ge ma et kinon	*Are we not alike?*

6.4. Chichén Itzá: The Temple of Kukulcan as seen from the Group of the Thousand Columns (photograph by author).

Tix kan thixal ti tun/e	*And of the ripe gleanings (?) of this tun?*
Mac u cobol y utztacil uinic	*Who is the corn-mold of the good people?*
Yn nok ynu ex y alah oua	*"My clothes and my pants" he said OUA*
Kue	*O deity*
Balac au oktic	*You mourn for this thing*
Yx cijx mamace	*And nobody better?*
V munalen u chii cħeen	*I am a servant of the Mouth of the Well*
Cen ti uli	*For me, when it arrived*
O Chuc lum	*O To conquer the earth*
Dzidz v tah katun aya	*To vanquish the warlord AYA*
(59) T u chi cħeen ytza	*At the Mouth of the Itza's Well*
O Antan he yao	*O Stomp now YAO*
Y ulu / u ayano	*The moon arrives (?) AYANO*
O [H]e ti hun imix u kijnil chuc / caan	*O This One Imix is the day of heaven's capture*
Bin ahau t u chiken cħeene	*According to the king to the west of the Well*

[H]e taba/ech yane	*Where will you be?*
Kue	*O deity*
[H]e tun hun ymix v kin	*Then this day One Imix*
Y alah t u chi cħeen ytza oa	*It declared to the Mouth of the Itza's Well OA*
Anta here yao	*Stomp now YAO*
Y ulu u ayano	*The moon arrives (?) AYANO*
Muclam muclam	*Burial ground, burial ground*
Cijx y aua/t	*And so he shouts*
O Muclam muclam	*O Burial ground, burial ground*
Ci xan y ohelob thun	*So they also know the slit drum*
Ci y aue	*So he shouts*
Ci xan y awat	*So also it shouts*
O T u hun te yaxkine	*O In the first dry season*
Chichil kinij ca te	*A strong sun for the second time*
Ak yabil ti tali	*There were many tongues when it came*
O Ayano ayano ayano	*O AYANO AYANO AYANO*
Y ulu u ayano	*The moon arrives (?) AYANO*
Yan / xin macxin	*Who is it really?*
Ahan uale	*A defender, perhaps?*
Chichil ni ca te / ayano	*A strong tip the second time AYANO*
Ox ten c acan v kine	*Three times we bewail the day*
Kue	*O deity*
C ah/ualob c ahualob	*Our enemies, our enemies*
Vui yao	*Listen! YAO*
Ma xan / ulom t u chi cħeen ytza oa	*Will not arrive also at the Mouth of the Itza's Well OA*
Anta here yae	*Stomp now YAE*
Y ulu u ayano	*The moon arrives (?) AYANO*
Ox te caan u kin	*The sun of the third heaven*
He macen ua	*If I am this man*
T u than tan y ol vinice	*In the word before the heart of the people*
Cen u mac	*I am the man*
Lee eya	*LEE EYA*
Macen ua	*If I am the man*
T u than tan / y ol putun	*In the word before the heart of the Putun*

Men a nate oeyan	*Because you may understand it OEYAN*
Cħaben / akaben	*I am genesis, I am night*
Coon ua sihij oeya	*Is it we who are born? OEYA*
Alakon / miscit ahau	*We are comrades, Miscit King*
Ho atal	*Five are paid*
Tix vlu	*And arrive*
Max / ela	*Who burned it?*
Bin yn kacuntah t in kay be	*I was going to remember in my song thus*
Antan here yao	*Stomp now YAO*
Y ulu u ayano eya	*The moon arrives (?) AYANO EYA*
Ci/milen y alah	*He said "I am dead*
T u men u kin cah oeya	*Because of the town's day" OEYA*
Ca/tacen y alahe	*He said "I am two*
T u men u sat cah	*Because the town is lost"*
O U ti u / lah ti y ol	*O It all belongs to him in his heart*
U tuclah t u pucsikale	*He thought it in his core*
Men u / sat cah	*Because the town is lost*
O Vali kacuntan in kay	*O It stood memorialized in my song*
O Antan / here yao ayano	*O Stomp now YAO AYANO*
Y ulu v ayano	*The moon arrives (?) AYANO*
Lay kay t u lacal lae	*This is all of the song*
V dzoc lukanil y anu/mal ahau dios lae.	*The perfection of God the King's news.*

(CHUMAYEL 58.22–60.2)

The setting of the "Song of the Fall of Chichén Itzá" is the feast (*uilim*) of the *ahau* Hunac Ceel (Chumayel 58.23). In the Códice Pérez (pages 135.23–25), Hunac Ceel is known as a *halach uinic* of Mayapán whose scheming led to the overthrow of his fellow *halach uinic* at Chichén Itzá. Texts elsewhere in the Chumayel manuscript relate how Cauich Hunac Ceel became co-ruler of Chichén Itzá with Ah Mex Cuc (Chumayel ms. pages 10–11), suggesting that the *ah mex cuc uinicob* mentioned in the Morley Manuscript is a reference to Itzá people of Yucatán, who are often (although not always; cf. Restall 2004) differentiated from the *maya uinicob* "Maya people" in Classical Yucatecan documents (Knowlton 2010).

In the song itself, we find a voice within a voice, the voice of a "servant of Chichén" framed by that of the compiler who is *bin yn kacuntah t in kay be* 'going to remember in my song thus' (Chumayel 59.21). Prior to the beginning of the song, a drum of the *thunkul* or *teponaztli* type "is sounded" (*pecnahi*), indicating that the song is set to music (Ciudad Real 2001:485; Alfonso Lacadena, personal communication, October 2006). The song is divided into six stanzas by a recurring litany. In the first stanza, this Itzá singer appeals on the basis of common ancestry (Chumayel 58.24, 59.19–20) against those who have come "to conquer the earth" and "vanquish the warlord" (Chumayel 58.28). In the second stanza, we learn that One Imix is the fated day of "heaven's capture," as determined by the "king to the west." The third stanza invokes a transition from "the first dry season" to a second period, with frequent references to shouting and to *muclam*, the "burial ground." The fourth stanza invokes a shift from a second period to the third time period in which "we bewail the day." In the fifth stanza, during "the sun of the third heaven," the Itzá singer identifies himself with the Classic period metaphor for generative sacrifice ("I am genesis, I am darkness") in his appeal to a *miscit* (Nahuatl: Misquitl) king, who is perhaps the "king to the west" mentioned earlier. From Chumayel 59.21 in the sixth and final stanza, the voice switches between that of the Itzá singer and the reported speech of the compiler. We learn that the Itzá singer is dead upon the fall of Chichén Itzá, the song being a ghostly elegy paralleling "the perfection of God the King's news" (Chumayel 60.1–2).

It is interesting that this song follows an illustration of Death and the account of the creation of the First Father and First Mother and their children, who "entered [the world] in the presence of laments" (Chumayel 58.10). The song has the character of an elegy for a shared Mesoamerican identity. I say "elegy," because when the narrative voice again comes to the foreground near the end of the song, we learn that the Itzá singer is dead and the song is to "memorialize" the fallen city. It is the fulfillment of prophecy, as "the perfection of God the King's news" (Chumayel 59.25–60.2). Amid the song are appeals to comradeship (*alak*; Chumayel 59.19) and common origin (*et kin*; literally, "of the same sun/day"; Chumayel 58.24–25) for help against *c ah ualob c ah ualob* 'our enemies, our enemies' (Chumayel 59.12–13). Although the song is ostensibly about an event from several centuries earlier in the pre-Hispanic past, the final line "the perfection of God the King's news" suggests that the hearer should draw a parallel between past conquests and present circumstances.

The song is punctuated with non-lexical particles (vocables) expressing sorrow. These vocables, virtually nonexistent in extant examples of Classical Yucatecan Maya song, are ubiquitous elements of Classical Nahuatl song and thus seem to derive from a Central Mexican tradition, the implications of which I discuss elsewhere (Knowlton 2010).[8] Also of interest is a common refrain throughout the song, *o muclam muclam* 'O burial ground, burial ground.' In the K'iche' *Popol Vuh*, the First People were assembled for the First Dawn at the mythological site of Tulan Zuyva, variations of whose name are shared throughout the traditions of Late Postclassic Mesoamerica. Following the First Dawn at Tulan Zuyva, the languages of the First People change and consequently they split into the various nations or *amac* populating Postclassic Mesoamerica. There the ancestors of the K'iche' sang a song titled *ca mucu* "Our Burial," which explicitly calls to memory "the Yaqui people," or Central Mexicans, one of many nations from whom they split there at Zuyva (Christenson 2003a:230–232; Christenson 2003b:191–192, 303–304).[9] Thus, the "Song of the Fall of Chichén Itzá" in the Chumayel manuscript and the song of the K'iche' ancestors in the *Popol Vuh* share the themes of elegizing a lost shared identity, are connected to the mythic-legendary past, and allude to connections with Central Mexico either directly (the "Yaqui" people) or indirectly (the *miscit* king and presence of Nahua vocables in this Maya song).

Therefore, both the indigenous, likely Postclassic song traditions and Maya-language Christian doctrinal texts contributed to a colonial discourse that emphasized the shared origins of Mesoamerican peoples. However, although appeals to common descent from the First Father and First Mother by the Defender of the Indians were enough according to Spanish law to curb some of the excesses of the encomienda system, they apparently were not sufficiently conducive to the sense of identity needed for a pan-Indian alliance. When read in the contemporaneous colonial context in which the song is framed, these appeals by the ghost of "the Itzá" of Chichén Itzá are against these same forces of Death portrayed by the illustration introducing the section (Figure 6.1).

A final observation on the language used in the song's appeals bears notice. In appealing to common origin against the forces of suffering and death mentioned before, the "Itzá" resorts to in-group language (Chumayel 59.18–20):

> Because you may understand it OEYAN
> I am genesis (*ch̄ab*), I am night (*akab*)
> Is it we who are born (*sih*)? OEYA
> We are comrades, Miscit king.

This appeal to common ancestry uses the reproductive (*sih*) understanding of the ancient Maya diphrastic kenning *ch̄ab akab* 'genesis and night' (see Chapter 2). This constitutes the single known use of this Classic period couplet in the colonial Books of Chilam Balam. However, there is another Classical Yucatecan document in which the couplet appears frequently and prominently in reference not to the birth and descent of people but to the birth and descent of the forces of sickness and death on the date of

Creation itself. This text is the collection of medical incantations known as the *Ritual of the Bacabs*.

THE SURVIVAL OF PRE-HISPANIC METAPHYSICS

Although there are numerous medical documents in colonial Maya literature, there is no text that parallels the types of discourses found in the *Ritual of the Bacabs*. Dating to the late eighteenth century, the extant copy has nonetheless often been cited as evidence for pre-Hispanic Maya medical belief and practice (Roys 1965; Arzápalo Marin 1987; Gubler 1996).[10] This claim is likely to be for the most part accurate, but it is difficult to verify independently, as no distinctively medical texts have been successfully identified in the entire Maya hieroglyphic corpus (V. Bricker and Miram 2002:63).[11] The organization and wording of the texts of the *Ritual of the Bacabs* do provide a dramatic contrast to the tomes of Maya astrological medicine and medical prescriptions recorded in the Books of Chilam Balam, as the latter are now known to be organized fundamentally along the principles of Hippocratic-Galenic-Arabic medicine, inherited by medieval Spain (V. Bricker and Miram 2002:23–30, 35), which is documented throughout the Americas (Foster 1994).

What makes the *Ritual of the Bacabs* unique is that it contains medical "incantations" (literally, 'its word,' or *v thanil* in Maya) and few references to medical concepts of obvious European derivation. The Spanish loanwords that do occur in the text are one-word invocations of Jesus, Maria, Dios, and the ubiquitous conclusion "Amen." It is the only known representative of the genre of medical incantations written in the Classical Yucatecan Maya language. This fact, along with its terse style and esoteric subject matter, has made these texts notoriously difficult to understand, and I make no attempt at a comprehensive interpretation in what follows. What I would like to discuss, however, are two specific features pertinent to our discussion of Classical Yucatecan Maya cosmogonic myths. First, I will address the text's frequent use of the *ꜩhab akab* 'genesis and night' couplet, which constitutes (with a single exception) all known instances of its use in Colonial period Maya documents. Second, I consider the possibility that the colonial text of the *Ritual of the Bacabs*, while steeped in Postclassic Maya lore, was in fact composed in dialogue with European concepts of illness and healing, although not those belonging to the Hippocratic-Galenic-Arabic tradition of humoral medicine.

As discussed in Chapter 2, in Classic times the diphrastic kenning *ꜩhab akab* could refer, among other things, to the gendered complementary dualism metaphysically required for ritual efficacy. As documented from

Classic inscriptions at Palenque, this ritual efficacy could be invoked in discourses on the births of the gods (theogony). In the text of the Ritual of the Angels (Chapter 5), we saw that *c̄hab* appears in some colonial cosmogonies that refer to the birthing (*sihsah*) of the angels. When Spanish clergy elicited meanings of *c̄hab* from Maya speakers in the sixteenth century, it was already marked as a "vocablo antiguo" when used in reference to pre-Hispanic penitence (Ciudad Real 2001:207). It seems fabulous, then, that this expression of complementary dualism would appear so frequently and prominently in a text dated to no earlier than the late eighteenth century, with contextual meanings so compatible with its use in hieroglyphic texts of the Classic period.

The majority of the incantations in the *Ritual of the Bacabs* involve the recollection of events occurring on the traditional Maya creation date 4 Ahau: *can ahau kin can ahau c̄hab* '4 Ahau is the day, 4 Ahau is the genesis' (Arzápalo Marín 1987; ms. page 208). The text also shares with pre-Hispanic sources and some Classical Yucatecan texts a division of the cosmos into four cardinal directions with their own deities and color associations. The principal events on the 4 Ahau creation date being recalled are the birth and lineage of the illness-spirit the healer is exorcising (Roys 1965:xii). An extension of its usage in reference to the "conjuring" (*tzac*) of supernatural beings *tu c̄hab ti y akabil* 'in genesis, in darkness' in pre-Hispanic discourses (Chapter 2), this theogonic use accounts for the ubiquitous presence of *c̄hab akab* in association with the creation date in the introductory lines of the incantations. Roys (1965:xv) observes:

> In a considerable number of these incantations the origin of the evil spirit is ascribed to "the lust of creation [*ch'ab*]" and "the lust of darkness [*akab*]." From the various contexts it seems plain that *ch'ab* is the male principle and *akab*, the female. Although the phrase is often a stereotyped one, slight variations sometimes occur, when these two forces are cited.

Roys backs this argument with the substitution pattern in elements of semantic and structurally parallel lines, with *al* 'woman's offspring' sometimes substituted for *akab*, and *mehen* 'man's offspring' sometimes substituted for *c̄hab* (Roys 1965:xv). The birth reckoning of the illness-spirit accords with traditional Maya principles of double-descent kinship, although their names often identify them with animals and their progenitors are invariably Maya deities. It seems, then, that we have a close adaptation of a pre-Hispanic metaphysical trope in a colonial ritual discourse, committed to alphabetic writing at least 1,200 years after the trope was used in the elite public discourse recorded in Maya hieroglyphs.

However, is it appropriate to refer to *c̄hab akab* (or any discursive element for that matter) as a pre-Hispanic "survival"? In the case of poetic elements, from a Bakhtinian perspective this might be. Bakhtin (1981:285) saw poetry as "by convention suspended from any mutual interaction with alien discourse," a literary convention that stripped language from its natural social context of dialogic tensions in a movement toward monoglossia and standardization. Couplets and diphrastic kennings as standardized poetic devices, although not static, do "reflect lengthier social processes, i.e., those tendencies in social life requiring centuries to unfold" (Bakhtin 1981:300).[12]

The Itzá singer says before using the ancient trope, [*tu*]*men a nate* 'because you may understand it' (Chumayel 59.18); because of their common Mesoamerican heritage, the song's audience "may understand" the use of the ancient trope in the appeal to subvert "our enemies." Whereas "at any given moment, languages of various epochs and periods of socio-ideological life cohabit with one another," as we have seen in the heteroglossia of colonial Maya cosmogonic myths, the poetic device of couplets and diphrastic kennings "depersonalizes 'days' in language" (Bakhtin 1981:291) in their conventionalized forms. Therefore, in my opinion those ethnohistorians and other scholars concerned primarily with discovering survivals of pre-Hispanic ideology in Classical Yucatecan Maya literature would profit more from attention to poetic devices than from those other areas of discourse that are more responsive to the historical dialogic of composition.[13]

But again, the frequent use of the ancient Maya trope *c̄hab akab* in the *Ritual of the Bacabs* does not dictate that the meanings of these texts are not rejoinders in dialogue with European concepts of illness and healing. Certainly, there is little evidence in this particular Maya text of the Hippocratic-Galenic-Arabic medicine established in Spain at the time. But humoral theory was not the sole model of illness and healing either. Christian doctrinal discourse promoted a view of illness and healing tied particularly to the Judeo-Christian cosmogony, in which moral transgression of the First People and the activities of benevolent and malevolent supernaturals all contributed to one's sickness and well-being on a cosmological scale.

ORIGINAL SIN, ORIGINAL SICKNESS

Commentaries on Judeo-Christian cosmogonies that appear in Classical Yucatecan texts attribute the ultimate origin of sin and sickness not simply to the actions of the First People but also to the animosity of the fallen angels toward them. As discussed in Chapter 5, one cosmogony in the Chumayel describes how, following a battle with Parrot in Heaven, *ca dzab caan corporales ti ojales tumenel u yax papa* 'then heavenly bodies were placed in holes (?) by the First Pope' (Chumayel 53.8, 53.19–20). The Genesis commentary in the Book of Chilam Balam of Kaua complements the Chumayel account, describing how the rebellious angels fell with Lucifer to earth, where they entered numerous plants, holes in the earth (*holob ti lum*), and winds (*ik*) that *cu chucic uinic ca kohanac* 'capture someone so that he may become sick' (V. Bricker and Miram 2002:292; Kaua ms. page 154). According to the accounts of the creation of Adam and Eve in the Morley Manuscript, *u lobil espiritus yanob mitnale* 'the bad spirits that are in Hell' plotted the Fall of the First People because God had promised these First People the *sillas kanche dzamobe* 'chairs, seats, and thrones' in Heaven left vacant by Lucifer's angels (Whalen 2003a; ms. pages 205–206).

The Morley Manuscript contains extensive textual material in Classical Yucatecan Maya regarding the First People, texts that provide a significant amount of evidence that the illness etiology linked to Christian cosmogony was current among Mayas of colonial Yucatán. Although the Chumayel cosmogonies recount that the First Father was placed in Paradise (Chumayel 58.3) and that his children (*mehen*) entered the world *y icnal acanob* 'in the company of laments,' it does not explicitly detail what transpired to produce the transition from Paradise to the sad condition of humanity in the world. The Morley Manuscript accounts roughly follow the medieval Christian lore on the First People with some interesting expropriations of colonial Maya language, expropriations that, like their counterparts in Nahuatl doctrinal literature (Burkhart 1989), may show up in the dialogic construction of Maya cosmogonic myths.

According to the Morley Manuscript, Paradise is the site of the *yax cheil cab* 'First Tree of the World.' This is the same tree that in Maya cosmology stands at the world's center, and the term has been mistakenly identified with the Christian cross by some scholars (Freidel, Schele, and Parker 1993:39). In Classical Yucatecan Maya literature, the *yax cheil cab* is identified less often with the cross than with the cross's binary opposite, the tree of the forbidden fruit from which Original Sin results (Knowlton and Vail 2010). For the Maya, the pairing of the First Mother and First Father beneath the *yax cheill cab* in "Paradise" would likely have resonated with Late Postclassic beliefs, as the center of the cosmogram on pages 75–76 of the Madrid Codex depicts an aged creator couple beneath a tree at the center of the cosmos (Figure 6.5). Furthermore, Landa (1978 [ca. 1566]:57–58) reports:

6.5. Aged creator couple seated beneath a tree at the center of a Postclassic Maya cosmogram. Detail from Madrid Codex, pages 75–76 (reproduced by permission of the Museo de América, Madrid).

> The future life they said was divided into good and evil, into pains and delights. . . . The delights they said they would come into if they had been of good conduct, were by entering a place where nothing would give pain, where there would be abundance of food and delicious drinks, and a refreshing and shady tree they called *yaxché*, the Ceiba tree, beneath whose branches and shade they might rest and be in peace forever.

In the Morley Manuscript, Dios commands Adam and Eve not to eat *u uich u yax cheil cab u cheil grasia . . . u cheil cuxtal y toh olal* 'the fruit of the First Tree of the World, the Tree of Grace . . . the Tree of Life and Health' (Whalen 2003a; ms. page 205.4–7; see also 209.3–4). It is at the *yax cheil cab* where the *cisin zerpiente* 'devil serpent' sent by the fallen angels deceives Eve into eating the fruit (ms. page 207). Convinced by the serpent and disobediently eating from the "Tree of Life (*cuxtal*) and Health (*toh olal*)," *noh kinam* 'great throbbing pain' comes upon Eve (ms. page 212). Instead of Life and Health, by eating the fruit of the *yax cheil cab*, the First People introduced Death and Sickness into the world.

It is important to note that the term used in relation to Eve's fall, *kinam* 'throbbing pain,' appears more than sixty times in the incantations of the *Ritual of the Bacabs* (Arzápalo Marín 1987:494). It is used throughout the Morley Manuscript in discourses of pain resulting from the Original Sin.[14] *Ocij u kinam keban ti yol* 'the throbbing pain of sin entered the heart' of Eve (Whalen 2003a; ms. page 130.3–4). Adam and Eve "came to know the aching pain (*yail*) and the throbbing pain (*kinam*) of worldly wisdom" taught to them by "Hun Ahau Lucifer" (ms. page 130.10–11). Recalling the statement in the Chumayel mythography that the children of Adam and Eve "entered [the world] in the presence of laments" (Chumayel 58.10), this *yax keban* 'original sin' is *u chun ca yail* 'the origin of our aching pain' and *u chun xotcij u kinob ti cimil* 'the reason the days end with death' for *con y al u mehen* 'we who are the children of women, the children of men' (ms. page 130.12–13, 16–17). However, *u kinam u cilich numyail* 'the throbbing pain, the blessed suffering' of Dios Mehenbil 'God the Son,' reopens *u hool caan toon* 'the entrance of heaven for us' (ms. page 131).

Colonial period Maya-language discourses on moral forgiveness and the ritual of confession (Morley Manuscript pages 70–100) are cast explicitly in the language of illness and healing, a discursive phenomenon shared in some respects with colonial Nahuatl doctrinal literature (Burkhart 1989: chapter 6). Confession of immorality was a healing practice among the pre-Hispanic Maya of Yucatan according to Landa (1978 [ca. 1566]:45), so it should perhaps come as no surprise that the use of *v thanil* 'its word' in combating illness stands out on the dialogical frontier of Maya and Spanish religious belief. Expanding upon a quote from Saint Augustine, the author notes that *keban* 'sin' brings upon the offender *kohanil* 'sickness' and *cimil* 'death.' Persons 'fall' *lubul* into *kak* 'illness; pustule' just as they 'fall' into *keban* 'sin' (ms. page 82.10).[15] The priest as confessor is the *ah dzac yah* 'healer of wounds' to whom the sick person should tell *bix chunpahanil v kohanile* 'how this sickness has begun' in order to return to *toh olal* 'health' (Whalen 2003a:ms. page 83).

So what do these discourses of the origins of people, sin, and sickness and their cure through confession have to do with the medical incantations of the *Ritual of the Bacabs*? I suggest that looking at the *Ritual of the Bacabs* in light of colonial dialogue can illuminate the aspect of these enigmatic texts that most perplexed Roys (1965:xxv):

> Discussions with Professor Verne F. Ray, who has made a special study of shamanism in the Pacific Northwest, has led me to realize the unusual significance of the absence in the Maya incantations of prayers to the deities, although the deities are frequently cited. The Bacabs are given orders, admonished, and sometimes even cursed; but I can find no instance of a deity being supplicated.

I wish to raise the possibility here that the Maya deities who are cited as the progenitors of the illnesses in the *Ritual of the Bacabs* are the Maya deities as reinterpreted in dialogue with Euro-Christian cosmogony. As with the deity Hun Ahau (Whalen 2003a:ms. pages 125–130), they have become the fallen angels, the bringers of sickness; and the medical incantations of the *Ritual of the Bacabs* are Maya exorcisms to some extent hybridized in rejoinder to these discourses promoted by the Franciscans. As noted above, spiritual healing according to the Christian model given in Maya-language doctrinal literature involves speaking forth *bix chunpahanil v kohanile* 'how this sickness has begun' (Whalen 2003a:ms. page 83). As argued below, viewing the *than* 'words' of the *Ritual of the Bacabs* as Maya Christian exorcism texts may be a productive approach to understanding this esoteric document.

The majority of the incantations begin by invoking both Can Ahau (4 King, the date of creation) and Hun Ahau (1 King). As mentioned earlier, the *Bacabs* text identifies *can ahau kin can ahau c̄hab* '4 Ahau is the day, 4 Ahau is the genesis' (Arzápalo Marín 1987; ms. page 208), but reference to Hun Ahau complicates this picture.[16] Just as the Franciscans in Central Mexico identified Nahuatl deities with the fallen angels who became demons (Burkhart 1989; Cervantes 1994), Hun Ahau is identified in the Morley Manuscript with Lucifer (Whalen 2003a:ms. pages 125–130).

In both the 1620 *Discursos Predicables* of Juan Coronel (ms. page 13v) and the Genesis commentary of the Book of Chilam Balam of Kaua, Lucifer fell (*lubi*) to *metnal* 'hell' *tu dzu lum* 'in the center of the earth.' The Kaua account goes on to state that the angels following him entered (*oci*) various things on earth in order to plague people with sickness (V. Bricker and Miram 2002:292; ms. pages 153–154). Likewise, in the *Ritual of the Bacabs*, the origin of the illness-spirits frequently recalls what they entered (*oci*) and where they fall (*lubul*), sometimes with the word (*than*) of the exorcism sending the illness back to *metnal* (Arzápalo Marín 1987).

Furthermore, although most of the deity names are likely of pre-Hispanic derivation, a few of their appellations are suggestive of the Christian discourses of the origins of people and the animosity of the fallen angels. The titles *Hun y ahual cab, Hun y ahual anom* 'First Enemy of the World, First Enemy of *anom* (ms. page 123) and *Hun y ahual uinicob, hun y ahual anomobe* 'First Enemy of the Peoples, First Enemy of the *anomob*' (ms. page 176) are suggestive for several reasons. Maya-language sermon material appearing in both Juan Coronel's *Discursos Predicables* and the Morley Manuscript (ms. page 234) refer to the Devil as the *ahual* 'enemy' of human beings.

Furthermore, the term *anom* rarely appears in Classical Yucatecan Maya texts outside the (probably late sixteenth-century) Morley Manuscript, where it is always used in reference to Adam. The Motul Dictionary glosses *anom* as 'el primer hombre, Adán' (Ciudad Real 2001:64), but I believe this is likely the appropriation of a pre-Hispanic term for the First People. Although rare, this term is shared with the creation mythology of K'iche' Maya. In the *Popol Vuh*, the gods ordain the creation of the wooden people who preceded the creation of the people of maize, who are referred to as *vinac anom* (Christenson 2003b:29, 267). Christenson (2003a:80n100) notes that Fray Domingo Basseta's 1698 dictionary of K'iche' defines *anom* as a "model or form" as well as a "buffoon, or someone who is lightminded and unserious." One cannot help but wonder if the Yucatec Maya informants from whom the friars' elicited *anom* provided the term as a form of sarcasm or criticism of the Christians' beliefs regarding the first man, likening the First People of the Christian account to that failed, destroyed race of people from a previous creation.

There is also a link between *anom* and the *yax cheil cab*, not only in the Classical Yucatecan Maya texts of the Morley Manuscript but also in Fray Andrés de Avendaño y Loyola's account of the beliefs of "pagan" Peten Itzá before their final conquest in 1697:

> The king and all of his family and followers worship together at this stone column. They call this same column, which is the title by which they give homage to it, *yax cheel cab*, which means in their language "the first tree of the world," and as I have understood in their ancient songs (there are few who understand them). They want it to be understood that they give homage to it because this is the tree of whose fruit our first father Adam ate, who in their language is called Ixanom. (Avendaño y Loyola 1997 [1696]:35; translation mine)

Thus by the late seventeenth century, the Peten Itzá had incorporated the equation of *yax cheel cab* with the tree in Eden involved in the temptation of *yax anom Adán* into their own "pagan" religious practices (see Knowlton and Vail 2010). Perhaps unique to Avendaño's account is the attachment of the female agentive prefix *ix-* to the term *anom*. This suggests a belief in the androgyny of the first person(s), like that documented by Dennis Tedlock in the contemporary K'iche' "Story of Evenadam" (D. Tedlock

1992b:414). So a century before the extant copy of the *Ritual of the Bacabs* was put to paper, even the "pagan" Peten Itzá had adapted some variation of the Judeo-Christian myth of the Devil's temptation of First People into their beliefs and rituals.

Finally, the *Ritual of the Bacabs* has a distinct antisyncretic slant to its presentation of Oxlahun-ti-ku ("Thirteen-As-Deity"). Alternate redactions in the Book of Chilam Balam of Tizimín (14v.26–28) and the Códice Pérez (117.16–18) of the Katun 11 Ahau cosmogony explicitly identify Oxlahun-ti-ku with the Christian Dios, who is even referred to as Oxlahun-ti-Citbil ("Thirteen-As-Father") at one point in the Book of Chilam Balam of Chumayel (36.8). In the *Ritual of the Bacabs*, this often Christianized deity is instead "polytheisized" by being referred to in the plural Oxlahun-ti-kuob. Although both singular and plural forms of the name are used in the text, the plural form is more common, appearing eleven times. The reason I suspect this as an intentional "polytheizing" of Oxlahun-ti-ku, instead of simply reflecting a pre-Hispanic polytheistic conception of the deity, is that no such pluralization is found in the name of his antagonistic counterpart Bolon-ti-ku ("Nine-As-Deity") in the text. The Bacabs, who are referred to in all three known redactions of the Katun 11 Ahau myth as *can tul ti ku* 'Four who are deity,' are likewise explicitly pluralized as *can tul tii kuob* in the *Ritual of the Bacabs* (ms. page 183; see also ms. page 26). It appears that, for some reason, the scribe felt it necessary to emphasize their plurality as multiple "deities," or polytheism, rather than multiple aspects of one "deity." This latter discursive approach was more readily compatible with the Christian Trinity. Certainly some deities, like the Lords of Xibalba in the *Popol Vuh*, were thought to play a role in Maya illness etiologies during pre-Hispanic times. Polytheizing the more ambiguous Maya deities, however, may mark a discursive strategy meant to represent *all* Maya deities as supernatural agents of sickness and death (i.e., as devils), a discursive strategy that also occurs in colonial Nahuatl doctrinal literature (Burkhart 1989).

CONCLUSION

This discussion of the elegiac *kay* 'song' of a historical disaster (the fall of Chichén Itzá) within a narrative of the creation of the First People has analyzed this in terms of the contemporary context of comparable discourses on Original Sin and sickness in the Maya-language doctrinal literature, as well as in the *Ritual of the Bacabs*. Colonial Maya discourses of the historical disasters of the pre-Hispanic and Colonial periods as well as those crises of individual sickness are not disconnected events but result from the same entropic processes at work since the beginnings of the world. Maya *katun* history, which had since pre-Hispanic times recorded historical wars and pestilences, in the Colonial period was being made intelligible in light of the Judeo-Christian cosmogony promoted by the Franciscans. Rather than simply isolated instances occurring in the distant past, the events of the cosmogony establish the basic human condition and, by extension, those events that follow. The Maya account of the First People and later catastrophes is a rejoinder to the extensive doctrinal literature in which the Fall of Humanity and the origin of sickness-bearing malevolent angels are juxtaposed with the old gods and ancient discourses of *ȼhab* 'genesis' and *akab* 'darkness.'

NOTES

1. The legendary Zuyua is known as Tulan Zuyua in highland Maya mythology. Tulan is a reference to the Central Mexican Tullan or Tollan, the "Place of Reeds," where the inventors of the arts and sciences, the Toltecs, resided in the legendary past (Sullivan and Knab 1994:18–19; Christenson 2003a:80–81). In the K'iche' Maya *Popol Vuh* (Christenson 2003a:231–232) and the Annals of the Kaqchikels (Maxwell and Hill 2006), Tulan Zuyua is the place where the original unity of the first peoples was divided and the gods differentiated their languages, creating the diversity of peoples that populate Mesoamerica.

2. The reading of Cimil for the name of God A is not as well established phonetically as the name Xib. The latter name is related to various terms for "fright" in Mayan languages. It appears in Classical Yucatecan Maya as Xibalba, glossed as "Devil" in the Motul Dictionary (Ciudad Real 2001:587), and Xibalba is also the name of "the Place of Fright," the name of the K'iche' Maya underworld in the *Popol Vuh*. The name of another underworld denizen that frequently appears in Classical Yucatecan literature, Cisin, is more likely the name of God Q rather than God A (Vail 1998:172).

3. Perhaps it should not surprise us that an educated Maya author in the Colonial era was familiar with the Latin poets, even if imperfectly. As Gruzinski (2002: chapter 6) discusses, works by Latin authors, such as Horace's contemporary Ovid, had been published in Mexico City since 1577. Mexican Indian painters depicted Greco-Roman mythological creatures such as centaurs in church murals, and Ovid's *Metamorphoses* "was part of general knowledge, being one of the most published, discussed, translated, and imitated books of the day" (Gruzinski 2002:90).

4. The name Ix Cab Tun, which may be a combined form of this paired appellative, appears in the Postclassic Dresden Codex, where it is paired with the name of Goddess O, Chac Chel (Dresden 69:E3–F3, 70:A3–B3), and the title Bacab (Dresden 74:A3–B3) (Gabrielle Vail, personal communication, August 2008).

5. U Colel Cab is also a name that in contemporary Yucatec Maya communities refers to the native stingless bee (Sosa 1985:330, 367); bees played an important role in other Maya creation myths already discussed.

6. We have already encountered this in our discussion of the couplet *tu ba tu hunal* in relation to the Maya interpretation of the "oneness" of the Christian Dios in Chapter 5.

7. We should note here that the title of the Latin translation of Aristotle's treatise *On the Soul* is *De Anima*, from which the Spanish word *ánima* 'soul' is derived. Furthermore, the term for the three-part soul in Kaqchikel, *ranima*, is actually the possessed form of the Spanish loanword *ánima*, prefixed by the third-person pronoun *r-* (Hill and Fischer 1999:320).

8. Interestingly, although these Nahua vocables here are rare for Maya song, they also appear in colonial Zapotec songs from Oaxaca transcribed alphabetically around the beginning of the eighteenth century (Tavárez 2000; Tomlinson 2007:91). This may suggest that in music, like the codices, intercultural exchange and even a shared intellectual culture were well developed during the Late Postclassic period in Mesoamerica.

9. For alternative translations of the title of the K'iche' song *ca mucu*, see D. Tedlock 1985:182; 1996:305, 309; Colop 1999:148; 2008:159.

10. The last two manuscript pages are written on the back of a printed Indulgence, which is dated 1779 (Roys 1965:vii).

11. Thompson's (1958) article on divinatory almanacs for diseases in the Maya codices was published prior to significant advances in the syllabic decipherment of the writing system; since then, his essentially iconographic argument has been found to have no basis in the actual content of the accompanying texts.

12. Maxwell and Hanson (1992:36) refer to similar devices as "fossilized" in their study of the Nahuatl metaphors recorded in Andrés de Olmos's 1547 *Arte*.

13. The problem and promise of approaching the history of literary transmission through the poetic devices it contains are familiar to students of epic literature; one good example is the analysis of panegyric in West African *tariku* 'history' of the medieval ruler Sunjata (Austen 1999; Wilks 1999).

14. Yucatec Maya language distinguishes among *kinam* 'throbbing pain,' *yail* 'aching pain,' and *chibal* 'sharp pain.'

15. *Kak* 'illness' or 'pustule' is among the major illness types treated in the *Ritual of the Bacabs* and appears in that manuscript more than 100 times (Arzápalo Marín 1987:489–490).

16. Roys (1965:3) is inconsistent in interpreting this as a reference to either the date or the deity by that name. These two interpretations are not mutually exclusive, as Ahau dates in *kahlay* texts are personified by taking the *ah-* prefix (e.g., Chumayel 47.19; Tizimín 14v.26).

CHAPTER SEVEN

The Calendar and the Catechism

The final cosmogony contained in the Chumayel mythography is an especially beautiful narrative, titled here, following Edmonson (1986), the "Birth of the Uinal," *uinal* being the twenty-day Maya week (V. Bricker 2002b).[1] While the preface presents the purpose of the Chumayel mythography as an answer to the questions of origin posed to the Maya by their colonial interlocutors (42.19–21), this final text answers these interlocutors with an assertion of the compatibility of Maya and Spanish cosmologies presented in the hybrid voice of both Maya and Spanish Christian traditions' most ancient authorities.

THE DIALOGISM OF RECEIVED TRADITION

This creation narrative known as the "Birth of the Uinal" begins by relating the genre of the cosmogony as the Maya scribe identified it and by asserting its source as an ancient received tradition:

Bay tzolci yax ah miatz merchise	*Thus it had been chronicled by the first sage Melchizedek*

Yax ah / bouat na puc tun	*The first diviner Na Puc Tun*
Sacerdote	Sacerdote
Yax ah kin	*The first day-keeper*
Lay kay uchci v sihil vinal	*This song is how the birth of the uinal had come to pass*
Ti ma to ahac / cab cuchie.	*when it had not yet dawned back then.*

(CHUMAYEL 60.3–6)

The cosmogonic narrative of the "Birth of the Uinal" is presented as deriving from received tradition, a "song" (*kay*) relating how this cosmogony had been "chronicled" (*tzol*), which means literally "to put in order." *Tzol* is also used to refer to counting, particularly in ritual processions and land surveys, the *tzol peten* and *tzol pictun*, respectively (Hanks 2000:258, 267). This creation song is attributed to the first sage (Yucatec: *yax ah miatz*) and *sacerdote* of Judeo-Christian tradition, Melchizedek. It is simultaneously attributed to a Maya religious leader who is listed in both clandestine Maya books and published Spanish sources as among the traditional companions of the Chilam Balam, Na Puc Tun, here called both the first diviner (Yucatec: *yax ah bouat*) and first day-keeper (Yucatec: *yax ah kin*), as a parallel to the Spanish title for "priest."

Both semantic couplets and bilingualism are well-documented features of Maya discourse style from the pre-Hispanic period (V. Bricker 2000). The use of bilingual semantic couplets occurs often in Maya documents, from the listing of everyday objects of Colonial period notarial documents (Restall 1997:241–242, 301–302) to the naming of cosmological phenomena in the various redactions of a Ptolemaic-Christian Genesis commentary (Knowlton 2008). In the present context, these bilingual couplets form an example of the discursive strategy of *syncrisis*, the juxtaposition of various points of view on a single object, in this case, the traditional author of the cosmogony being related.

The names attributed to the "First Priest" relating this song of creation is quite significant. Na Puc Tun is the first of a series of four diviners whose proclamations accompany the prophecy of the Chilam Balam published in the Franciscan Lizana's 1633 chronicle of the "spiritual conquest" of Yucatán (Lizana 1995 [1633]). This is the same published text discussed earlier (Chapter 3), in which the Maya-language prophecies it contained were later hand-copied into numerous Maya community books, including the Book of Chilam Balam of Chumayel (ms. page 104). As an indigenous priest whose prophecies have been, in a sense, "legitimized" as *poesia* by their publication in "orthodox" Franciscan sources,

Na Puc Tun is an intriguing character in the religious imagination of colonial Yucatán.

Perhaps even more intriguing is the identification of this enigmatic Maya priest Na Puc Tun with the equally enigmatic Judeo-Christian figure of Melchizedek. Regarding the "historical" figure, he is virtually unknown besides his brief appearance in the Hebrew Bible as king of Salem (later Jerusalem) and the priest of El Elyon ("God Most High"), who both blesses and receives tithes from the patriarch Abraham (Genesis 14.18–20). Over the centuries, a mystique grew up around this Melchizedek among the religious communities of the eastern Mediterranean, and by the time of Christ, Melchizedek had acquired a messianic character in the lore. A first-century BC document recovered from among the Dead Sea Scrolls identifies him as a heavenly priest and eschatological deliverer (Vermes 1997:500–502). Toward the end of the first century AD, the author of the New Testament Epistle to the Hebrews produced an exegesis arguing for the preeminence of the Christian Gospel over Mosaic Law and its priestly line through Aaron by presenting Jesus Christ as priest in the primordial and timeless priestly line of Melchizedek (Hebrews 7.1–19).

Evidence suggests that some Maya educated by the Franciscans were aware of this lore surrounding Melchizedek. Melchizedek is mentioned in the Morley Manuscript as the *yax ah kinhij ti bal cahe* 'first day-keeper / priest of the entire world' (ms. page 38.11–13). To refer to the Melchizedek as the *first* priest and not just priest of Salem, but of the *entire world,* is to confer on this figure the attributes not of the "historical" figure of the Hebrew Bible but the messianic personage of the Christian New Testament. In the dialogical frontier of colonial Yucatán, to equate Melchizedek with Na Puc Tun would be one rhetorical avenue of asserting the legitimacy of the traditional calendrical divination practiced by Maya *ah kin* in the context of Spanish *sacerdotes'* attempts to extirpate it. Deriving from so prominent a character as Na Puc Tun–Melchizedek, the received tradition of this cosmogony may have been perceived as of far more weight than the "orthodox" Genesis commentaries published in works like the *Discursos Predicables* that were preached by the Spanish clergy.

THE JOURNEY OF THE CREATOR GODS

Ca hoꝑi u ximbal t u ba / t u hunal	*So the [the divine being] began to walk by himself, alone*
Ca y alah u chich	*Then his maternal grandmother said*
Ca y alah u dzenaa	*Then his father's brother's wife said*
Ca y alah u mim	*Then his paternal grandmother said*
Ca y alah u muu	*Then his brother's wife said*

Bal bin / c alab	*"What shall we say*
Ca bin c ylab vinic ti be	*"when we shall see a human being on a road?"*
C u thanob / tamuk u ximbalob cuchie	*Thus they speak while they walk back then*
Minan uinic cuchi.	*There was no human being back then.*

(CHUMAYEL 60.6–11)

The point at which the creation song proper begins, a divine being is walking alone, followed by a group of four elder female relatives who discover his footprints *ti be* 'on a road.' (Figure 7.1). Roads, represented by series of footprints in pre-Hispanic iconography, are particularly potent cosmological symbols of Yucatec Maya, past and present. The often-cited cosmogram of pages 75–76 of the Madrid Codex (Figure 7.2) depicts alongside the path of day signs a series of footprints in the intercardinal spaces, all leading to the central tree flanked by the aged creator deities (see also Paxton 2001). In contemporary Yucatec Maya ritual discourse, "the day, state of being and destiny of the individual" are said to be that individual's "road" (Hanks 2000:243).

The temporal setting of the "song" is during a time before time, before the creation of the world and before the days of the *uinal*, or Maya week, had their names. As discussed in Chapter 2, the *uinal* was the week composed of thirteen numbers and twenty named days observed by the Maya and was symbolically associated with its near homophone *uinic* 'human being,' both of which share the same logogram in the pre-Hispanic writing system. This association is apparently of considerable antiquity: as several scholars have noted, the terse accounts in the pre-Hispanic Dresden Codex (61:A8–B8 and 69:C8–D8) relating that *patah ah uinac* 'the man / 20-day period was formed' on the Classic period creation date of 4 Ahau 8 Cumku are followed closely by additional texts relating various peregrinations (*y octah*) of different manifestations of the rain god Chac and other supernatural entities. Likewise, the peregrinations of these five figures, the as-yet-unnamed divine being and his four elder female relatives, are themselves ritual acts of creation, as will become clearer as the text moves along.

Ca tun kuchiob te ti likine	*And then they arrived there in the east*
Ca / hopi y alicob	*and they began to say*
Mac ti mani vay lae	*"Who passed by here?*
He y ocob / lae	*"These are his footprints."*

7.1. Postclassic representation of the Maya deity Chac "on a road" (*ta bih*) represented by footprints. Dresden Codex, page 65b (Förstemann 1880).

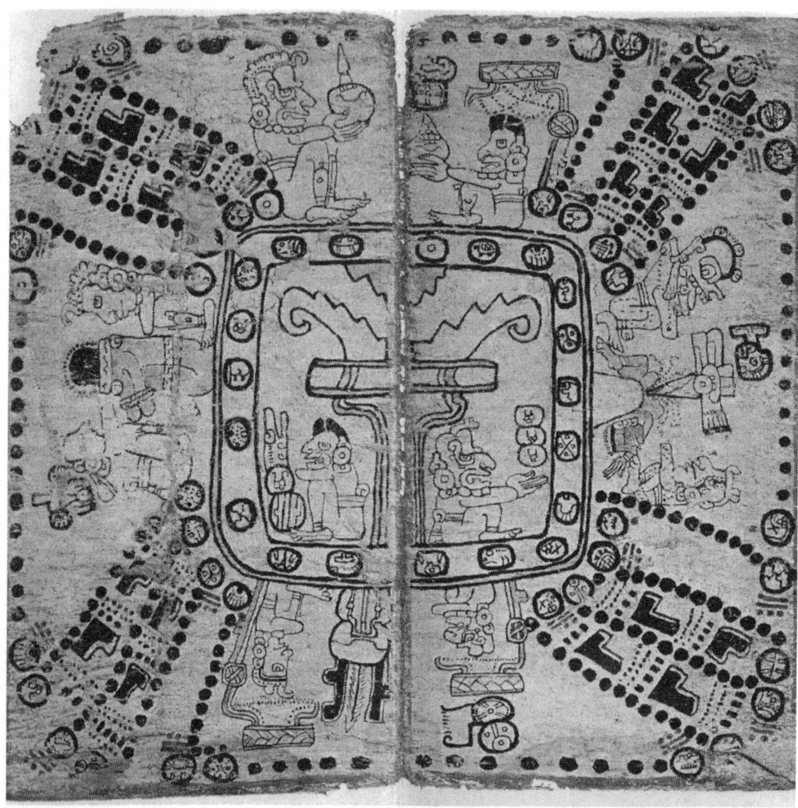

7.2. Postclassic Maya cosmogram outlining in space the days of the 260-day *tzolkin* with footprints in the intercardinal directions. Madrid Codex, pages 75–76 (reproduced by permission of the Museo de América, Madrid).

Ꝑis t au oci	*"Measure with your foot there"*
Ci bin u than u colel cab	*goes the word of U Colel Cab*
Ca bin u ꝑisah y oc ca yumil ti d[io]s citbil	*Then going she measured the foot of Our Lord who is God the Father*
Lay u / chun y alici	*"This is the beginning" she said there*
Xoc lah cab oc lae	*This foot accounts for the whole world*
Lahca oc	*Twelve footprints*
Lay tzolan sihci t u men oxlahun oc	*It is chronicled that he had been born by thirteen footprints [13 Oc]*

Uchci / u nup tan ba y oc	*It had come to pass that the image of his foot was encountered*
Likciob ti likine	*They had risen from the east*
Ca / y alah u kaba	*Then she said his name*
Ti minan u kaba kin cuchie	*when there was no name for the day-sun back then*
Ximbalnahci y v chiich	*He walked with his maternal grandmother*
y u dzenaa	*With his father's brother's wife*
y v mim	*With his paternal grandmother*
y v muu.	*With his brother's wife.*

(CHUMAYEL 60.11–18)

The elder female relatives proceed to measure the footprints as they trek across the entire world (Yucatec: *lah cab*) following twelve (Yucatec: *lahca*) footprints (note the characteristically Maya wordplay between *lah cab* and *lahca*; Roys 1967:116). Upon completion of this journey, they are again in the east, where they encounter the thirteenth footprint, which is also the first named day of the Maya week in the myth: Oxlahun Oc ("13 Foot"). At this point the myth-singer divulges one name of the divine being creating the footprints: *ca yumil ti dios* or the Christian God. Yet note that the sojourns and rising in the east make it clear that we are not dealing with a conception of Dios that would likely be smiled upon by the good friars and the extirpators of idolatry. What the elder female relatives have been following and what U Colel Cab ultimately names is in fact *kin*, meaning both "day" and the "Sun." The identification of the Spaniard's Dios as a Postclassic Maya Sun deity (Ahau Kin) will become even more explicit as the myth proceeds.

Likewise, note that the women elders tracking the Dios-Sun find the first footprint in the east and then finally conclude their peregrination by rising in the east, indicating that their journey has completed an entire circuit. Given that there are five individuals walking, the four females and the Dios-Sun, with a total of thirteen steps each, this gives us implicitly a total of sixty-five (13 × 5), a number that we will see is of considerable importance for understanding the conclusion of the myth.

Sih uinal	*The uinal was born*
Sihci kin / v kaba	*The name of the day-sun had been born*
Sihci caan y luum	*Heaven and earth had been born*
Eb haa luum	*The stairway of water [to the] earth*
Tunich y che	*The stone and the tree*

Sihci v bal kaknab y luum.	*The things of the sea and the earth had been born.*

(CHUMAYEL 60.19–22)

At this point, the myth-singer catalogs the cosmos that emerges from the peregrinations of those first divinities. Having established an overview of the framework of the Maya cosmos, units of time, sky, earth, and the steps that connect them, and the plants and animals, the myth-singer now transitions to a mode of divinatory interpretation that has parallels with the practices of Maya day-keepers to this day.

DIVINING THE DAYS OF CREATION

At this point, the Maya myth-singer proceeds to count a series of twenty days and account the specific episode of creation that occurred on each of the days of the first *uinal* as reckoned in the 260-day *tzolkin* divinatory calendar composed of thirteen numbers and twenty named days ($13 \times 20 = 260$ possible day name combinations). As Barbara Tedlock (1982) noted briefly in an article on contemporary Maya divination, the exegesis of the day names in this passage from the Book of Chilam Balam of Chumayel parallels the hermeneutics of speech play through metaphor and poetic sound texture (paronomasia) that she documented during ethnographic fieldwork among K'iche' (Quiche) day-keepers in the community Momostenango in highland Guatemala. As is obvious from the content of the surviving pre-Hispanic codices, Maya calendar priests have for many centuries used the *tzolkin* calendar (called the *cholq'ij* in contemporary K'iche') in divination with respect to a multitude of activities, public or private, seasonal or quotidian. According to Tedlock (1982:270), among contemporary K'iche' *ajq'ija'* (the highland Maya religious title equivalent to the Yucatecan *ah kinob*), "calendrical experts interpret a given day name by means of phrases that frequently include the sounds of its name but not the name as such; that is to say, the names are 'read' not as words in themselves, but as a kind of *oral rebus* for quite other words." More recently, Victoria Bricker (2002b) documented many of the numerous puns, metaphors, and other devices the colonial myth-singer of the "Birth of the Uinal" employed in his interpretation, which at times parallel the practices of contemporary highland Maya calendar priests observed by Tedlock. In this section, I provide my own observations of the myth-singer's cosmogonic interpretations of the days of the *uinal*, supplemented at times by those already made by Bricker (2002b). As we shall see, the exegesis employed by the myth-singer involves the emergence of meaning in a dialogue with multiple religious discourses, near and far, ancient and novel.[2]

Hun chuen v hoksici u ba t u kuil	*On One Chuen ["Artisan"] he revealed there the image of the divinity*
V ment/ci caan y luum.	*Heaven and earth had been made.*

(CHUMAYEL 60.23–24)

On the first day in our list, Hun (or "One") Chuen, is interpreted by the myth-singer as the day of the making of the sky and the earth. In Classical Yucatecan, *ah chuen* referred to a "craftsman, or an official of some art" (Ciudad Real 2001:41; see also Edmonson 1986:11). The Postclassic Yucatec Maya were part of a pan-Mesoamerican network or "world system" that involved cultural interchange with both non-Maya groups and Mayan language groups to the south (Kepecs and Masson 2003). In various areas occupied by speakers of Mayan languages, Hun Chuen is not simply a day name but the name of a supernatural personage, the patron of craftsmen. For instance, in the sixteenth century, Las Casas (1967 [1559]:506; in Christenson 2003a:147) reports that

> all the skilled artisans, such as painters, featherworkers, carvers, silversmiths, and others like them, worshiped and made sacrifices to those younger sons called Huncheven and Hunahan, so that they would grant them the skill and mastery to carry out their work in an accomplished and perfect way; but although they worshiped them as divine men, they were not held as gods in general, nor superior to all others.

In the K'iche' *Popol Vuh*, the half brothers of the Hero Twins are Hun Batz and Hun Chouen, who are characterized as the inventors and patrons of the various arts, including carving (Christenson 2003a:113, 147); the day corresponding with the Yucatec Chuen in the K'iche' calendar is Batz ("howler monkey").[3] As patrons of these arts, the image of the divinity said to have been revealed on Hun Chuen could well be a divine image of the kind the Spanish clergy referred to as an "idol."

It is important to distinguish, then, that the Maya myth-singer attributes to the day Hun Chuen not the "creation" of the cosmos per se. Creation statements in Classical Yucatecan myths involve verbs with gendered, procreative overtones such as *c̄hab* or *sih*, like "birth" of sky and earth mentioned a few lines earlier. Instead, what occurs on Hun Chuen is their "making" or fashioning, based on the word *men* 'deed.' This continued fashioning of the original created stuff is then the activity of a divine artisan, as artisans are also known in the Classical Yucatecan language as *ah men* (Ciudad Real 2001:49). Perhaps not coincidentally, in contemporary Yucatán, *(a)h men* refers to native curers or shamans (V. Bricker, Po'ot, and Dzul de Po'ot 1998:183). Thus, Hun Chuen is an especially appropriate date for inaugurating the fashioning of the cosmos via a divine exegesis of the days of the divinatory calendar.

Ca eb v mentci yax eb	*On Two Eb ["Stairway"], the first stairway had been made*
Emci likul tan y ol caan	*It had descended from before the Heart of Sky*
Tan y ol haa	*before the Heart of Water*
Minan luum y tunich y che	*There is no earth and stone and tree*
Ox [b]en v / mentci t u lacal bal	*On Three Ben ["Made"] all things had been made*
Hibahun bal v bal / caanob	*However many things are the things of the heavens*
y u bal kaknab	*and the things of the sea*
y v bal luum.	*and the things of the earth.*

(CHUMAYEL 60.24–28)

Succeeding One Chuen is Two Eb, *eb* being the term for "stairway." The stairway fashioned on this day reaches down from *tan y ol caan, tan y ol haa* 'the Heart of Sky, the Heart of Water,' a likely reference to the *eb ha luum* that was "born" a few lines earlier. This *eb* apparently served as a conduit between the waters of the celestial dome thought to come down to the earth as rain. Legal records of proceedings in Yucatán against suspected idolaters from the close of the sixteenth through the late seventeenth centuries note that Maya paid homage to the deity Tan Y ol Caan Chac, especially during times of drought (Chuchiak 2000:264–265). This Chac's image was placed in the center of altars surrounded by other god images in the four corners, and it was the one believed to be responsible for the fertility of the fields and to actually empty the gourd of rain to the earth, an activity often depicted in the surviving Postclassic Maya codices.

In the myth-singer's account, the descent of the stairway of rain and fertility from the Heart of Sky and Heart of Water necessarily preceded the continued shaping of "earth and stone and tree." The succeeding day name Ox (3) Ben ("to lack") is apparently confused by the scribe with the phonetically similar day name Men 'to make' (V. Bricker 2002b:10), as both day names begin with bilabial consonants. This is the day for the making of all the things of the sky, the sea, and the earth that had previously been lacking in the cosmos up to that point, and thus the confusion of the day names at some point in the process of redaction might not have done violence to content of the exegesis.

Can ix uchci u nixpahal caan y luum	*On Four Ix, the tilting of heaven and earth had come to pass*

Ho / men uchci u meyah t u lacal	*On Five Men ["Deed"] all his work had come to pass*
Vac cib uch/ci u mentci yax cib	*On Six Cib ["Candle"] it had come to pass the first candle had been made*
Uchci u sasilhal	*It had made things bright*
Ti minan kin ɏ v	*when there was no sun and moon*
V[u]c caban yax sihci / cab	*On Seven Caban the world had first been born*
Ti minan toon cuchi	*when we did not exist back then*
Vaxac edznab / edzlahci u kab ɏ y oc	*On Eight Edznab had established his hand and his foot*
Ca u cħicħaah y o/kol luum.	*when he gathered upon the earth.*

(CHUMAYEL 61.1–7)

The myth-singer's exegesis of the divinatory calendar continues to reference phonetic and semantic aspects of each day name. As Bricker (2002b:10) has discussed, the play between the day name Ix and the verb *nix* 'to tilt' likely refers to the pre-Hispanic iconographic convention of representing daybreak as involving the tilting of the sky as the Sun emerges between it and the earth. The interpretation of the following day, Ho (5) Men, as "all his work had come to pass" involves a relatively straightforward wordplay, with the word for "work" (*meyah*) being derived from the verb *men*. However, there is an additional layer of meaning here, as the number 5, as the "minimum totality of human space" made up of four corners and a center, can signify wholeness among contemporary speakers of Yucatec in other domains as well (Hanks 2000:215). Therefore, the myth-singer's simple single-utterance exegesis is actually operating on phonetic, morphological, and numerological levels simultaneously.

The following day names continue to build upon one another, with Vac Cib ("Six Candle") providing light for the birth of the *cab* 'world' on Vuc Caban. As Bricker (2002b:10) also notes, the pre-Hispanic glyph for the day name Caban is also the logograph for the word *cab*. To her iconographic observation, I wish to add that in Classical Yucatecan, *cab* also refers to a "town or region" (Ciudad Real 2001:94), the four boundary markers and central plaza of a Maya community serving as a microcosm of the world. Recognizing this helps us understand the particular human-centeredness of this exegesis, as evident in its use of the first-person plural "the *cab* had first been born when *we* did not exist back then." The following day name, Vaxac (8) Edznab, involves both a soundplay with *edz* 'to establish,' as Bricker (2002b:10) has already noted, and a semantic play between the second part of the day name *nab*. *Nab* refers to a "handspan" as a unit of measurement, playing on the activities of the "hand" (*kab*) of the deity explicitly referenced in the myth-singer's interpretation.

Bolon cauac yax tumtabci / metnal	*On Nine Cauac, Metnal had first been deliberated*
Lahun ahau uchci v binob v / lobil vinicob ti metnal	*Ten Ahau ["King"] it had come to pass the bad peoples went to Metnal*
T u men d[io]s citbil ma chicanac cuchie	*because God the Father had not yet appeared back then*
Bulu [im]yx uch/ci u patic tunich y che	*Eleven Imix it had come to pass the formation of stone and tree*
Lay u mentah / ychil kin.	*This he made within a day.*

(CHUMAYEL 61.7–12)

As mentioned earlier, Metnal or Mitnal is the name of the Yucatecan Maya underworld, which although often referred to in the scholarly literature as comprising nine layers (Thompson 1970), in Classical Yucatecan language sources is actually said to be composed of ten (see Chapter 4). Landa (1978 [ca. 1566]:38) identifies Mitnal as "hell," as do Classical Yucatecan language sources such as the Morley Manuscript. The day name Cauac has no obvious meaning in Classical Yucatecan, and there is no phonetic wordplay obvious in the interpretation of the day. However, Cauac is derived from the proto-Mayan **kahoq*, which means "lightning" and "thunder" (Kaufman and Norman 1984:117). Spero (1991) notes multiple ethnographic cases in modern Mayan language-speaking communities in which deities whose names are linguistically related to the Yucatec Cauac are associated with lightning, thunder, mountain caves, and sinkholes. In an incantation in the *Ritual of the Bacabs*, an *actun* 'cave' or 'cavern' leads to *tan y ol metnal tan y ol haa* 'before the heart of Metnal, before the heart of water' (ms. page 204; Arzápalo Marín 1987:413). Chuchiak (2000:267) cites an 1807 document referring to the Chacs and Pauahtuns as being located in caves and cenotes. The association of Cauac with lightning, thunder, and openings in the earth may provide the rationale for the myth-singer's exegesis linking the day to Metnal. A Ptolemaic-Christian Genesis commentary penned in Classical Yucatecan and appearing in various redactions in the Morley Manuscript and the Books of Chilam Balam of Kaua and of Chan Kan (Knowlton 2008) relates how Lucifer fell from heaven to *metnal t u dzu lum* 'Metnal in the center of the earth.' This and several other Classical Yucatecan language texts attest to the fact that the Maya were being educated in the fall of the Christian devil and that the missionaries equated *metnal* with the Christian hell. In the New Testament, Jesus states that he saw "Satan fall like lightning from Heaven" (Gospel of Luke 10.18), and this might account for why a Maya exposed to the Spanish missionaries would associate Cauac with hell.

The reference to the first act of deliberating (*tumtab*) related to the underworld on this day also makes sense in light of Classical Yucatecan-language accounts in the Morley Manuscript (ms. pages 205–208) of the *audienciaob* 'high courts' held in Mitnal. It was in these meetings that *u lobil espiritus* 'bad spirits' and the *cizin*, the latter being the pre-Hispanic supernatural beings (Vail 1998) identified in the Colonial period with the Christian "devils," first "deliberated" (*tumtic*) how to deceive the First People into eating from the *yax cheil cab* (Morley ms. page 206). Thus with the underworld in place on Nine Cauac, on the following day, Lahun Ahau 'Ten King,' the "bad people" (*v lobil vinicob*) went to Metnal. The events on this day could refer to either the lore regarding the fall of Lucifer and the devils or the medieval Christian lore regarding the fate of the dead in the pre-Christian period, prior to Christ's death and subsequent descent into Hell to rescue them. In any event, it is clearly indicative of the transformation of Old World diabolism in the New (Cervantes 1994), as well as its effect on the cosmology of the Colonial period Maya. Following the placement of Metnal and its inhabitants, trees and wood are "formed" (*pat*) on the day named Imix, which recalls the various *imix che* established in the five partitions of the world after the destruction of the previous world, as recounted in the Katun 11 Ahau myth (Chapter 4).

Lahcabil yk uchci sih/sic yk	*Twelve Ik ["Wind, Breath"] it had come to pass breath had been born*
Lay u chun u kabatic yk	*This is the origin of calling it "breath"*
T u men mi/nan cimil ychil lae	*because there is no death within this*
Oxlahun akal uch/ci u cħaic haa	*Thirteen Akal ["Lagoon"] it had come to pass he grasps water*
Ca y aksah luum ca u patah / ca uinichi[l]	*Then he dampened the earth and he formed our bodies*
Hunnil kan v yax mentci u lep̧el / y ol	*One Kan ["Ripe"] he had been furious for the first time*
T u menel v lobil u sihsah	*because of the evil it gave birth to*
Ca chicchan / uchci u chictahal v lobil hibal	*Two Chicchan it had come to pass he discovered the evil thing*

Y ilah ychil u uich / cahe	*He saw it with his own eyes*
Ox cimil v tusci cimil	*Three Cimi ["Death"] he had invented Death*
Uchci u tus/ci yax cimil ca yumil ti d[io]s.	*It had come to pass Our Lord who is God invented the first death.*

(CHUMAYEL 61.12–20)

As Bricker (2002b:11) noted, the myth-singer's cosmogonic interpretation of the days beginning with Lahcabil Ik ("Eleven Wind-Breath") through the day Ox Cimil ("Three Death") recounts the steps in the origin of the First People, with clear allusions to the story of the Garden of Eden in the Judeo-Christian tradition.

One should note, however, that the importance of *ik* in pre-Hispanic Mesoamerican concepts of life and being is well established by iconographic and textual evidence, from the Olmec to Classic Maya to Aztec (see Houston and Taube 2000:265–273 for an overview with emphasis on Classic Maya hieroglyphic examples). Although alluding to the Judeo-Christian tradition, the myth-singer's account contains idiosyncrasies best understood in reference to other Classical Yucatecan documents. For example, the myth-singer refers to the following day as Akal, instead of the usual name for the day, Akbal, meaning "night." *Akal*, however, means 'lagoon' or 'to become moist' (Ciudad Real 2001:60). The resulting creation of human beings by Dios not only include *luum* 'earth' and *yk* 'breath' but also liquid. The use of a liquid is not mentioned in the biblical account (Genesis 2.7), but earth, breath, and moisture all appear as elements in the Maya-language account of the creation of *yax anom Adan* in the Morley Manuscript (ms. page 168). In another indigenous account, the K'iche' *Popol Vuh*, the use of water (to make blood) was one of the characteristics distinguishing the creation human beings from the wooden people of the previous world (Christenson 2003a:194; see also D. Tedlock 1996:288 and Colop 2008:129).

The image of the forbidden fruit of Judeo-Christian tradition is evoked by reference to *kan*, which is used to refer to ripened fruit (Ciudad Real 2001:325). Then follows the day Chicchan, corresponding to "Serpent" in Maya calendars. This, as Bricker (2002b:11) notes, is the serpent of the Garden of Eden. Called the *cisin zerfiente* of the Morley Manuscript (ms. page 207.13), the Serpent appears before the origin of Death, paralleling the fall of Judeo-Christian tradition that occurs on Ox Cimi ("Three Death").

Ho lamat lay u tusci vuc lam chac haal kak/nab	*On Five Lamat he had invented these seven deluges, the oceans*

Vac muluc uchci v mucchahal kopob / t u lacal	*Six Muluc it had come to pass he caused all the valleys to be buried*
Ti ma to ahac cabe.	*when it had not yet dawned.*

(CHUMAYEL 61.21–23)

The scribe recording the myth fails to record what should be the following day, Four Manik. As there is an empty line in the original manuscript at this point, this might indicate that perhaps the scribe was transcribing the "Birth of the Uinal" from another manuscript that was damaged in which this line was defective, although with the evidence available to us, this is purely speculation. Within the text itself, the myth-singer resumes the account with the establishing of natural features, first with reference to deluges (*lam*) on the day Lamat, followed by the burying (*muc*) of valleys on the day Muluc.

In completing the cycle of day names, this Colonial period myth-singer concludes his account with a method of interpretation through paronomasia that is very much like that employed in divinations by contemporary Maya day-keepers of the Guatemalan highlands. But despite the similarities in methods of exegesis, what are we to make of the unusual purpose to which this was employed, the relation of a cosmogony? To better understand this aspect of the "Birth of the Uinal," we proceed from ethnographic analogy back to the sociohistorical context of those who would have performed and transcribed the myth.

COSMOGONY AS COUNTER-CATECHISM

Lay uchci y ocol v tusthanil ca yumil ti d[io]s t u lacal	*This had come to pass beneath the commandments of Our Lord who is God to all*
Ti / minan tun than ti caan	*when there was no speech then in heaven*
Ti minan tunich / y che cuchi	*when there was no stone and tree back then*
Ca tun binob u tum t u baob	*So then they went and examined it themselves*
Ca y alah tun	*And he said then*
Bay la / oxlahun tuc vuc tuc hun	*"Thus these thirteen heaps and seven heaps are one"*
Lay y alah	*He said this*
Ca hok / v than ti minan than t i	*Then speech was released when there was nothing spoken to him*

Ca katab u chun t u men yax / ahau kin	*Then its origin was desired by Yax Ahau Kin*
Ma ix hepahac v nucul than ti ob	*As the instruments of speech had not been opened for them*
Vchebal / v thanic u baobe.	*so that they speak to each other.*

(CHUMAYEL 61.23–62.4)

Following the cosmogonic interpretation of the days of the Maya divinatory calendar, the narrative turns to the origin of speech. Yet, despite the obvious influence of the friars' teaching on the myth-singer's narrative, the ideology presented here, including that of speech, differs from that of the Judeo-Christian tradition. As Tedlock (1979) notes, unlike the divine monologues of the Christian God, creation stories of the speakers of Mayan languages are often framed in the form of dialogues. The dialogism of Maya cosmogonies subverts and confounds the dichotomies of missionaries and scholars alike. In the origin of speech related above, the *deus faber* of the text is called by both the Spanish name Dios and the Maya name Yax Ahau Kin ("First King Sun"). Named simply Ahau Kin in the hieroglyphic texts of the Postclassic Maya codices, he is known to scholars as God G (Taube 1992:50–56), the Sun god associated with the domains of both creation and death (Vail 2000b:124–125, 133–135) (Figure 7.3). The statement that in fact initiates speech is "thus these thirteen heaps and seven heaps are one," a phrase interpreted by Bricker (2002b:11–12) as a correlation of the count of thirteen days of the divinatory calendar with the seven-day biblical week to complete the sum of one *uinal* (twenty-day Maya week) as the concluding act in the creation of the *vinic* 'human being.' Even before speech existed, a dialogue in the form of the correlation between Maya and European systems was required "so that they [human beings] speak to each other."

Dialogic processes are fundamental to how Maya cosmogonies order the universe. Thus, the "Birth of the Uinal" is in some respects the cultural mirror image of the Genesis commentaries of the Morley Manuscript and in Yucatec-language Christian doctrinal texts of the *Discursos Predicables*. Although both narratives employ the syncrisis of Maya and European cosmogonies and cosmologies, the rhetorical goal of those Genesis commentaries is to present Christian-Ptolemaic cosmology with comparable Maya terms (Knowlton 2008), whereas the Birth of the Maya Week presents the cosmogonic activity of Maya calendrical divination with a comparable exegesis in the Judeo-Christian cosmogonic tradition. That this narrative is attributed to the *yax ah kin* 'first day-keeper' Na Puc Tun, who is simultaneously the original *sacerdote* Melchizedek, suggests the possibility that the

7.3. God G, a Postclassic depiction of the Sun deity Ahau Kin. Madrid Codex, page 108b (reproduced by permission of the Museo de América, Madrid).

Maya-Christian pedigree of this cosmogony is meant to trump the claims of the Counter-Reformation catechists. This possibility appears even more likely once we examine other texts in which the Maya *tzolkin* calendar is adapted to missionary discursive devices to serve as a counter-catechism.

There are significant differences between Maya-language dialogues given in published catechismal documents such as the 1620 *Doctrina Christiana en la Lengua de Maya* (Coronel 1620b) and those dialogues attested to in the underground manuscript traditions of the Maya Books of Chilam Balam. In her translation and commentary on the Morley Manuscript, Whalen (2003b:8) was able to identify the Christian question-and-answer dialogue appearing on manuscript pages 22–70 as a Maya translation of *Las preguntas que el emperador hizo al infante Epitus*, published in 1540 but subsequently banned by the Inquisition in 1559. The sorts of differences inherent in the language of published official books versus those of a popular and/or clandestine nature exist in those examples of formal question-and-answer dialogues in colonial Maya literature. In Bakhtinian terms, a formal dialogue may involve the device of *anacrisis*, the "means for eliciting and provoking the words of one's interlocutor, forcing him to express his opinion and express it thoroughly" (Bakhtin 1984:110). In his discussion of the Socratic notion that knowledge or "truth is not born nor is it to be found inside the head of the individual person, it is born *between people* collectively searching for truth, in the process of their dialogic interaction," anacrisis is to Bakhtin one of two devices (the other being syncrisis) by which thought is dialogized. But it is possible to have a formal dialogue that is not functionally dialogic but monologic; a dialogue in which the words provoked of one's interlocutor are not the interlocutor's words at all but all belonging to the same voice. Examples of formal dialogues in Colonial period Maya documents suggest the formal dialogues of the *cartapacios* are also functionally dialogic, while those of published works of the religious are functionally monologic.

The dialogues in the Books of Chilam Balam and the Morley Manuscript, whether of strongly autochthonous content (the riddles of the "Language of Zuyua") or of historically Old World derivation (the "Tale of the Wise Maiden," as well as "The Questions that the Emperor Hadrian Asked the Infant Epitus"), all exhibit what Bakhtin calls the ironic, "carnivalesque" character of dialogized thought (Bakhtin 1968, 1984:132). Rather than examples of the rote memorization characteristic of some colonial educational regimes, each of the above dialogues involves the contradictions and inversions of social statuses, in which the socially subordinate characters of *mehen* 'son,' *suhuy* 'maiden,' and *paal* 'child' exhibit uncharacteristic wisdom in dialogue with their socially superior interlocutors: *yum* 'father, lord,' *ah miyatz* 'wise man,' and *emperador* 'emperor,' respectively. In his interpretation of the "Language of Zuyua" contained in the Book of Chilam Balam of Chumayel, Allen Burns (1991:35) also asserts, drawing on field research on contemporary Yucatec Maya oral literature, that such riddles "function to question and mock authority, not celebrate it."

Circulating in the clandestine *cartapacios*, one element that is so intriguing about these dialogues is the extent to which they contrast with the public, published dialogues available in the Yucatec Maya language at that time. In addition to the *Discursos Predicables*, Fray Juan Coronel published in 1620 the *Doctrina Christiana en Lengua de Maya*, which contains a large *diálogo* composed of *kat* 'questions' for the Spanish catechist and *kam* 'answers' to be memorized by the Maya neophyte. Whereas the dialogues contained in the handwritten copybooks provided examples of inverted social statuses, the "Exposition of Christian Doctrine" in Coronel's 1620 work strongly reinforces them. In his study of the Maya-language Franciscan *diálogos*, Hanks (1995:250) concludes: "In performing the *diálogo*, the neophyte becomes a subordinate speaker whose answers are pre-scripted by the very one questioning him. He submits to judgment of his knowledge, acquiesces to the authority of the church, ventriloquates the talk of a Christian." In place of a carnivalesque anacrisis dialogizing thought, in which true knowledge emerges only in the dialogic interaction between people, we have a discourse in the form of a dialogue but exhibiting the functional qualities of a monologue (D. Tedlock and Mannheim 1995:4). Thus, Bakhtin (1984:110) cites the catechism as the ultimately degenerate form and fate of the Socratic dialogue.

Therefore, the dialogues of the published catechisms, although formally dialogues but functionally monologues (D. Tedlock and Mannheim 1995:4), establish hierarchical relationships favoring the Inquisitor (Hanks 1995). The dialogues redacted by hand in Maya community books, by contrast, are structured according to the carnivalesque inversion of statuses: the child who is wiser than the emperor, the maiden who is wiser than the wise men, the interrogated inferior who is actually heir to titles of authority.

It is not the ultimate historical derivation of the manuscript dialogues that accounts for their difference with the published catechisms; many, although by no means all, of the dialogue texts mentioned above have European antecedents. The difference is instead to be found in the orientation of their reproduction. For their part, the colonial Maya produced discourses like those of the question-and-answer of the published catechisms but as a way of incorporating the divinatory calendar into practices that were, for many Spanish clergy and their catechumens, rote drills of so many articles of faith.

In the pages following the mythography in the Book of Chilam Balam of Chumayel, there is a dialogue section organized much like the dialogues of the "Language of Zuyua" found on the pages that immediately precede the Chumayel mythography. As with the "Language of Zuyua" section of the manuscript, these posterior dialogues are composed of questions asked by a person addressed as *yum* 'father,' an honorific title applicable to a Maya of higher social status or to a Catholic priest. This "father" in turn addresses questions or riddles to a *mehen* 'son,' which can likewise apply to a social inferior or a catechumen. These parallels drawn, one can observe the similarities of the following lines to those of a Christian catechism:

Bax u kinil takci tu nak suhui cħuplale	"What is the day this virgin maiden conceived in her womb?"

Yume / Canil Oc takci tu nak	"Father, Four *Oc* [Foot; To Enter] she had conceived in her womb."
Mehene balx kinil hok/ci	"Son, what day had he come forth?"
Oxil Oc hokcii	"Three *Oc* he had come forth."
Bal kinil cimci	"What day had he died?"
Hun / Cimil cimci be	"One *Cimil* [Death] he had died thus
Tijx oci tu mucnal ti Hun Cimie.	"and then entered into the grave on this One *Cimil* [Death]."

(CHUMAYEL 67.25–28)

Here we find a catechism-like dialogue covering the topics of the Immaculate Conception, birth, death, and burial of Christ, just as we find in the published *Expossicio de la Doctrina Christiana en la Lengua de Maya* (Coronel 1620b:17, 22). But in place of the Counter-Reformation concerns crystallized in "orthodox" Maya-language publications such as the *Discursos Predicables* (Coronel 1620a:32–42), we have in this handwritten manuscript a counter-catechism, a genuine dialogic syncrisis of Christian doctrine (the question) and Maya divinatory calendrics (the response).

Both the dialogue cited above and the discourse of the "Birth of the Uinal" juxtapose the Maya divinatory calendar with elements of Christian doctrine. This syncrisis is consistent with the autochthonous metaphysics of correlative monism that oriented the practice of divinatory calendrics in Classic Maya civilization (Chapter 2). Simultaneously, by placing divinatory traditions and Christian doctrine on equal footing, these texts exemplify a Maya rejection not of Christianity itself but of the monologic ideal Spanish Christendom attempted to impose on religious culture in the dialogical frontier that was colonial Yucatán.

RITUAL, SCRIPT BILINGUALISM, AND THE DIALOGIZED SIGN

Ca binob tan y ol caan	*Then they went before the Heart of Sky*
Ca u machaah / v kab t u ba tan baobe	*and they grasped one another's hands*
Ca tun ualah tan chumuc peten	*and then stood facing the middle of the peninsula*
Heklayob lae	*These are they*
Heklaobi ah toocob can tulob lae	*These there are the Burners, there are four of them*

Chan chicchan	⊙	ah toc E2:	*Four* Chicchan	⊙	*Burner* E2:
Canil	OC	ah toc Pio	*Four*	OC	*Burner* Pio
Ca men	⊙	ah toc MER	*Four* Men	⊙	*Burner* MER
Can ahau	⊙	ah toc	*Four* Ahau	⊙	*Burner*

Lay ahauob can tulob lae	*These are the kings, there are four of them*

Vaxac muluc	Hoil cauac	*Eight Muluc*	*Five Cauac*
Bolon oc	Vac ahau	*Nine Oc*	*Six Ahau*
Lahun chuen	2 Vay ymix	*Ten Chuen*	*2 uay Imix*
Buluc eb	Vacxacil yk	*Eleven Eb*	*Eight Yk*
Lahca men	4 Bolon akabal	*Twelve Men*	*4 Nine Akabal*
Oxlahun yx	5 Lahun kan	*Thirteen Yx*	*5 Ten Kan*
Hun men	6 Buluc chicchan	*One Men*	*6 Eleven Chicchan*
Ca cib	Laca cimiy	*Two Cib*	*Twelve Cimiy*
Ox caban	7 Oxlahun manik	*Three Caban*	*7 Thirteen Manik*
Can edznab	Hun lamat	*Four Edznab*	*One Lamat*

Lay sihci vinal	*This uinal had been born*
y uchci y ahal cab	*and the dawn had come to pass*
Tzolci / caan y luum y cheob y tunich	*Sky and earth and trees and stone had been chronicled*
Sihci t u la/cal t u men ca yumil ti d[io]s lae	*All of this had been born by Our Lord who is God*
Lay citbil / ti minan caan y luum	*This Father, when there was no heaven and earth*
Ti bay yanil t u diosil / t u muyalil	*who is thus in his Godhood in the clouds*
T u ba t u hunal	*by himself, alone*
Ca u sihsah balcah t u sinil	*And he gave birth to all the things in the world*
Ca pecnahi t u caanil t u kuil	*and that moved in the heavens by his divinity*
Ti bay noh / u chucil yanil ah tepale	*Thus when the great sign of the Sovereign appears*
V tzolan kin sansamal	*He chronicles the day-sun every day*
Licil u xocol v chun ti likine	*He counts its beginning in the east*
He bix tzolanile.	*In whatever way it is chronicled.*

(CHUMAYEL 62.4–63.6)

Perhaps one of the most fascinating features of the "Birth of the Uinal" text is its script bilingualism. The author of this portion of the Chumayel

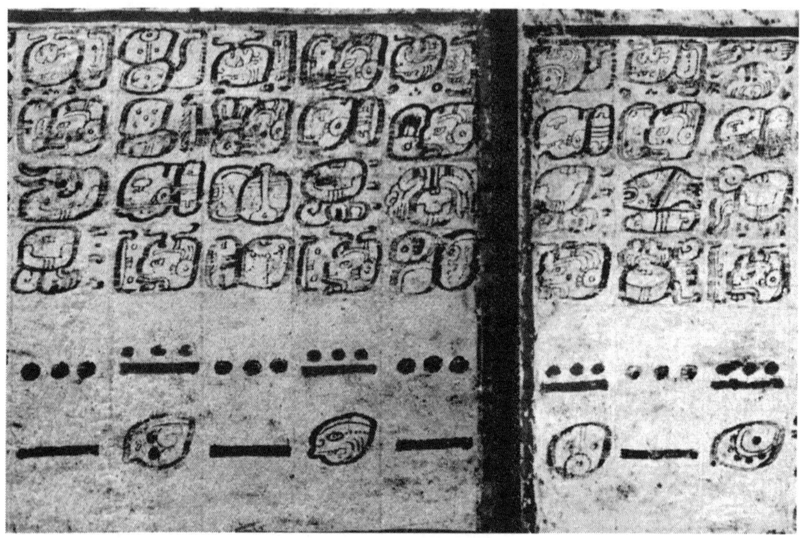

7.4a. Postclassic Maya Burner almanac. Dresden Codex, pages 30b–31b (Förstemann 1880).

mythography juxtaposes alphabetic and logographic script, further undermining the miscast distinction between form and content.

On page 62 of the Chumayel manuscript, the linear narrative text is interrupted by a table designating four *tzolkin* dates: 4 Chicchan, 4 Oc, 4 Men, and 4 Ahau. Each of these dates is spaced sixty-five days apart, just as the five divine beings walking each thirteen steps at the beginning of the myth preceded the naming of the *kin* 'day/Sun' in the east. Together, these four periods of sixty-five days encompass one full cycle of the 260-day divinatory calendar. As attested to in both pre-Hispanic hieroglyphic books and Colonial period sources, certain ceremonies associated with the Maya rain deity Chac were performed (V. Bricker 1991; V. Bricker and Miram 2002: 49–58) (Figures 7.4a and 7.4b). The ritual specialists who performed these ceremonies were four *ah tocob* 'Burners.' In the Chumayel text, each *tzolkin* date is followed by the title *ah toc* 'Burner,' the four collectively referred to at the end of the table as *ahauob* 'kings.' Following scholarly convention, I will refer to the four *tzolkin* day names (Chicchan, Oc, Men, Ahau) as the "Burner days," the combination of numeral and Burner day name as given above as "Burner dates," and the four sixty-five-day ceremonial periods these dates delineate as "Burner periods."

Perhaps most striking about the presentation of the Burner days in this cosmogonic text is the appearance of the Western astronomical/astrologi-

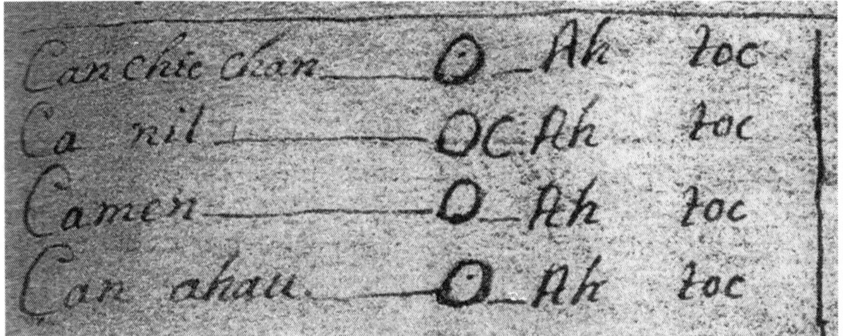

7.4b. Burner almanac with European Sun ideogram used as glyph for the Maya word *kin* 'sun' and 'day.' The Book of Chilam Balam of Chumayel, page 62 (reproduced by permission of the Princeton University Library, Princeton, New Jersey).

cal symbol for the Sun: ⊙. In its Western usage, this sign is an ideogram (a sign representing an idea, not specific to a particular language), although it originated as the ancient Egyptian logograph (a sign signifying a specific word) for *r'e* 'sun' (Zauzich 1992:24–25). It is difficult to see the relevance of the ⊙ symbol as an ideogram meaning Sun in the Burner table. While the table is embedded in a cosmogonic narrative in which the first dawn of the Sun is important, the Burner dates themselves have no obvious referent to any solar phenomenon. The *tzolkin* calendar, of which the Burner periods are a part, is composed of 260 days, nowhere near approximating the solar year, as opposed to the 365-day *haab* calendar. Therefore, *tzolkin* dates do not regularly coincide with any regularly occurring patterns in the apparent movement of the Sun. *Tzolkin* dates constantly vary as to where they will fall within a solar year, their divinatory import derived from the number and name of the day, as opposed to any seasonal phenomena.

Why, then, does the author incorporate the Sun sign into the Burner table? To answer this question, I suggest that the ⊙ symbol is not being used as an ideogram but as a logograph. Within the table itself, the ⊙ symbol appears following only three out of four of the Burner dates, the numeral and day name of each written in Yucatec Maya language in the Latin alphabetic script brought by the Spaniards. While in these three instances the symbol follows the written numeral and day name, the ⊙ symbol is substituted for by the day name itself, Oc (Knowlton 2006).

If the ⊙ symbol is functioning in its European sense, it would only represent the Sun or, even if read in a particular European language such as Spanish, would represent the word *sol*, simply meaning "Sun." But if the ⊙ symbol is functioning as a logograph for the Maya word *kin*, it would mean both "Sun" and "day." This meaning of "day" as well as "Sun" is specific to Maya and not shared by Spanish or the Western ideographic usage of the ☉ symbol and makes sense of why this symbol could be substituted for the day name itself. In this case, although its form is of Old World historical derivation, the sign functions as a Maya hieroglyph. Just as Maya logographs for entire words could be substituted for with syllabic signs, Latin letters are substituted for the colonial logograph. The text therefore contains script bilingualism, with hieroglyphic and alphabetic writing systems used simultaneously to express, in this case, a single language, colonial Yucatec Maya (Knowlton 2006).

The ☉ symbol is neither the first nor the only example of a colonial Maya hieroglyph whose form is of Old World historical derivation. Victoria Bricker (2000) has recognized that, in European-style illustrations, king heads represent the *tzolkin* day name Ahau 'King' in the Books of Chilam Balam, replacing pre-Hispanic glyphic forms of the Ahau glyph. One motivation for using European-derived symbols in place of traditionally Maya ones for logographs is obvious: the Spanish clergy actively sought to repress the use of the autochthonous logosyllabic writing system, including seizing and burning those books found written in the ancient script (Chuchiak 2004). This repression had the effect of disrupting the at least 1,500-year-old Maya calligraphic tradition to the point that by the time page 23 of the extant version of the Book of Chilam Balam of Chumayel was written, the *tzolkin* day-sign glyphs are almost entirely illegible (Gordon 1993 [1913]:23). However, there is ample evidence that the principles of the ancient writing system were still being transmitted late into the Colonial period (Landa 1978 [ca. 1566]:83; V. Bricker 1989, 2000; Chuchiak 2004), despite claims that Maya glyphic writing was already obsolescent perhaps even centuries prior to the arrival of the Spaniards (Houston, Baines, and Cooper 2003).

Just as the colonial Maya cosmogonies we have examined in this study are examples of dialogized language, the ☉ symbol is an example of the dialogized sign, in which the arbitrary referents of ideas and language (writing systems) are themselves subjected to a renegotiation of meaning in the context of the colonial encounter.

CONCLUSION

As we have seen, the creation myth of the "Birth of the Uinal" is grounded in ritual practices of the Postclassic Yucatecan Maya, such as calendrical divination using the *tzolkin* and the fire rites surrounding important periods of the Burner cycle. Yet, the cosmogony is a thoroughly colonial work, a rejoinder to missionary activities of the Christian clergymen. The chronicling of the days of creation takes the form of a counter-catechism, an account whose authority supersedes that of the catechist by appeal to even more ancient, fundamental authorities. By equating the prophetic voices of both the Maya world of the *peten* and the Old World biblical mythology, the myth-singer subverts the catechists' distinction between the activities of the missionary and missionized and in doing so challenges the hierarchical relationship that relegated Maya ways of knowing to the demonized category of *idolatría*. The myth-singer's position is that these differences are simply a matter of syncresis. Their object is the same Sun that travels the heavens each day, regardless of whether one calls it a sign of Dios or the Yax Ahau Kin and whether it is measured in periods of seven days or of twenty, and the symbols of Western astrology can be adopted to serve the function of the hieroglyphic writing system that the Christian extirpators so brutally suppressed.

NOTES

1. Roys (1967) refers to this text as "The creation of the uinal," and V. Bricker (2002b) calls it "The Creation of the Maya Week."

2. The day names are of ancient origin, and a few have little obvious semantic content in Classical Yucatecan Maya language. However, the majority of the day names still maintained some meaning even in Classical Yucatecan. Furthermore, since this text itself results from an attempt by a colonial Maya author to provide an exegesis of these archaic day names, I think it is justifiable in this particular case to analyze the names as if they have meaning in Classical Yucatecan Maya.

3. Bricker (2002b:9) noted that the first day, 1 Chuen, corresponds to the day Monkey in related Mesoamerican calendars. She further reasons, based on the fact that the profile of a monkey head is one form of the glyph for *ku* 'deity' in the pre-Hispanic Maya logosyllabic script, that "here 1 Chuen is described as the day when the Mayan god (*ku*), not the Biblical God (*dios*), manifested himself in his divinity."

CHAPTER EIGHT

"In Whatever Way It Is Chronicled"

The final myth of the Chumayel mythography concludes on a hopeful note, remarking that the same Sun of the same creator travels across the sky to mark the day "in whatever way it is chronicled" (63.6). This statement, and the discourse of the entire cosmogony in fact, while subverting the monologues of the missionary catechists, argues for the mutual compatibility if not interdependence of the Maya and Spanish systems in the colonial world they both now inhabited.

Throughout the course of this study, I have interpreted the multiple cosmogonies contained in the Book of Chilam Balam of Chumayel in terms of the multiple voices or "languages" employed. Grounded in a dialogic theory of language and culture, the various methods I have employed to aid in the interpretation of these creation myths ranged from analyses of multiple redactions of the same myth to individual instances of deictic markers, reported speech, and evidentiality, all of which shed light on the hidden world of these clandestine colonial creations. Where possible, I have compared multiple versions of a Classical Yucatecan Maya cosmogony to highlight how the voices of the text are adopted and adapted Postclassic

Mesoamerican mythological discourses to the realities of life in colonial Yucatán (Chapter 4). Where multiple versions were not available, I have drawn on contemporaneous sources to provide a documentary context for the production and redaction of a particular cosmogony, highlighting its possible rhetorical intent through juxtaposition with those discourses it was likely composed in rejoinder to.

Also throughout, I have kept in mind how a strict polarity between supposedly static "tradition" and authorial "innovation" has plagued the interpretation of other complex compositions, such as Homeric epic (Peradotto 2002). As classicists like Nagy (2002) have discovered in their own work on the social forces of canon formation, alternate traditions may be just as legitimate and meaningful in the cosmology of the narrative, and the mythico-legendary past is made contemporary in the performance of the teller. Sources such as the Postclassic Maya codices and even Classic period inscriptions can give us insight into the possible content of indigenous mythologies, from isolated tropes to characters and narrative themes that the Maya scribes of the Colonial period wrote in rejoinder to, as well. But such archaicisms, from the millennium-long documented use of the diphrastic kenning *c̄hab akab* to a Nahua-influenced song recounting the fall of the Terminal Classic city of Chichén Itzá, were nonetheless recorded for colonial purposes in rejoinder to a colonial context. In what follows, I summarize a few observations that can be drawn from this investigation of the creation myths of the Book of Chilam Balam of Chumayel and related documents.

First, there is the issue of native genres in which creation myths fall. The issue of the application of genres not only as literary forms but as social practices during the colonial period is a salient one. It is productive to consider the cases of the Maya creation myths presented here in relation to Mignolo's (2003) arguments regarding Renaissance genres as tools of European colonialism and the indigenous hybrid genres that emerged to sustain cultural traditions. As discussed in the most depth in Chapter 3, the writer(s) who compiled the Chumayel mythography called it a *kahlay* 'history.' *Kahlay* is also the self-identified genre of at least one of the sources of extant versions of the Katun 11 Ahau creation myth (Chapter 4). However, both the Ritual of the Angels (Chapter 5) and the "Birth of the Uinal" (Chapter 7) identify themselves as *kayob* or 'songs.' Yet the reason for this attribution is different in each case. The Ritual of the Angels refers to *kay* as it likens itself to a sung Catholic Mass (*kaybil missa*). In contrast, the activity of the myth-singer of the "Birth of the Uinal" is *tzol* 'to chronicle; put in order' the events of creation through an exegesis of days like the reading of an almanac or table by a Maya *ah kin* 'day-keeper.' In Chapter 6, however, we find another *kay* (the song of the fall of Chichén Itzá) embedded in an otherwise untitled creation narrative, this song divided into stanzas by a recurring litany, a structure quite unlike the *kay* of the "Birth of the Uinal."

It appears that the unmarked generic category into which what we call creation myths fall is the *kahlay*. As the narratives of things remembered, this genre also includes primordial titles (Restall 1998) and the *katun* 'prophecies' that make up many of the indigenous historical narratives contained in the Books of Chilam Balam. Earlier, the narratives that survive in ancient Maya monumental inscriptions link accounts of mythological characters and events of the past to the history of kings in the present (e.g., see Stuart's [2005] exegesis of the Temple XIX inscriptions at Palenque). For the ancient and colonial Maya, myth and history are not separate discourses and their worlds are ultimately not separate realms. Other colonial Mesoamerican narratives documenting the primordial to Postclassic history of a people, including the Nahuatl *Historia Tolteca-Chichimeca* and the K'iche' *Popol Vuh* (Christenson 2003a:230–231), include sung interludes. These songs may have had a separate life apart from the narrative, but their place within a mythological narrative likely formed part of the implicit knowledge of their audience that enriched understanding, edification, and enjoyment of the myth in performance.

At the same time that the Chumayel mythographer utilized these preexisting genres, he also reframed these myths in novel ways. Compared to the preoccupations with specific locales and patronym groups (*chibal*) that mark the mythology of the Katun 13 Ahau myth, the Chumayel mythography, as *u kahlay cab tu kinil* 'the World History of the Era,' only explicitly divides author and audience by social class, between *con ah tepal uinicob* 'we the sovereign people' and *maya uinicexe* 'you Maya people.' The geographical scope of the mythography, however, is the entire *peten*. And rather than a focus on the arrival of this or that patronym group like the Canul or on a city like Mayapán, as we find so often in other *katun* histories, the Chumayel mythography represents a shift from more provincial to more universal concerns. This is remarkable in light of the fact that other Mesoamerican mythologies often served provincial functions as primordial titles, including the *Popol Vuh*, which was itself compiled by members of a noble lineage in the context of a factional dispute (Van Akkeren 2003). As Restall (2004) has argued, and the preface of the mythography shows, the Maya of Yucatán did not consistently perceive themselves as all belonging to a single group. However, in this compilation, we see the stirrings of an indigenous, even "Maya" consciousness among the literati involved in the production of the Books of Chilam Balam, as is also suggested by the manner in which language comes to index ethnicity in the redactional history of some other cosmological texts in the Books of Chilam Balam (Knowlton 2008).

Another topic I wish to address is what these Colonial period myths suggest about the intellectual culture of Late Postclassic Yucatán. Scholars have amply documented in recent years the shared political, economic, and information networks that connected Postclassic Mesoamerica into a "world system" (Smith and Berdan 2003) and incidents of substantial intellectual interchange between northern Yucatán and highland Mexico in the Late Postclassic period (Vail and Hernández 2010). Something fascinating is the considerable extant to which documents of Classical Yucatecan mythological traditions were composed in dialogue not just with Christian missionary works (which are prominent) but with characters and narrative themes found among indigenous ethnic and linguistic groups elsewhere throughout the sphere of the Postclassic Mesoamerican world system. Among the most obvious examples are the names of the Mexican deities Macuil Xochitl and Piltzintecuhtli in the Katun 11 Ahau myth, whose presence is unsurprising given that Nahuatl deity names and perhaps even other loanwords are already known to be present in Postclassic and earlier Maya hieroglyphic texts (Whittaker 1986; Taube and Bade 1991; Taube 1992:chapter 3; Macri and Looper 2003). However, other parallels to my knowledge were previously unidentified, like the correspondence between the episode of the bats in the "Burden of the Flower King" with the cosmogony of the Borgia Codex and the account in the Codex Magliabechiano (Chapter 4). And perhaps less immediately obvious evidence of intellectual interchange can be found in the domain of song and music. This includes similar phrases in the "Itzá"-language song of the fall of Chichén Itzá and a song in the K'iche' *Popol Vuh* (Chapter 6, this volume) and the presence of Nahua vocables in the song of the fall of Chichén Itzá (Knowlton 2010), a feature also shared by colonial Zapotec songs from Oaxaca (Tavárez 2000; Tomlinson 2007:91).

Other evidence connects the mythology of the lowland Yucatecan Maya with that of the highland Maya. Of course, these include long-recognized and widely shared motifs like the cosmogonic sacrifice of a reptilian earth monster (Taube 1989a). But correspondences also include shared characters like Ix Kukil Ix Yaxun ("Lady Quetzal–Lady Lovely Cotinga") whose K'iche' Achi namesake also appears in the *Rabinal Achi* as Uchuch Q'uq' Uchuch Raxon (Chapter 4). Perhaps even more intriguing are rare shared lexemes like *anom*, which appears in Classical Yucatecan texts in relation to the First People but is applied in the *Popol Vuh* to the senseless wooden people of the previous creation (Chapter 6). Even nonsense words (Chapter 5) representing the unpronounceable "otherness" of foreign languages are shared between the Classical Yucatecan Ritual of the Angels (ms. page 53.13) and the *Annals of the Kaqchikels* (ms. page 25.2; Otzoy 1999; Maxwell and Hill 2006). Of course, outlining parallels among the myths of lowland Maya, highland Maya, and highland Mexican cultures, particularly in a structuralist mode, is nothing new. But given recent scholarly interest in reevaluating the *historical* interchange among different groups in Postclassic Mesoamerica, the question of whether it is possible to identify an "international style" not only in material culture but in Late Postclassic to early colonial Mesoamerican literature would benefit from further, especially philologically inclined, research.

What the Chumayel mythography provides the most direct evidence for, of course, is how the colonial Maya responded to the suppression of their indigenous cosmogonies and the autochthonous institutions involved in their maintenance, transmission, and performance. The mythography was compiled in the environment of a colonial society undergoing repeated renegotiations of familiar cultural categories of both Maya and Spaniard. And cosmogonies, being discourses of the foundation of the (culture-specific) categories against which experience is judged, provide an ideal position from which to examine colonial processes and politics of syncretism. In the previous chapters, we have seen how in the process of creating a compilation of creation myths, this anonymous Maya mythographer renegotiated categories of "divinity," "human being," and the "soul" in ways meaningful for the *maya uinicob* living in the colonial system. These emerging colonial categories at times corresponded with the ancient metaphysics and at other times departed from it significantly. In each case, the cosmogonic "tradition" innovated upon the Postclassic Maya and Euro-Christian sources that it emerged in dialogue with. In the case of the Spanish Christian interlocutors of the Chumayel mythographer's audiences, however, it is clear that in their insistence on suppressing the colonial Mayas' own religious compositions, the handwritten Books of Chilam Balam, they discarded an opportunity for genuine dialogue. The colonial catechists who compiled the *dialogos* in Classical Yucatecan both ask and answer the questions for their Maya charges, just as Dostoevsky's Grand Inquisitor does as he condemns a silent Christ. In the process of transforming dialogue into monologue, these clergy sacrificed both Maya civilization and the millennial dream that brought the first missionaries to Yucatán on the altar of their own idol: orthodoxy.

APPENDIX

Cross-Reference of Material in the Katun 11 Ahau Creation Myth Shared by Two or More Redactions

C = Chumayel ms.; T = Tizimín ms.; P = Pérez Códice

1)	C42.23	ychil buluc ahau
	T14v.26	ychil ah buluc ahau
	P117.16	ychil buluc ahau
2)	C42.23–24	tij ca hoki ah / mucen cab
	T14v.26	ca liki ah musen cab
	P117.16	ca liki ah musen cab
3)	C42.24–25	kaxic u uichob oxlahun / ti ku
	T14v.26–27	kaax ix / v uich oxlahun ti ku
	P117.16–17	kaxic u uich oxlahun / ti ku
4)	C42.25	ma yx y oheltahobi
	T14v.27	ma ix y oheltahob
	P117.17	ma ix uy oheltahob
5)	C42.25–26	v kaba halili / v cic y̦ v mehenobe
	T14v.27–28	u kaba cilich / citbil
	P117.17–18	u kaba cilich yumbili yetel me/henbil yetel espiritu santo

6)	C42.26	y alahob t i
	T14v.28	lai u kaba y alahob t i
	P117.18	lay u kaba y alob t i
7)	C42.26–27	ma ix chacanhij v uich tiob xan
	T14v.28–29	ma ix chicanhi v uich ti/ob xan
	P117.18–19	ma ix chi/canpahi u uich tiob xani
8)	C42.27	tuchi yx ca dzoci vy ahal cabe
	T14v.29	ca dzoci y ahal cab
	P117.19	tuchi ix ca dzoci uy ahal cab tiobi
9)	C42.28	ma yx y oheltahob binel v lebal
	T14v.29–30	ma ix y oheltahob binil / v lebal
	P117.20	ma ix y ohel binil u lebal
10)	C42.28–29	ca ix chuci oxla/hun ti ku t u menel bolon ti ku
	T14v.30	ca ix cihi oxlahun ti ku ti bolon ti ku
	P117.20	ca ix cihii oxlahun ti ku
11)	C42.29–30	ca emi / kak ca emi tab
	T14v.30–31	ca emi [ ] / ca emi tab
	P117.20–21	ca / emi kak ca emi tab
12)	C42.30	ca emi tunich y che
	T14v.31	ca emi tunich y̱ chee
	P117.21	ca emi tunich ca emi che
13)	C	
	T14v.31–32	ca tali u baxal che y̱ / tunich
	P117.21–22	ca tali u / baxal che yetel tunich
14)	C43.1	y ca ix paxi v pol ca ix lahi v uich
	T14v.32–33	ca paxi u pol ca la/hi v uich
	P	
15)	C43.2	ca ix tubabi ca ix cuchpachhi xan
	T14v.33	ca tubabi
	P117.22	ca ix tubabi
16)	C43.2–3	ca ix colabi / v cangel y v holsabac
	T14v.33	ca colpahi cangel y̱ hosabac
	P	
17)	C43.3–4	ca cħabi yx kukil / yx yaxun
	T14v.33–34	ca / cħabi ix kukil ix yaxum
	P	yx kukil yx yaxum

18)	C43.5	y+ v pucsikal puyem sicil
	T14v.34	v ꝑuyem sicil
	P117.23	yetel ix ꝑuyem sicil
19)	C43.5	y+ puyem top
	T14v.34–35	v ꝑuyem / toꝑ
	P117.23	yetel ix ꝑuyem toꝑ
20)	C43.6	v tepah ynah yax bolon dzacab
	T14v.35	v teꝑah uy inah yax bolon dzacab
	P117.23–24	u teꝑah / uy inah yax bolon dzacab
21)	C43.7	ca bini t uy oxlahun tas caan
	T14v.35–36	ca bini t uy oxla/hun tas caan
	P117.24	ca bini ti oxlahun taz caan
22)	C43.7–8	ca yx tun culhij / v madzil
	T14v.36	ca culhi u madzil
	P117.25	ca ix culhi u madzil
23)	C43.8	y v ni v baclili vay y okol cabe
	T14v.36	ɏ u ni u baclili
	P117.25	yetel u ni bacalil
24)	C43.8–9	ca / tun bin u pucsikal t u menel oxlahun ti ku
	T14v.36–37	ca bi/ni [u] pucsikali t u menel oxlahun ti ku
	P117.25–26	ca ix tun bini u / pucsikal t u menel oxlahun ti ku
25)	C43.10	ma ix y oltahob binci v pucsikal viil lae
	T14v.37–38	ma ix y ohel/tah bi[n-c]i u pucsikal viil lae
	P117.26–118.1	ma ix uy oheltahob / binci u pucsikal uiil lae
26)	C43.10–11	ca ix / hullahi
	T14v.38	ca hutlahi
	P118.1	ca ix hutlahi
27)	C43.11–12	ixma yumob y ah numyaob ix/ma ychamob
	T14v.38–15r.1	ixma / yumob ah numyaob ixma ichamob
	P118.1–2	ixma yumob yetel ah ma / yumob yetel ah numyaab yetel ichamob
28)	C43.12–13	cuxanob ix ti minan u pucsika/lob
	T15r.1–2	cuxanob ix ti / manan u pucsikal
	P118.2–3	cuxanob ix ti / minan u pucsikal
29)	C43.13	ca yx mucchahij
	T15r.2	ca mucchahiob
	P118.3	ca ix mucchahiob

30)	C43.13–14	t u men v yam tzuc t u yam / kaknab
	T15r.2–3	t u yam sus t u yam / kaknab
	P118.3	t u yam zuz t u yam kaknab
31)	C43.14	hun vadz hail hulom haail
	T15r.3	hun vadz hail
	P118.4	hun uadz hail
32)	C43.14–15	tij / ca u chi col cangelili
	T15r.3	ti u chi u col canhel
	P118.4	ti u chi col canheel
33)	C43.15	ti homocnac canal
	T15r.3–4	ti homoc/nac canal
	P118.4	ti homocnac canal
34)	C43.16	homocnac ix ti cab
	T15r.4	homocnac ix cabal
	P118.4–5	homocnac ix / cabal xan
35)	C	
	T15r.4	t u katunil u nup
	P118.5	t u katunil u nup
36)	C	
	T15r.4–5	u vudz / cimci u thupil mehen
	P118.5	u vudz cimci u thupil mehen
37)	C	
	T15r.5	lai u vudz u katunil oxil oc
	P118.6	la ix u vudz u katunil oxil oc
38)	C	
	T15r.5–6	u ki/nil ulci vaye
	P118.6	u kinil ulci uaye
39)	C	
	T15r.6	hun cimi u kinil
	P118.7	hun cimi u kinil
40)	C	
	T15r.6	dzocci u than katun
	P118.7	dzocci u than katun
41)	C43.16–17	valic can tul ti ku / can tul ti bacab
	T15r.7	ca ualhi can tul ku can tul bacab
	P118.7–8	ualcil ix can tul ku can / tul bacab

42)	C43.17	lay hayesob
	T15r.7	lai hayesob cab
	P118.8	lay hayesob lae
43)	C43.17–18	tuchij / tun ca dzoci hay cabil
	T15r.7–8	ca / dzoci hai cabile
	P118.8	tuchi tun ca dzocii hai cabile
44)	C	
	T15r.8	ca valhi chac imix che
	P118.9	ca ix ualhii chac ymix che
45)	C43.20–21	ca ix ualhi y ocmal caan
	T15r.8	lai y ocmal can
	P118.9	lai uy ocmal caan
46)	C43.21	v chicul hay cabal
	T15r.9	lai u chicul u hayal cab
	P118.11	la ix u chicul / uy ahal cab lae
47)	C	
	T15r.9	lai u coic inah che bacab
	P118.10	la ix u coic inah che bacab
48)	C43.19	ca tzolic kan xib yui
	T15r.9–10	ua/lic kan xib yuy
	P118.10–11	ualic kan-xib / yuyum
49)	C43.19–20	ca ualhi sac imix che / ti xaman
	T15r.9	ca ualhi sac imix che ti xaman
	P118.12	ca ualhii zac ymix che ti xaman
50)	C	
	T15r.10–11	lai / valic sachic v chicul hai cabil
	P118.11–12	lay ualic zac / chic lay u chicul hai cabil
51)	C43.22–23	ca yx ualhi ek ymix / che
	T15r.11–12	ca ix ualhi ek imix che / t u chikin peten
	P118.12–13	ca ix ualhi ek imix che t u chi/kin peten
52)	C	
	T15r.12	u chicul hai cabil
	P118.13	u chicul hai cabil
53)	C43.23	cu[lic] ek tan pidzoy
	T15r.12–13	lai ek imix che culic / ek tam picdzoy
	P118.13	culic ah ek tan pixoy

54)	C43.23–24	ca yx ualhij kan ymix / che
	T15r.13	culic kanal imix che t u nohol peten
	P118.13	ca ix / ualhii kanal kanal ymix che t u nohol peten
55)	C43.24	v chicul hay cabal
	T15r.14	u chicul u hayal cab
	P118.14–15	u chicul hai / cabil
56)	C43.25–26	cumlic ix kan xib yui yx kan oyal / mut
	T15r.14	culic kan oyal mut
	P118.15	lay culic ah kaan oyal mut
57)	C43.26	ca ix ualhij yax imix che t u chumuc
	T15r.14–15	ca culhi yax / imix che t u chumuc cab
	P118.15–16	ca ix ualhi yax ymix che / t u chumuc cab
58)	C43.27	u kahlay hay cabal
	T15r.15	u kahlai hai cabil
	P118.16	u chicul hai cabil lae
59)	C43.27–28	cum/tal v cah v lac
	T15r.15–16	cumtal / u cah u lac
	P118.16–17	licil u cumtal u / lac u luch

---

60)	C45.21–22	tij ca/ca u hekah y oc ah buluc ahau
	T15r.17	buluc ahau u kinil
	P118.18	buluc ahau u kinil
61)	C45.22–23	tij / ca emi u than bolon dzacab
	T15r.17	y emel u than bolon dzacab
	P118.18	uy emel u than ah bolon dzacab
62)	C	
	T15r.17–18	miatz / t i
	P118.18–19	ah mi/yatz te
63)	C	
	T15r.18	t u vudz
	P118.19	t u vudz zutup t u katunil
64)	C45.24	ca emi katal v cah u cuch katun
	T15r.18	u katal u cuch katun
	P118.19	u katal u cuch katun
65)	C45.24–25	katun / bolon te u cuch
	T15r.18	bolon te u cuch
	P118.20	bolon te u cuch

66)	C45.25	ca emi ti caanil
	T15r.18	ca emi ti canil
	P118.20	ca emi ti canil
67)	C45.25–26	kan ix / u kinil kaxci u cuch
	T15r.19	kan u kinil uale ca hau u cuch
	P118.20–21	u kinil uale ca hau / u cuch
68)	C45.26	tij ca emi haa
	T15r.19	ca emi
	P118.21	ca t i emi
69)	C45.27	tali tan y ol caan
	T15r.19	tali tan y ol caan
	P118.21	tali tun tali tan y ol caan
70)	C45.27	vchebal u ca put sihil
	T15r.20	u ca put sihil
	P118.21	u ca put zihil
71)	C45.28	bolon haaban y otoch
	T15r.20	bolon haban y otoch
	P118.22	bolon aban uy otoch
72)	C45.28–29	y et emcij bo/lon mayel
	T15r.20	y et emci bolon mayel
	P118.22	y et emci bolon mayel
73)	C45.29	cħahuc u chi v ni y ak
	T15r.21	cħahuc u chi cħahuc u ni y ak
	P118.22–23	cħahuc u chi / cħahuc u ni yak
74)	C45.30	cħahuchi u dzomel
	T15r.21	cħahuc ix u dzomil
	P	
75)	C45.30	ti ca emi can tul chaac
	T15r.21–22	ca emi / ca tul chac
	P118.23	ti ca emi ca tul chac
76)	C	
	T15r.22	uayab sodz
	P118.23	uayab zoodz lae
77)	C45.31	lay u cabilob nicte lae
	T15r.22	lai dzudze u cabilob nicte
	P118.24	la ix la ix dzudze t u kabil nicte

78)	C46.1	tij ca hokij yx chac hoch kom t i
	T15r.22–23	ti ca hoki ix chac hocħ kom
	P118.24	ti ca hoki ix chac choch kom
79)	C46.1–2	y yx / sac hoch kom t i
	T15r.23	ix sac hocħ kom
	P	
80)	C46.2	y yx ek hoch kom
	T15r.23	ix ek hocħ kom
	P118.25	yx ek choch kom
81)	C46.2–3	y yx / kan hoch kom
	T15r.23–24	ix kan / hocħ kom
	P118.25	ti ix kan choch kom
82)	C46.3	y yx hau nal y yx huk nab
	T15r.24	ix hau nab ix hudz nab
	P118.25–26	ti ix hau nab ix / hudz nab
83)	C	
	T15r.24	ix kuk nab
	P118.26	ix kuk nab
84)	C46.4	y et hokci tun yx hoyal nicte
	T15r.24–25	hokci / tun ix oyal nicte
	P118.26	hokci tun ix oyal nicte
85)	C46.5	y yx ni nicħ cacau
	T15r.25	ix ni nich cacau
	P118.26–119.1	ix ni nich ca/cau
86)	C46.5–6	y yx chauil / tok
	T15r.25	ix chabi tok
	P119.1	ix chabil tok
87)	C46.6	y yx macuil xuchite
	T15r.25–26	ix ma/bil xuchit
	P119.1	ix macuil xuchit
88)	C46.7	yx hobon y ol nicte
	T15r.26	ix hobon y ol nicte
	P119.1	hobon y ol nicte
89)	C	
	T15r.26	ix kouol y ol nicte
	P119.1–2	ho/uol y oc nicte

90)	C46.8	lay hokob nicte
	T15r.26–27	lai / hokciob nicte lae
	P119.2	lay hokiob nicte lae
91)	C46.8–9	laob / ix ah comayelob
	T15r.27	ah conmayelob lae
	P119.2	ah comayelob
92)	C46.9	lay v naa nicte
	T15r.27	u na nicteob
	P119.2–3	lay u / na nicteob
93)	C46.9–10	ca ho/kiob
	T15r.27–28	hok/ci
	P119.3	hokiob
94)	C46.10–11	y udzub ah kin y udzub ahau y u/dzub holcan
	T15r.28	y udzub ah kin y udzub ahau y udzub holcan
	P119.3–4	uy udzub ah kin y udzub ahau y udzub / hoolcaan y udzub halach uinic
95)	C46.11	lay u cuch nicte ahau
	T15r.28–29	lai u cuch / nicte ahau
	P119.4	lai u cuch nicte ahau
96)	C46.12	ca emi
	T15r.29	ca emi
	P119.4–5	ca / emi
97)	C	
	T15r.29–30	ma ix uah u cuch nicte katun t u ki/nil
	P119.5	u cuch katun t u kinil
98)	C	
	T15r.30	ma ix kuchi
	P119.5	ma ix kuchi
99)	C46.16–17	cħabnaci ku mit/nali bolon dzacab
	T15r.30	u cħabnaci ku mitnali bolon dzacab
	P119.5–6	cħabnaci ku / metnali bolon dzacab
100)	C46.17	ca emi t u chun nicte pilim te
	T15r.30–31	ca / emi u cħab nicte pislim tee
	P119.6	ca emi u cħab nicte islim te
101)	C46.18	yax bac dzunun ix v uayinah
	T15r.31	yax bac dzunun ix v uayinah
	P119.7	yax bac dzunun ix u uayintah

102)	C46.18	ca emi
	T15r.32	ca emi
	P119.7	ca emi
103)	C46.18–19	ca u dzudzah / u cabil bolon yal nicte t u ychil
	T15r.32	ca u dzudzah u kabil nicte bolon yal nicte
	P119.7–8	ca u dzudzaah u / kabil nicte bolon yal nicte
104)	C46.20	ca tun hoki u pucsikal nicte lae
	T15r.32–33	ca tun / hoki u pucsikal nicte
	P119.8–9	ca tun hoki u puczikal nicte / lae
105)	C46.21	can hek ix u lac nicte lae
	T15r.33	can hek ix u lac nicteob
	P119.9	can hek ix u la[c] nicteob
106)	C46.22	ti yx culan ah kin xocbil tun chumuc
	T15r.33–34	tix culan / ah kin xocbil tun
	P119.9–10	ti ix culan ah kin xocbil / tun
107)	C46.22–23	tij ca / uchi u huhu y ol oxlahun ti ku
	T15r.34	ti ca uchi u hokol oxlahun ti ku
	P119.10	ca uchi u hokol oxlahun ti ku
108)	C46.23	ma yx y oheltah
	T15r.34–35	ma / ix y oheltahob
	P119.10	ma ix y oheltahob
109)	C46.24	y emel u keban u pop ti ku
	T15r.35	y emel u keban pop
	P119.11	y emel u keban pop
110)	C46.24	ix tathan cuchie
	T15r.35	kuchi t u than cuchi
	P119.11	ti kuchi ix t u than cuchi
111)	C46.25	nicte yx v pop
	T15r.36	nicte ix u pop
	P119.11–12	nicte ix / u pop
112)	C46.25	nicte ix v kanche
	T15r.36	nicte ix u kanche
	P119.12	nicte ix u kanche
113)	C46.26	sauin culic sauin u ximbal
	T15r.36	sauin culic
	P119.12	zauin culuc

114)	C46.26–27	sauin u lac sauin u / luch
	T15r.36–37	sauin u / luch [sa]uin u lac
	P119.12–13	zauin u lac za/uin u luch
115)	C46.27	sauin u pucsikal
	T15r.37	sauin u pucsikal
	P119.13	zauin u puczikal
116)	C46.28	sauin u chi
	T15r.37	sauin u chi
	P119.13	zauin u chi
117)	C46.28	cool u than ti y ahaulili
	T15r.37–15v.1	hach / coil u than ti y ahaulil
	P119.13–14	coo u / than ti y ahaulil
118)	C46.28–19	t u kin / uat uil
	T15v.1	t u kinil auat viil
	P119.14	t u kinil auat uil
119)	C46.29	t u kin uaat vkul
	T15v.1	auat ukul
	P119.14	auat ukul
120)	C46.29–30	t u xay u chi lic u ha/nal
	T15v.2	t u xai u chi lic u hanal
	P119.14–15	t u / xai u chii lic u hanal
121)	C46.30	t u pach u xau lic u uil
	T15v.2	t u pac u xau c u uiil
	P119.15	u uil
122)	C46.32	sip u than sip u can
	T15v.3	sip u than ti culic sip u can
	P119.15	zip u than ti culic
123)	C46.33	kaxan u uich
	T15v.3	kaxan u uich
	P119.15–16	ka/xan u uich
124)	C46.33–47.1	ti culic chac cah / v pop
	T15v.3–4	ti culic cħa u / cah tza u cah pop
	P119.16	ti culic cħaa u caah tza u cah t u pop
125)	C47.1	culic tamuk y ahaulil
	T15v.4	culic t uy ahaulic
	P119.17	tamuk uy ahaulil

126) C47.1	t u ban u yum t u ban v naa
T15v.4–5	t u ban u yum t u ban / u naa
P119.17	t u ban u yum t i t u ban u na t i
127) C47.2	ma ix y ohel
T15v.5	ma ix y ohel u yum mehen te
P119.17–18	ma / ix uy ohel u yum t[i] mehen
128) C47.2	ma v naa alin tee
T15v.5	ma ix y ohel u na sihese
P119.18–19	ma ix uy ohel u naa alin / tei
129) C	
T15v.6	halili yan t u ni y ak dzedzece
P119.19	halili yan t u ni y ak dzedzece
130) C	
T15v.6	v hauat cuch
P119.19	u hauat cuch
131) C	
T15v.6–7	ma u / matan ti bolon ti ku
P119.19–20	ma u / matan ti bolon ti ku
132) C	
T15v.7	emi ix vuc satai
P119.20	emi ix vuc zatay
133) C	
T15v.7	ca ix sati y ol
P119.20–21	ca ix ti zati / y ol
134) C	
T15v.8	ca ix sati y ik
P119.21	ca ix ti zati uy ik
135) C	
T15v.8	ca cħaci v cal
P119.21	ca cħaci u cal
136) C	
T15v.8	v hicħ u cal
P119.21	lai hicħ u cal
137) C	
T15v.8	t u ba t u hunal
P119.21–22	t u ba t u hunal

138) C
T15v.9 sip u than ah bobat lae
P119.22 zipi ix u than ah bobat lae

139) C
T15v.9 sip ix ah kin lae
P119.22–23 zipi ix ah kin / lae

140) C
T15v.9 si sip ahau
P119.23 tit zipi ahau

141) C
T15v.10 sipob ix holcan lae
P119.23 sipob ix hoolcanob lae

142) C
T15v.10 ti haulahi t u thubob
P119.23–24 ti haulahi / u thanob

143) C
T15v.10–11 ti noclahi chi/mal
P119.24 ti noclah ix u chimaob

144) C
T15v.11 ti noclahi nabte
P119.24–25 ti noclah ix u nab/teob

145) C
T15v.11 lahun yal yah ual uincob
P119.25 lahun yal u yah ual uincob

146) C
T15v.11–12 ix ca / ualhi
P119.25 ix ca ualhi cuchi

147) C
T15v.12 ma ix ti y oheltahob
P119.26 ma ix t uyoheltahob

148) C
T15v.12–13 u talel u dzocol u than katun / holcani
P119.26–27 u talel u dzocol u than katun / hoolcanobi

149) C
T15v.13 uil likciob cuchie
P119.27 uil ca lukob cuchie

150) C
T15v.13 u cħuimaob ix tab t u kab
P119.27–28 u cħuimaob ix tab t u kab / cuchi

151) C
T15v.14 ma ix kaxan v uich
P119.28 ma ix kaxan u uich katun cuchie

152) C
T15v.14 u dzahob ix u tan
P119.28–120.1 t u dzahob ix / u tan

153) C
T15v.14–15 ti lomol / nicte
P120.1 ti lomol nicte

154) C
T15v.15 ix cimci ah kinob ah miatzob
P120.1 ix cimciob ah kinob ah miatzob

155) C
T15v.15–16 ahauob holca/nob
P120.1–2 yetel / ahauob yetel holcanob

156) C
T15v.16 hokanob ix than ichil u yanal katune
P120.2–3 hokanob ix u than ichil u yanal / katun

157) C
T15v.16–17 t u bolon / tune
P120.3 ichil bolon tune

158) C
T15v.17 ti vil uchom
P120.3 t u uil bin uchuc

159) C
T15v.17 v xotom batabil
P120.3–4 u yantal t u bata/bil

160) C
T15v.17–18 ti y ahaulil y al / v mehen
P120.4 t uy ahauil yala u mehen

161) C
T15v.18 ah kinchil coba y ah miscit
P120.4–5 ah kinchil coba yetel ah mis/cit uale

162) C
T15v.18–19 vale u than / oxlahun ti ku
P120.5 uale u than oxlahun ti ku

163) C
T15v.19 mai t in than
P120.5 mai t in than

164) C
T15v.19–20 cat uchi ox vadz katun t u uini/cil vale
P120.5–6 cat uchi ox uadz / ti uincilil uale

165) C
T15v.20 y okol cab ca uchi ox vadz katun vale
P120.6 y okol cab ca ti uchi ox uadz ti katun uale

166) C
T15v.20–21 t u kin / naclah vitz
P120.6–7 t u / kiniil naclah uitz

167) C
T15v.21 chuchul chuch vale
P120.7 t u kinil cħucħul cħucħ uale

168) C
T15v.21–22 t u kin chac tun num/ya uy al u mehen ah num ytza
P120.7–8 t u kinil u / chacil numya ti yala u mehen ah num itza

169) C
T15v.22–23 ma setel bin dzocbal / nicte uinicil nicte katun
P120.8–9 hach ma / u cetel bin dzocbali nicte katun nicte uinicil

170) C
T15v.23 ichil christianoil uale
P120.9–10 t u hidz cris/tianoil uale mta.

References

Acuña, René

1993 *Bocabulario de Maya Than*. Universidad Nacional Autónoma de México, Mexico.

2001 Escritos Mayas Inéditos y Publicados Hasta 1578: Testimonio del Obispo Diego de Landa. *Estudios de la Cultura Maya* 21:165–179.

Adorno, Rolena

1982 *From Oral to Written Expression: Native Andean Chronicles of the Early Colonial Period*. Maxwell School of Citizenship and Public Affairs, Syracuse University, Syracuse, New York.

Andrews, Anthony P., E. Wyllys Andrews, and Fernando Robles Castellanos

2003 The Northern Maya Collapse and Its Aftermath. *Ancient Mesoamerica* 14:151–156.

Arzápalo Marín, Ramón

1987 *El Ritual de los Bacabes: Edición Facsimilar con Transcripción rítmica, traducción, notas, índice, glosario y cómputos estadísticos*. Universidad Nacional Autónoma de México, Mexico.

Austen, Ralph A.

1999 The Historical Transformation of Genres: Sunjata as Panegyric, Folktale, Epic, and Novel. In *In Search of Sunjata: The Mande Oral Epic as*

History, Literature and Performance, ed. Ralph A. Austen, 69–87. Indiana University Press, Bloomington.

Avendaño y Loyola, Fray Andrés de
1997 [1696] *Relación de las dos entradas que hice a la conversión de los gentiles ytzáex, y cehaches*. Ed. Temis Vayhinger-Scheer. Fuentes Mesoamericanas 1. Verlag Anton Saurwein, Möckmühl, Germany.

Aveni, Anthony
2002 *Empires of Time: Calendars, Clocks, and Cultures*. University Press of Colorado, Boulder.

Aveni, Anthony F., Susan Milbrath, and Carlos Peraza Lope
2004 Chichén Itzá's Legacy in the Astronomically Oriented Architecture of Mayapán. *RES* 45:123–143.

Baeza, D. Bartolomé del Granado
1845 [1813] Los Indios de Yucatan. In *Registro Yucateco*, 165–178. Impreso de Castilla y Cia, Mérida.

Bakhtin, Mikhail
1968 *Rabelais and His World*. Trans. Hélène Iswolsky. Indiana University Press, Bloomington.
1981 *The Dialogic Imagination: Four Essays*. Trans. Caryl Emerson and Michael Holquist. University of Texas Press, Austin.
1984 *Problems of Dostoevsky's Poetics*. Trans. Caryl Emerson. University of Minnesota Press, Minneapolis.

Barrera Vásquez, Alfredo
1944 Transcription of the Book of Chilam Balam of Tusik. Manuscript in the Latin American Library. Tulane University, New Orleans.

Barrera Vásquez, Alfredo, Juan Ramón Bastarrachea Manzano, William Brito Sansores, Refugio Vermont Salas, David Dzul Gógora, and Domingo Dzul Poot
1995 *Diccionario Maya Cordemex: Maya-Español, Español-Maya*. 3rd ed. Editorial Porrúa, Mexico.

Barrera Vásquez, Alfredo, and Silvia Rendón
1948 *El Libro de los Libros de Chilam Balam*. Fondo de Cultura Económica, Mexico.

Barth, Fredrik
1987 *Cosmologies in the Making: A Generative Approach to Cultural Variation in Inner New Guinea*. Cambridge University Press, Cambridge.

Bassie-Sweet, Karen
2008 *Maya Sacred Geography and the Creator Deities*. University of Oklahoma Press, Norman.

Behrens, Daniel Graña, Nikolai Grube, Christian M. Prager, Frauke Sachse, Stefanie Teufel, and Elisabeth Wagner (editors)

2004 Continuity and Change: Maya Religious Practices in Temporal Perspective. *Acta Mesoamericana* vol. 14. Verlag Anton Saurwein, Markt Schwaben, Germany.

Bierhorst, John (translator)

1992 *History and Mythology of the Aztecs: The Codex Chimalpopoca*. University of Arizona Press, Tucson.

Blom, Jan-Petter, and John J. Gumperz

1972 Social Meaning in Structure: Code-Switching in Norway. In *Directions in Sociolinguistics*, ed. John J. Gumperz and Dell Hymes, 407–434. Holt, Rinehart and Winston, New York.

Bolles, David

2001 *Combined Dictionary-Concordance of the Yucatecan Maya Language*. FAMSI, Crystal River, Florida. http://www.famsi.org/reports/96072/corodoc torg.htm, accessed January 12, 2004.

Boone, Elizabeth

2003 A Web of Understanding: Pictorial Codices and the Shared Intellectual Culture of Late Postclassic Mesoamerica. In *The Postclassic Mesoamerican World*, ed. Michael E. Smith and Francis F. Berdan, 207–221. University of Utah Press, Salt Lake City.

2007 *Cycles of Time and Meaning in the Mexican Books of Fate*. University of Texas Press, Austin.

Bricker, Harvey M., and Victoria R. Bricker

1992 Zodiacal References in the Maya Codices. In *The Sky in Mayan Literature*, ed. Anthony Aveni, 148–183. Oxford University Press, New York.

2007 When Was the Dresden Codex Venus Table Efficacious? In *Skywatching in the Ancient World: New Perspectives in Cultural Astronomy*, ed. Clive Ruggles and Gary Urton, 95–120. University Press of Colorado, Boulder.

Bricker, Victoria R.

1981 *The Indian Christ, the Indian King: The Historical Substrate of Maya Myth and Ritual*. University of Texas Press, Austin.

1986 *A Grammar of Mayan Hieroglyphs*. Publication No. 56. Middle American Research Institute, New Orleans.

1989 The Last Gasp of Maya Hieroglyphic Writing in the Books of Chilam Balam of Chumayel and Chan Kan. In *Word and Image in Maya Culture: Explorations in Language, Writing, and Representation*, ed. William F. Hanks and Don Rice, 39–50. University of Utah Press, Salt Lake City.

1991 "Faunal Offerings in the Dresden Codex." In *Sixth Palenque Round Table, 1986*, vol. 8, ed. Merle Greene Robertson and Virginia M. Fields, 285–292. University of Oklahoma Press, Norman.

1995 Advances in Maya Epigraphy. *Annual Review of Anthropology* 24:215–312.

1997 What Constitutes Discourse in the Maya Codices? In *The Language of Maya Hieroglyphs*, ed. Martha J. Macri and Anabel Ford, 129–143. Pre-Columbian Art Research Institute, San Francisco.

2000 Bilingualism in the Maya Codices and the Books of Chilam Balam of Chumayel. *Written Language and Literacy* 3:77–115.

2002a Evidencia de Doble Descendencia en las Inscripciones de Yaxchilán y Piedras Negras. In *La organización social entre los mayas prehispánicos, coloniales y modernos*, ed. Vera Tiesler Blos, Rafael Cobos, and Merle Greene Robertson, 1:126–145. Universidad Autónoma de Yucatán, Mérida.

2002b The Mayan *Uinal* and the Garden of Eden. *Latin American Indian Literatures Journal* 18:1–20.

2004 Mayan. In *The Cambridge Encyclopedia of the World's Ancient Languages*, ed. Roger D. Woodard, 1041–1070. Cambridge University Press, Cambridge.

N.d. Quotatative Markers. Unpublished manuscript in possession of the author.

Bricker, Victoria R., and Helga-Maria Miram (translators)

2002 *An Encounter of Two Worlds: The Book of Chilam Balam of Kaua*. Publication No. 68. Middle American Research Institute, New Orleans.

Bricker, Victoria R., Eleuterio Po'ot Yah, and Ofelia Dzul de Po'ot

1998 *A Dictionary of the Maya Language as Spoken in Hocabá, Yucatán*. University of Utah Press, Salt Lake City.

Brinton, Daniel G.

1882 *The Maya Chronicles*. Library of Aboriginal American Literature 1. D. G. Brinton, Philadelphia.

Burkhart, Louise M.

1989 *The Slippery Earth: Nahua-Christian Moral Dialogue in Sixteenth-Century Mexico*. University of Arizona Press, Tucson.

Burns, Allan F.

1983 *An Epoch of Miracles: Oral Literature of the Yucatec Maya*. University of Texas Press, Austin.

1991 The Language of Zuyua: Yucatec Maya Riddles and Their Interpretation. In *Past, Present, and Future: Selected Papers on Latin American Indian Literatures*, ed. Mary H. Preuss, 35–40. Labyrinthosm Lancaster, California.

Cervantes, Fernando

1994 *The Devil in the New World: The Impact of Diabolism in New Spain*. Yale University Press, New Haven, Connecticut.

Chan Kan, Book of Chilam Balam of

N.d. Photographic copy in the Middle American Research Institute, Tulane University, New Orleans. (Original in Museo Nacional de Antropología, Mexico, DF.) See also Hires 1981.

Chinchilla Mazariegos, Oswaldo

2005 Cosmos and Warfare on a Classic Maya Vase. *RES* 47:107–134.

2006 The Stars of the Palenque Sarcophagus. *RES* 49/50:40–58.

Christenson, Allen (translator)

2003a *Popol Vuh: The Sacred Book of the Maya*. University of Oklahoma Press, Norman.

2003b *Popol Vuh: Literal Poetic Version*. University of Oklahoma Press, Norman.

Chuchiak, John F., IV

2000 The Indian Inquisition and the Extirpation of Idolatry: The Process of Punishment in the *Provisorato de Indios* in the Diocese of Yucatan, 1563–1812. Ph.D. diss., Latin American Studies / Latin American History Department, Tulane University, New Orleans. University Microfilms, Ann Arbor, Michigan.

2001 Pre-Conquest *Ah Kinob* in a Colonial World: The Extirpation of Idolatry and the Survival of the Maya Priesthood in Colonial Yucatán, 1563–1697. In *Maya Survivalism*, ed. Ueli Hostettler and Matthew Restall, 135–157. *Acta Mesoamericana* vol. 12. Verlag Anton Saurwein, Markt Schwaben, Germany.

2002 Toward a Regional Definition of Idolatry: Reexamining Idolatry Trials in the *Relaciónes de Méritos* and Their Role in Defining the Concept of *Idolatria* in Colonial Yucatán, 1570–1780. *Journal of Early Modern History* 6(2):1–29.

2004 The Images Speak: The Survival and Production of Hieroglyphic Codices and Their Use in Post-Conquest Maya Religion (1580–1720). In *Continuity and Change: Maya Religious Practices in Temporal Perspective*, ed. Daniel Graña Behrens, Nikolai Grube, Christian M. Prager, Frauke Sachse, Stefanie Teufel, and Elisabeth Wagner, 167–183. *Acta Mesoamericana* vol. 14. Verlag Anton Saurwein, Markt Schwaben, Germany.

2005 Ah Otochnalob yetel Ah Chun Kaxob: Indios de Campana, Indios Idolatras, and the Colonial Re-construction of Maya Ethnic Identity, 1590–1700. A paper presented at the symposium Peoples and Institutions of the Colonial Americas, Gulf Coast Consortium of Latin American Colonialists, New Orleans, February 2005.

2006 Yaab Uih Yetel Maya Cimil: Colonial Plagues, Famines, Catastrophes and Their Impact on Changing Yucatec Maya Concepts of Death and Dying, 1570–1794. In *Jaws of the Underworld: Life, Death, and Rebirth among the Ancient Maya*, ed. Pierre Robert Colas, Geneviève Le Fort, and Bodil Liljefors Persson, 3–18. *Acta Mesoamericana* vol. 16. Verlag Anton Saurwein, Markt Schwaben, Germany.

Chumayel, Book of Chilam Balam of

N.d. Original manuscript in the Princeton Collection of Mesoamerican Manuscripts. Manuscripts Division, Department of Rare Books and Special Collections, Princeton University Library, Princeton, New Jersey. See also Edmonson 1986; Gordon 1993 [1913]; Roys 1967.

Ciaramella, Mary M.

2002 *The Bee-Keepers in the Madrid Codex.* Research Reports on Ancient Maya Writing, No. 52. Center for Maya Research, Washington, DC.

Ciudad Real, Antonio de

2001 *Calepino Maya de Motul,* ed. René Acuña. Plaza y Valdes Editores, Mexico.

Clendinnen, Inga

1987 *Ambivalent Conquests: Maya and Spaniard in Yucatan, 1517–1570.* Cambridge University Press, Cambridge.

Códice Pérez

N.d. Photographic copy of original manuscript in Tozzer Library at Peabody Museum, Harvard University, Cambridge, Massachusetts. (Original is lost.) See Miram 1988.

Coe, Michael

1973 *The Maya Scribe and His World.* Grolier Club, New York.

1978 *Lords of the Underworld: Masterpieces of Classic Maya Ceramics.* Princeton University Press, Princeton, New Jersey.

1999 *Breaking the Maya Code.* 2nd ed. Thames and Hudson, London.

Cogolludo, Fr. Diego López de

1867 [1688] *Historia de Yucathan.* Juan García Infanzón, Madrid.

2006 [1688] *Historia de Yucatán.* Linkgua ediciones S.L., Barcelona.

Colop, Sam

1999 *Popol Wuj: Versión Poética K'iche'.* Cholsamaj, Guatemala City.

2008 *Popol Wuj: Traducción al español.* Cholsamaj, Guatemala City.

Coronel, Fr. Juan

1620a *Discursos Predicables.* (Photographic copy in Ayer Collection, Newberry Library, Chicago.) La Imprenta de Diego Garrido por Pedro Gutiérrez, Mexico. See also Bolles 2001.

1620b *Expossicio de la Doctrina Christiana en Lengua de Maya.* (Photographic copy in Latin American Library, Tulane University, New Orleans.) La Imprenta de Diego Garrido por Pedro Gutiérrez, Mexico.

Craine, Eugene R., and Reginald C. Reindorp

1979 *The Codex Pérez and the Book of Chilam Balam of Mani.* University of Oklahoma Press, Norman.

Demarest, Arthur A., Prudence M. Rice, and Don S. Rice

2004 *The Terminal Classic in the Maya Lowlands: Collapse, Transition, and Transformation*. University Press of Colorado, Boulder.

Dresden Codex

1998 *Kumatzim Wuj Jun: Códice Dresde*. Editorial Cholsamaj, Guatemala City, Guatemala. See also Förstemann 1880.

Edmonson, Munro S.

1992 The Middle American Calendar Round. In *Supplement to the Handbook of Middle American Indians*, vol. 5: *Epigraphy*, ed. Victoria R. Bricker and Patricia A. Andrews, 154–167. University of Texas Press, Austin.

1993 The Mayan Faith. In *South and Meso-American Native Spirituality: From the Cult of the Feathered Serpent to the Theology of Liberation*, ed. Gary H. Gossen and Miguel León-Portilla, 65–85. Crossroad Publishing Company, New York.

Edmonson, Munro S. (translator)

1982 *The Ancient Future of the Itza: The Book of Chilam Balam of Tizimin*. University of Texas Press, Austin.

1986 *Heaven Born Merida and Its Destiny: The Book of Chilam Balam of Chumayel*. University of Texas Press, Austin.

Farris, Nancy M.

1984 Maya Society under Colonial Rule: The Collective Enterprise of Survival. Princeton University Press, Princeton, New Jersey.

Förstemann, Ernst Wilhelm (editor)

1880 *Die Mayahandschrift der Königlichen öffentlichen bibliothek zu Dresden*. A. Naumann, Leipzig.

Foster, George M.

1994 *Hippocrates' Latin American Legacy: Humoral Medicine in the New World*. Gordon and Breach, Amsterdam.

Freidel, David, Linda Schele, and Joy Parker

1993 *Maya Cosmos: Three Thousand Years on the Shaman's Path*. Quill / William Morrow, New York.

Furst, Jill L.

1995 *The Natural History of the Soul in Ancient Mexico*. Yale University Press, New Haven, Connecticut.

1998 The *Nahualli* of Christ: The Trinity and the Nature of the Soul in Ancient Mexico. *RES* 33:208–224.

Garibay K., Angel Maria

1953–1954 *Historia de la literature nahuatl*. 2 vols. Porrúa, Mexico City.

1965 *Teogonia e Historia de los Mexicanos: Tres Opusculos del Siglo XVI*. Editorial Porrua, Mexico.

Garza, Mercedes de la

1983 *Relaciones histórico-geográficas de la gobernación de Yucatán*. 2 vols. Universidad Nacional Autónoma de México, Mexico City.

Gordon, George B.

1993 [1913] *The Book of Chilam Balam of Chumayel*. Aegean Park Press, Laguna Hills, California.

Graham, Ian

1977 Yaxchilan. *Corpus of Maya Hieroglyphic Inscriptions* 3(1). Peabody Museum of Archaeology and Ethnology, Harvard University, Cambridge, Massachusetts.

Greenleaf, Richard E.

1965 The Inquisition and the Indians of New Spain: A Study in Jurisdictional Confusion. *The Americas: A Quarterly Review of Inter-American Cultural History* 22(2):138–166.

Grube, Nikolai

1994 Hieroglyphic Sources of the History of Northwest Yucatan. In *Hidden among the Hills: Maya Archaeology of the Northwest Yucatan Peninsula*, ed. Hanns J. Prem, 316–358. Verlag Von Flemming, Möckmühl.

Grube, Nikolai, and Ruth J. Krochock

2007 Reading between the Lines: Hieroglyphic Texts from Chichén Itzá and Its Neighbors. In *Twin Tollans: Chichén Itzá, Tula, and the Epiclassic to Early Postclassic Mesoamerican World*, ed. Jeff Karl Kowalski and Cynthia Kristan-Graham, 205–249. Dumbarton Oaks, Washington, DC.

Grube, Nikolai, Alfonso Lacadena, and Simon Martin

2003 Chichén Itzá and Ek Balam: Terminal Classic Inscriptions from Yucatan. *Notebook for the XXVII Maya Hieroglyphic Forum at the University of Texas*. Maya Workshop Foundation, Austin, Texas.

Grube, Nikolai, and Werner Nahm

1994 A Census of Xibalaba: A Complete Inventory of *Way* Characters in Maya Ceramics. In *The Maya Vase Book*, vol. 4, ed. Justin Kerr, 686–715. Kerr Associates, New York.

Gruzinski, Serge

2002 *The Mestizo Mind: The Intellectual Dynamics of Colonization and Globalization*. Routledge, New York.

Gubler, Ruth

1996 The Ritual of the Bacabs: Spells and Incantations for Ritual Healing. In *Beyond Indigenous Voices: LAILA/ALILA 11th International Symposium on Latin American Indian Literatures* (1994), ed. Mary H. Preuss, 37–41. Labyrinthos, Lancaster, California.

Guss, David M.

1981 Historical Incorporation among the Makiritare: From Legend to Myth. *Journal of Latin American Lore* 7(1):23–35.

Hanke, Lewis

1970 *Aristotle and the American Indians: A Study in Race Prejudice in the Modern World.* Indiana University Press, Bloomington.

Hanks, William

1988 Grammar, Style, and Meaning in a Maya Manuscript. *International Journal of American Linguistics* 54(3):331–369.

1995 Dialogic Conversions and the Field of Missionary Discourse in Colonial Yucatan. In *Les Rituels du Dialogue: Promenades Ethnolinguistiques en Terres Amérindiennes,* ed. Monod Becquelin and Philippe Erikson, 235–254. Société d'Ethnologie, Nanterre.

2000 *Intertexts: Writings on Language, Utterance, and Context.* Rowman & Littlefield, Lanham, Maryland.

Heaney, Seamus (translator)

2000 *Beowulf: A New Verse Translation.* W. W. Norton & Company, New York.

Heist, William

1952 *The Fifteen Signs before Doomsday.* Michigan State College Press, East Lansing.

Heller, Monica (editor)

1988 *Codeswitching: Anthropological and Sociological Perspectives.* Mouton de Gruyter, Berlin.

Heywood, Thomas

1635 *The Hierarchie of the Blessed Angells; Their Names, Orders and Offices; The Fall of Lucifer with His Angells.* Adam Islip, London.

Hill, Jane H.

1992 The Flower World of Old Uto-Aztecan. *Journal of Anthropological Research* 48:117–144.

Hill, Robert M.

1992 The Social Uses of Writing among the Colonial Cakchiquel Maya: Nativism, Resistance, and Innovation. In *Columbian Consequences,* vol. 3, ed. David Hurst Thomas, 283–299. Smithsonian Institution Press, Washington, DC.

Hill, Robert M., and Edward F. Fischer

1999 States of Heart: An Ethnohistorical Approach to Kaqchikel Maya Ethnopsychology. *Ancient Mesoamerica* 10:317–332.

Hires, Marla Korlin (translator)

1981 The Chilam Balam of Chan Kan. Ph.D. diss., Department of Anthropology, Tulane University, New Orleans. University Microfilms, Ann Arbor, Michigan.

Hofling, Charles A., and Félix Fernando Tesucún

1997 *Itzaj Maya-Spanish-English Dictionary.* University of Utah Press, Salt Lake City.

Houston, Stephen D.

2000 In the Minds of the Ancients: Advances in Maya Glyph Studies. *Journal of World Prehistory* 14:121–201.

Houston, Stephen, John Baines, and Jerrold Cooper

2003 Last Writing: Script Obsolescence in Egypt, Mesopotamia, and Mesoamerica. *Comparative Studies in Society and History* 45(3):430–479.

Houston, Stephen D., and David Stuart

1989 The *Way* Glyph: Evidence for "Co-Essences" among the Classic Maya. *Research Reports on Ancient Maya Writing* 30. Center for Maya Research, Washington, DC.

1992 On Maya Hieroglyphic Literacy. *Current Anthropology* 33:589–593.

1996 Of Gods, Glyphs, and Kings: Divinity and Rulership among the Classic Maya. *Antiquity* 70:289–312.

1998 The Ancient Maya Self: Personhood and Portraiture in the Classic Period. *RES* 33:73–101.

Houston, Stephen D., David Stuart, and John Robertson

2000 The Language of Classic Maya Inscriptions. *Current Anthropology* 41(3): 321–356.

2004 Disharmony in Maya Hieroglyphic Writing: Linguistic Change and Continuity in Classic Society. In *The Linguistics of Maya Writing*, ed. Søren Wichmann, 83–101. University of Utah Press, Salt Lake City.

Houston, Stephen D., David Stuart, and Karl Taube

1989 Folk Classification of Classic Maya Pottery. *American Anthropologist* 91:720–726.

2006 *Memory of Bones: Body, Being, and Experience among the Classic Maya.* University of Texas Press, Austin.

Houston, Stephen, and Karl Taube

2000 An Archaeology of the Senses: Perception and Cultural Expression in Ancient Mesoamerica. *Cambridge Archaeological Journal* 10:261–294.

Hull, Kerry M.

2003 Verbal Art and Performance in Ch'orti' and Maya Hieroglyphic Writing. Ph.D. diss., Department of Anthropology, University of Texas at Austin, Austin.

Hymes, Dell H.

1980 Particle, Pause, and Pattern in American Indian Narrative Verse. *American Indian Culture and Research Journal* 4:7–51.

1981 *In Vain I Tried to Tell You: Essays in Native American Ethnopoetics.* University of Pennsylvania Press, Philadelphia.

Jackson, Sarah, and David Stuart

2001 The *Aj K'uhun* Title: Deciphering a Classic Maya Term of Rank. *Ancient Mesoamerica* 12:217–228.

Janowitz, Naomi

1993 Re-creating Genesis: The Metapragmatics of Divine Speech. In *Reflexive Language: Reported Speech and Metapragmatics*, ed. John A. Lucy, 393–405. Cambridge University Press, Cambridge.

Jones, Grant D.

1989 *Maya Resistance to Spanish Rule: Time and History on a Colonial Frontier.* University of New Mexico Press, Albuquerque.

1998 *The Conquest of the Last Maya Kingdom.* Stanford University Press, Stanford, California.

Joyce, Rosemary

1996 The Construction of Gender in Classic Maya Monuments. In *Gender and Archaeology*, ed. Rita P. Wright, 167–195. University of Pennsylvania Press, Philadelphia.

Justeson, John, William Norman, Lyle Campbell, and Terrance Kaufman

1985 *The Foreign Impact on Lowland Mayan Language and Script.* Publication No. 53. Middle American Research Institute, New Orleans.

Karttunen, Frances

1992 *An Analytical Dictionary of Nahuatl.* University of Oklahoma Press, Norman.

Kaua, Book of Chilam Balam of

N.d. Photostatic copy in Ibero-Amerikanisches Institut Preußischer Kulturbesitz in Berlin. (Original is lost.) See also V. Bricker and Miram 2002.

Kaufman, Terrence S., and William Norman

1984 An Outline of Proto-Cholan Phonology, Morphology, and Vocabulary. In *Phoneticism in Maya Hieroglyphic Writing*, ed. John S. Justeson and Lyle Campbell, 77–166. Institute for Mesoamerican Studies Publication No. 9. State University of New York, Albany.

Kepecs, Susan, and Marilyn A. Masson

2003 Political Organization in Yucatán and Belize. In *The Postclassic Mesoamerican World*, ed. Michael E. Smith and Francis F. Berdan, 40–44. University of Utah Press, Salt Lake City.

Knorosov, Yuri V.

1958 The Problem of the Study of the Maya Hieroglyphic Writing. *American Antiquity* 23:248–291.

Knowlton, Timothy

2002 Diphrastic Kennings in Mayan Hieroglyphic Literature. *Mexicon* 24: 9–14.

2006 From Old World Ideogram to Maya Hieroglyph: A Case Study of Writing Systems in a Colonial Context. In *The Bricker Almanac: A Festschrift in Honor of Harvey and Victoria Bricker*, special publication of *Human Mosaic: A Journal of the Social Sciences* 36(1):93–97.

2008 Dynamics of Indigenous Language Ideologies in the Colonial Redaction of a Yucatec Maya Cosmological Text. *Anthropological Linguistics* 50(1):90–112.

2010 Nahua Vocables in a Maya Song of the Fall of Chichén Itzá: Music and Social Memory in the Construction of Yucatecan Ethnicities. In *Astonomers, Scribes, and Priests: Intellectual Interchange between the Northern Maya Lowlands and Highland Mexico in the Late Postclassic Period*, ed. Gabrielle Vail and Christine Hernandez, 241–259. Dumbarton Oaks, Washington, DC.

Knowlton, Timothy, and Gabrielle Vail

2010 Hybrid Cosmologies in Mesoamerica: A Reevaluation of the *Yax Cheel Cab*, a Maya World Tree. *Ethnohistory* 57(4):709–739.

Kowalski, Jeff Karl, and Cynthia Kristan-Graham

2007 *Twin Tollans: Chichén Itzá, Tula, and the Epiclassic to Early Postclassic Mesoamerican World*. Dumbarton Oaks, Washington, DC.

Kropfinger–von Kügelgen, Helga

1973 Europäischer Buchexport von Sevilla nach Neuspanien im Jahre 1586. In *Das Mexiko-Projekt der Deutschen Forschungs-Gemeinschaft V*, ed. Wilhelm Lauer, 1–105. Franz Steiner Verlag, Wiesbaden.

Lacadena, Alfonso

1997 Bilingüísmo en el códice de Madrid. In *Los investigadores de la cultura maya*, 184–204. Universidad Autónoma de Campeche, Mexico.

2006 El origen prehispánico de las profecías katúnicas mayas coloniales: Antecedentes clásicos de las profecías de 12 Ajaw y 10 Ajaw. In *Sacred Books, Sacred Languages: Two Thousand Years of Ritual and Religious Maya Literature*, ed. Rogelio Valencia Rivera and Geneviève Le Fort, 201–225. Acta Mesoamericana Vol. 18. Verlag Anton Saurwein, Markt Schwaben, Germany.

Lacadena, Alfonso, and Søren Wichmann

2004 On the Representation of the Glottal Stop in Maya Writing. In *The Linguistics of Maya Writing*, ed. Søren Wichmann, 103–162. University of Utah Press, Salt Lake City.

Lakoff, George, and Mark Johnson

1980 *Metaphors We Live By*. University of Chicago Press, Chicago.

Landa, Fr. Diego de

1978 [ca. 1566] *Yucatan Before and After the Conquest*, trans. William Gates. Dover Publishers, New York.

Las Casas, Fr. Bartolomé de

1967 [1559] *Apologética Historia Sumaria*. 2 vols. Ed. Edmundo O'Gorman. Universidad Nacional Autónoma de México, Mexico.

León-Portilla, Miguel

1963 *Aztec Thought and Culture: A Study of the Ancient Nahuatl Mind.* Trans. Jack Emory Davis. University of Oklahoma, Norman.

1992 *Fifteen Poets of the Aztec World.* University of Oklahoma Press, Norman.

Li, Andrés de

1999 [1492] *Reportorio de los Tiempos.* Ed. Laura Delbrugge. Tamesis, London.

Lindberg, David C.

1992 *The Beginnings of Western Science: The European Scientific Tradition in Philosophical, Religious, and Institutional Context, 600 B.C. to A.D. 1450.* University of Chicago Press, Chicago.

Linden, John H.

1986 Glyph X of the Maya Lunar Series: An Eighteen-Month Lunar Synodic Calendar. *American Antiquity* 51:122–136.

1996 The Deity Head Variants of Glyph C. In *Palenque Round Table 1993*, vol. 10. Ed. Merle Greene Robertson, Martha Macri, and Jan McHargue, 343–356. Pre-Columbian Art Research Institute, San Francisco.

Lizana, Bernardo de

1995 [1633] *Devocionario de Nuestra Señora de Izamal y Conquista Espiritual de Yucatán.* Ed. René Acuña. Universidad Nacional Autónoma de México, Mexico.

Lois, Ximena

1998 Gender Markers as "Rigid Determiners" of the Itzaj Maya World. *International Journal of American Linguistics* 64:224–282.

Looper, Matthew G.

1995 The Three Stones of Maya Creation Mythology at Quiriguá. *Mexicon* 17:24–30.

Lounsbury, Floyd G.

1985 The Identities of the Mythological Figures in the Cross Group Inscriptions of Palenque. In *Fourth Palenque Round Table 1980*, vol. 6. Ed. Merle G. Robertson and Elizabeth P. Benson. Pre-Columbian Art Research Institute, San Francisco.

Love, Bruce

1994 *The Paris Codex: Handbook for a Maya Priest.* University of Texas Press, Austin.

Lovin, Robin W., and Frank E. Reynolds

1985 *Cosmogony and Ethical Order: New Studies in Comparative Ethics.* University of Chicago Press, Chicago.

Lucy, John A.

1993 Metapragmatic Presentationals: Reporting Speech with Quotatives in Yucatec Maya. In *Reflexive Language: Reported Speech and Metapragmatics*, ed. John A. Lucy, 91–125. Cambridge University Press, Cambridge.

Macri, Martha J., and Matthew G. Looper
2003 Nahua in Ancient Mesoamerica: Evidence from Maya Inscriptions. *Ancient Mesoamerica* 14:285–297.

Madrid Codex. See Tro-Cortesianus Codex.

Malinowski, Bronislaw
1948 *Magic, Science, and Religion and Other Essays.* Waveland Press, Long Grove, Illinois.

Martin, Simon
2006 Cacao in Ancient Maya Religion: First Fruit from the Maize Tree and Other Tales from the Underworld. In *Chocolate in Mesoamerica: A Cultural History of Cacao*, ed. Cameron McNeil, 154–183. University Press of Florida, Gainesville.

Martin, Simon, and Nikolai Grube
2000 *Chronicle of the Maya Kings and Queens.* Thames and Hudson, London.

Matthews, Peter
1979 The Glyphs on the Ear Ornaments from Tomb A-1/1. In *Excavations at Altun Ha, Belize, 1964–1970*, vol. 1, ed. David Pendergast, 79–80. Royal Ontario Museum, Toronto.

Mauss, Marcel
1990 [1925] *The Gift: The Form and Reason for Exchange in Archaic Societies.* Trans. W. D. Halls. W. W. Norton, New York.

Maxwell, Judith M., and Craig A. Hanson
1992 *Of the Manners of Speaking That the Old Ones Had: The Metaphors of Andrés de Olmos in the TULAL Manuscript.* University of Utah Press, Salt Lake City.

Maxwell, Judith M., and Robert M. Hill (translators)
2006 *Kaqchikel Chronicles.* University of Texas Press, Austin.

Maybury-Lewis, David, and Uri Almagor
1989 *The Attraction of Opposites: Thought and Society in the Dualistic Mode.* University of Michigan Press, Ann Arbor.

Mayer, Karl Herbert
1995 *Maya Monuments: Sculptures of Unknown Provenance*, Supplement 4. Academic Publishers, Graz, Austria.

McNeil, Cameron (editor)
2006 *Chocolate in Mesoamerica: A Cultural History of Cacao.* University Press of Florida, Gainesville.

Mediz Bolio, Antonio (translator)
1930 *Libro de Chilam Balam de Chumayel.* Imprenta y libreria Lehmann, San Jose, Costa Rica.

Mignolo, Walter D.

2003 *The Darker Side of the Renaissance: Literacy, Territoriality, and Colonization*. 2nd ed.University of Michigan Press, Ann Arbor.

Milbrath, Susan, and Carlos Peraza Lope

2003 Revisiting Mayapan: Mexico's Last Maya Capital. *Ancient Mesoamerica* 14:1–46.

Miller, Mary, and Simon Martin

2004 *Courtly Art of the Ancient Maya*. Thames and Hudson, New York.

Miller, Mary, and Karl Taube

1993 *An Illustrated Dictionary of the Gods and Symbols of Ancient Mexico and the Maya*. Thames and Hudson, London.

Miram, Helga-Maria

1988 Transcriptions of the Chilam Balam of Tusik, and the Códice Pérez. *Maya Texte II*, vol. 3. Toro Verlag, Hamburg.

Miram, Helga-Maria, and Victoria R. Bricker

1996 Relating Time to Space: The Maya Calendar Compasses. *Palenque Round Table 1993*, vol. 10. Ed. Merle Greene Robertson, Martha Macri, and Jan McHargue, 393–402. Pre-Columbian Art Research Institute, San Francisco.

Miram, Helga-Maria, and Wolfgang Miram

1988 *Concordance of the Chilam Balames*. 6 vols. Toro Verlag, Hamburg.

Monaghan, John D.

2000 Theology and History in the Study of Mesoamerican Religions. In *Supplement to the Handbook of Middle American Indians*, vol. 6: *Ethnology*, ed. Victoria R. Bricker and John D. Monaghan, 24–49. University of Texas Press, Austin.

Mora-Marín, David F.

2001 The Grammar, Orthography, Content, and Social Context of Late Preclassic Mayan Portable Texts. Ph.D. diss., Department of Anthropology, State University of New York at Albany, Albany. University Microfilms, Ann Arbor, Michigan.

2009 A Test and Falsification of the "Classic Ch'olti'an" Hypothesis: A Study of Three Proto-Ch'olan Markers. *International Journal of American Linguistics* 75(2):115–157.

Morley, Sylvanus G.

1916 The Supplementary Series in the Maya Inscriptions. In *Holmes Anniversary Volume: Anthropological Essays Presented to William Henry Holmes*, ed. F. Hodge, 366–396. J. W. Bryan Press, Washington, DC.

Morley Manuscript

[1576?] Original manuscript in the Library of the Laboratory of Anthropology, Museum of Indian Arts & Culture, Santa Fe, New Mexico. See also Whalen 2003a.

Myers-Scotten, Carol
1993 *Social Motivations for Codeswitching: Evidence from Africa.* Clarendon Press, Oxford.

Nagy, Gregory
2002 Reading Bakhtin Reading the Classics: An Epic Fate for Conveyors of the Heroic Past. In *Bakhtin and the Classics*, ed. R. Bracht Branham, 71–96. Northwestern University Press, Evanston, Illinois.

Okoshi, Tsubasa
1995 Revisión crítica de la organización política de la provincia de Ah Canul en vísperas de la invasión española. In *Memorias del Segundo Congreso Internacional de Mayistas, Mérida, Yucatán*, 60–69. Universidad Nacional Autónoma de México, Mexico City.

Otzoy C., Simón
1999 *Memorial de Sololá*. Comisión Interuniversitaria Guatemalteca de Conmemoración del Quinto Centenario del Descubrimiento de América, Guatemala City, Guatemala.

Paxton, Merideth
2001 *The Cosmos of the Yucatec Maya: Cycles and Steps from the Madrid Codex.* University of New Mexico Press, Albuquerque.

Peradotto, John
2002 Bakhtin, Milman Parry, and the Problem of Homeric Originality. In *Bakhtin and the Classics*, ed. R. Bracht Branham, 59–70. Northwestern University Press, Evanston, Illinois.

Popol Vuh
N.d. Original manuscript in the Ayer Collection, Newberry Library, Chicago. See also Christenson 2003a, 2003b; Colop 1999; D. Tedlock 1985, 1996.

Proskouriakoff, Tatiana
1960 Historical Implications of a Pattern of Dates at Piedras Negras, Guatemala. *American Antiquity* 25:454–475.
1973 The Hand-Grasping-Fish and Associated Glyphs on Classic Maya Monuments. In *Mesoamerican Writing Systems*, ed. Elizabeth P. Benson, 165–178. Dumbarton Oaks Research Library and Collection, Washington, DC.

Quezada, Sergio
1993 *Pueblos y caciques Yucatecos, 1550–1580.* El Colegio de México, Mexico City.

Restall, Matthew
1997 *The Maya World: Yucatec Culture and Society, 1550–1850.* Stanford University Press, Stanford.

1998 *Maya Conquistador.* Beacon Press, Boston.

2001 The People of the Patio: Ethnohistorical Evidence of Yucatec Maya Royal Courts. In *Royal Courts of the Ancient Maya,* vol. 2: *Data and Case Studies,* ed. Takeshi Inomata and Stephen D. Houston, 335–390. Westview Press, Boulder, Colorado.

2003 A History of the New Philology and the New Philology in History. *Latin American Research Review* 38(1):113–134.

2004 Maya Ethnogenesis. *The Journal of Latin American Anthropology* 9(1): 64–89.

Ringle, William M.

1988 *Of Mice and Monkeys: The Value and Meaning of T1016, the God C Hieroglyph.* Research Reports on Ancient Maya Writing, No. 18. Center for Maya Research, Washington, DC.

Ritual of the Bacabs

N.d. Original manuscript in the Princeton University Library. See also Arzápalo Marín 1987; Roys 1965.

Robertson, John, Stephen Houston, Marc Zender, and David Stuart

2007 *Universals and the Logic of the Material Implication: A Case Study from Maya Hieroglyphic Writing.* Research Reports on Ancient Maya Writing, No. 62. Center for Maya Research, Washington, DC.

Robertson, Merle Greene

1991 *The Sculpture of Palenque,* vol. 4: *The Cross Group, the North Group, the Olvidado, and Other Pieces.* Princeton University Press, Princeton, New Jersey.

Roys, Ralph L.

1957 *The Political Geography of the Yucatan Maya.* Publication, vol. 613. Carnegie Institution of Washington, Washington, DC.

Roys, Ralph L. (translator)

1965 *Ritual of the Bacabs.* University of Oklahoma Press, Norman.

1967 *The Book of Chilam Balam of Chumayel.* University of Oklahoma Press, Norman.

Russell, Jeffrey Burton

1986 *Lucifer: The Devil in the Middle Ages.* Cornell University Press, Ithaca, New York.

Sahlins, Marshall

1981 *Historical Metaphors and Mythical Realities: Structure in the Early History of the Sandwich Islands Kingdom.* University of Michigan Press, Ann Arbor.

Salomon, Frank

1982 Chronicles of the Impossible: Notes on Three Peruvian Indigenous Historians. In *From Oral to Written Expression: Native Andean Chronicles of the Early Colonial Period,* ed. Rolena Adorno, 9–39. Maxwell School of Citizenship and Public Affairs, Syracuse University, Syracuse, New York.

Sánchez de Aguilar, Pedro

1987 [1639] Informe Contra Idolorum Cultores del Obispado de Yucatan. In *El Alma Encantada: Anales del Museo Nacional de México*, ed. Fernando Benítez, 12–122. Instituto Nacional Indigenista / Fondo de Cultura Económica, Mexico.

Schele, Linda

1992 *The Proceedings of the Maya Hieroglyphic Workshop: The Origins Workshop.* Transcribed and ed. Phil Wanyerka. Maya Workshop Foundation, Austin, Texas.

1998 *Notebook for the XXII Maya Hieroglyphic Forum at Texas.* Maya Workshop Foundation, Austin, Texas.

Schele, Linda, and David Freidel

1991 *A Forest of Kings: The Untold Story of the Ancient Maya.* Quill/William Morrow, New York.

Schele, Linda, and Nikolai Grube

1997 *The Proceedings of the Maya Hieroglyphic Workshop: The Dresden Codex Workshop.* Transcribed and ed. Phil Wanyerka. Maya Workshop Foundation, Austin, Texas.

Schellhas, Paul

1904 Representation of the Deities of the Maya Manuscripts. *Papers of the Peabody Museum of American Archaeology and Ethnology, vol. 4, no. 1.* Harvard University, Cambridge, MA.

Seler, Eduard

1996 The Worldview of the Ancient Mexicans. In *Collected Works in Mesoamerican Linguistics and Archaeology*, trans. Charles Bodwich, 5:3–38. Labyrinthos, Lancaster, California.

Smith, Michael E., and Francis F. Berdan (editors)

2003 *The Postclassic Mesoamerican World.* University of Utah Press, Salt Lake City.

Sosa, John R.

1985 The Maya Sky, the Maya World: A Symbolic Analysis of Yucatec Maya Cosmology. Ph.D. diss., Department of Anthropology, State University of New York at Albany, Albany. University Microfilms, Ann Arbor, Michigan.

Spero, Joanne M.

1991 Beyond Rainstorms: The Kawak as Ancestor, Warrior, and Patron of Witchcraft. In *Sixth Palenque Round Table, 1986*, ed. Virginia M. Fields, 184–193. University of Oklahoma Press, Norman.

Stross, Brian, and Justin Kerr
1990 Notes on the Maya Vision Quest through Enema. In *Maya Vase Book*, vol. 2, ed. Justin Kerr, 348–361. Justin Kerr, New York.

Stuart, David
1984 Blood Symbolism in Maya Iconography. *RES* 7/8:6–20.
1998 "The Fire Enters His House": Architecture and Ritual in Classic Maya Texts. In *Function and Meaning in Classic Maya Architecture*, ed. Stephen D. Houston, 373–425. Dumbarton Oaks, Washington, DC.
2005 *The Inscriptions from Temple XIX at Palenque*. The Pre-Columbian Art Research Institute, San Francisco.

Sturluson, Snorri
2005 *The Prose Edda*. Trans. Jesse Byock. Penguin, New York.

Sullivan, Thelma, and Timothy Knab
1994 *A Scattering of Jades: Stories, Poems, and Prayers of the Aztecs*. University of Arizona Press, Tucson.

Tate, Carolyn
1992 *Yaxchilan: The Design of a Maya Ceremonial Center*. University of Texas Press, Austin.

Taube, Karl A.
1989a *Itzam Cab Ain: Caimans, Cosmology, and Calendrics in Postclassic Yucatan*. Research Reports on Ancient Maya Writing No. 26. Center for Maya Research, Washington, DC.
1989b The Maize Tamale in Classic Maya Diet, Epigraphy, and Art. *American Antiquity* 54(1):31–51.
1992 *The Major Gods of Ancient Yucatan*. Dumbarton Oaks, Washington, DC.
1993 *Aztec and Maya Myths*. University of Texas Press, Austin.
2004 Flower Mountain: Concepts of Life, Beauty, and Paradise among the Classic Maya. *RES* 45:69–98.
2005 The Symbolism of Jade in Classic Maya Religion. *Ancient Mesoamerica* 16:23–50.

Taube, Karl A., and Bonnie L. Bade
1991 *An Appearance of Xiuhtecuhtli in the Dresden Venus Pages*. Research Reports on Ancient Maya Writing No. 34. Center for Maya Research, Washington, DC.

Taussig, Michael
1984 History as Sorcery. *Representations* 7:87–109.

Tavárez, David
2000 De cantares Zapotecas a "libros de demonio": La extirpación de discursos doctrinales híbridos en Villa Alta, Oaxaca, 1702–1704. *Acervos* 17:19–27.

Tedlock, Barbara

1982 Sound Texture and Metaphor in Quiché Maya Ritual Language. *Current Anthropology* 23:269–272.

1992 Time and the Highland Maya. Rev. ed. University of New Mexico Press, Albuquerque.

1999 Maya Astronomy: What We Know and How We Know It. *Archaeoastronomy* 24(1):39–58.

Tedlock, Dennis

1979 The Analogical Tradition and the Emergence of a Dialogical Anthropology. *Journal of Anthropological Research* 35:387–400.

1986 Creation in the *Popol Vuh*: A Hermeneutical Approach. In *Symbol and Meaning beyond the Closed Community: Essays in Mesoamerican Ideas*, ed. Gary H. Gossen, 77–82. Institute for Mesoamerican Studies, State University of New York, Albany.

1992a On Hieroglyphic Literacy in Ancient Mayaland: An Alternative Interpretation. *Current Anthropology* 33:216–218.

1992b The Story of Evenadam. In *On the Translation of Native American Literature*, ed. Brian Swann, 406–425. Smithsonian Institution Press, Washington, DC.

1999 Dialogues between Worlds: Mesoamerica After and Before the European Invasion. In *Theorizing the Americanist Tradition*, ed. Lisa Philips Valentine and Regna Darnell, 163–180. University of Toronto Press, Toronto.

Tedlock, Dennis (translator)

1985 *Popol Vuh: The Definitive Edition of the Mayan Book of the Dawn of Life and the Glories of Gods and Kings*. Simon & Schuster, New York.

1996 *Popol Vuh: The Definitive Edition of the Mayan Book of the Dawn of Life and the Glories of Gods and Kings*. Rev. ed. Simon & Schuster, New York.

2003 *Rabinal Achi: A Mayan Drama of War and Sacrifice*. Oxford University Press, Oxford.

Tedlock, Dennis, and Bruce Mannheim (editors)

1995 *The Dialogic Emergence of Culture*. University of Illinois Press, Urbana.

Thompson, J. Eric S.

1958 Symbols, Glyphs, and Divinatory Almanacs for Diseases in the Maya Dresden and Madrid Codices. *American Antiquity* 23(3):297–308.

1962 *A Catalog of Maya Hieroglyphs*. University of Oklahoma Press, Norman.

1970 *Maya History and Religion*. University of Oklahoma Press, Norman.

Tizimín, Book of Chilam Balam of

N.d. Photostatic copy in the Latin American Library, Tulane University, New Orleans. (Original in the Museo Nacional de Antropología, Mexico City.)

Tomlinson, Gary

2007 *The Singing of the New World: Indigenous Voice in the Era of European Contact.* Cambridge University Press, Cambridge.

Tro-Cortesianus Codex

1967 *Codex Tro-Cortesianus (Codex Madrid): Museo de América Madrid.* Akademische Druck- u. Verlagsanstalt, Graz, Austria.

Tusik, Book of Chilam Balam of

N.d. Photographic copy in Tozzer Library at Peabody Museum, Harvard University, Cambridge, Massachusetts. (Original in Tusik, Quintana Roo, Mexico.) See also Barrera Vásquez 1944; Miram 1988.

Vail, Gabrielle

1994 A Commentary on the Bee Almanacs in Codex Madrid. In *Códices y documentos sobre México, Primer Simposio,* ed. Constanza Vega Sosa, 37–68. Instituto Nacional de Antropología e Historia, Serie Historia, Mexico.

1998 Kisin and the Underworld Gods of the Maya. *Latin American Indian Literatures Journal* 14:167–187.

2000a Issues of Language and Ethnicity in the Postclassic Maya Codices. *Written Language and Literature* 3:37–75.

2000b Pre-Hispanic Maya Religion: Conceptions of Divinity in the Postclassic Maya Codices. *Ancient Mesoamerica* 11:123–147.

2001 Bees and Honey. In *The Oxford Encyclopedia of Mesoamerican Cultures,* vol. 1, ed. Davíd Carrasco, 84–85. Oxford University Press, Oxford.

2006 The Maya Codices. *Annual Review of Anthropology* 35:497–519.

Vail, Gabrielle and Anthony Aveni (editors)

2004 *The Madrid Codex: New Approaches to Understanding an Ancient Maya Manuscript.* University Press of Colorado, Boulder.

Vail, Gabrielle, and Christine Hernández (editors)

2010 *Astronomers, Scribes, and Priests: Intellectual Interchange between the Northern Maya Lowlands and Highland Mexico in the Late Postclassic Period.* Dumbarton Oaks, Washington, DC.

Van Akkeren, Ruud W.

2003 Authors of the Popol Vuh. *Ancient Mesoamerica* 14:237–256.

Velásquez Garcia, Erik

2006 The Maya Flood Myth and the Decapitation of the Cosmic Caiman. *The PARI Journal* 7:1–10.

2007 Imagen, texto, y contexto ceremonial del "Ritual de los Ángeles": Viejos problemas y nuevas respuestas sobre la narrativa sagrada en los libros de Chilam Balam. Presented at the symposium The Maya and Their Sacred Narratives: Text and Context in Maya Mythologies, at the annual European Maya Conference, Geneva, Switzerland, December 10, 2007.

Vermes, Geza (translator)
1997 *The Complete Dead Sea Scrolls in English*. Allen Lane, New York.

Wald, Robert F.
2004 The Languages of the Dresden Codex: Legacy of the Classic Maya. In *The Linguistics of Maya Writing*, ed. Søren Wichmann, 27–60. University of Utah Press, Salt Lake City.

Whalen, Gretchen
2003a An Annotated Translation of a Colonial Yucatec Manuscript: On Religious and Cosmological Topics by a Native Author. FAMSI, Crystal River, Florida. http://www.famsi.org/reports/01017/index.html, accessed January 12, 2004.
2003b From the Morley Collection: The Book of a Maya *Maestro*. *El Palacio: The Magazine of the Museum of New Mexico* 108(2):6–13.

Whittaker, Gordon
1986 The Mexican Names of Three Venus Gods in the Dresden Codex. *Mexicon* 8:56–60.

Wichmann, Søren
2006 Maya Historical Linguistics and Epigraphy: A New Synthesis. *Annual Review of Anthropology* 35:279–294.

Wilks, Ivor
1999 The History of the Sunjata Epic: A Review of the Evidence. In *In Search of Sunjata: The Mande Oral Epic as History, Literature and Performance*, ed. Ralph A. Austen, 25–58. Indiana University Press, Bloomington.

Witt, Ronald G.
1977 Coluccio Salutati and the Conception of the *Poeta Theologus* in the Fourteenth Century. *Renaissance Quarterly* 30:542–544.

Zamorano, Rodrigo
1585 *Cronología y reportorio de la razón de los tiempos*. Andrea Pescioni y Juan de León, Seville.

Zauzich, Karl-Theodor
1992 *Hieroglyphs without Mystery: An Introduction to Ancient Egyptian Writing*. Trans. Ann Macy Roth. University of Texas Press, Austin.

Zender, Marc
2004 On the Morphology of Intimate Possession in Mayan Languages and Classic Mayan Glyphic Nouns. In *The Linguistics of Maya Writing*, ed. Søren Wichmann, 195–210. University of Utah Press, Salt Lake City.

Index

Page numbers in italics indicate illustrations